Developing and Testing Your Investing Beliefs

What are your investing beliefs? Most investors haven't taken the time to consider that question, let alone answer it. During the sharp stock market slide in 2008, some investors started following particular gurus who claimed to have predicted the financial crisis. And then the 2020 COVID-19 pandemic and government-mandated shutdowns really set investors on edge due to the surprising nature of that episode. These investors wanted to believe that someone out there could predict important financial events and tell folks how to time their investments to benefit from what was about to unfold.

Such market timing is a fool's errand. It sounds possible — and we'd like to believe that it is — but it's not possible on the scale various charlatans would have you believe. Furthermore, many of those who boast the loudest about their market-timing ability are worse than average at it.

It's challenging to work with someone on his investments when he has little in the way of background and beliefs. As someone seeking to educate yourself about investing, you may have a better idea of your investment beliefs than other investors do. To help you along in this process, here are some beliefs for you to consider:

>> **Your own personal comfort matters.** A wide range of investments are available to you, including stocks, exchange-traded funds (ETFs), mutual funds, real estate, and small business. Some folks are simply more comfortable with particular investments, so you shouldn't force yourself into a portfolio that's recommended as being best for you. Consider the value of your time and your investing skills and desires. Investing in stocks and other securities via the best mutual funds and ETFs is both time-efficient and profitable. Real estate investing and running a small business are the most time-intensive investments.

>> **Costs matter.** The more you pay in commissions and management fees on your investments, the greater the drag on your returns. And don't fall prey to thinking that you get what you pay for. Take advantage of tax-deductible retirement accounts, and understand the effect of your tax bracket when investing outside tax-sheltered retirement accounts. Minimize your trading. The more you trade, the more likely you are to make mistakes. Also, you suffer increased transaction costs and higher taxes for nonretirement-account investments.

» **Market timing is much harder to predict than folks realize.** Don't bail when things look bleak. The hardest time, psychologically, to hold on to your investments is when they're down. Even the best investments go through depressed periods, which is the worst possible time to sell. Don't sell when there's a sale going on; if anything, consider buying more. Ignore soothsayers and prognosticators. Predicting the future is nearly impossible.

» **There are better times than others to sell.** When you're really feeling good about an asset class like stocks, and those assets have had a multiple-year run and are getting widespread accolades, that's a good time to lighten up if you have other good reasons for doing so. By contrast, you can bump up your stock allocation if you're comfortable doing so after a major market decline.

» **Think long-term.** Because ownership investments like stocks, real estate, and small business are more volatile, you must keep your long-term perspective when investing in them. Don't invest money in such investments unless you plan to hold them for a minimum of five years and preferably for a decade or longer.

» **Diversify.** Diversification is a powerful investment concept that helps you reduce the risk of holding more-aggressive investments. Diversifying simply means that you hold a variety of investments that don't move in tandem in different market environments. When investing in stocks, for example, invest worldwide. You can diversify further by investing in real estate.

» **Emphasize value.** Over the long term, value-oriented investments tend to produce higher returns with less volatility than do pure growth-oriented investments.

» **Ignore the minutiae.** Don't feel mystified by or feel the need to follow the short-term gyrations of the financial markets. Ultimately, the prices of stocks, bonds, and other financial instruments are determined by supply and demand, which are influenced by thousands of external issues, including millions of investors' expectations and fears.

» **You are what you read and listen to.** Don't pollute your mind with bad investing strategies and philosophies. The quality of what you read and listen to is far more important than the quantity.

Praise for Eric Tyson

"Eric Tyson for president! Thanks for such a wonderful guide. With a clear, no-nonsense approach to . . . investing for the long haul, Tyson's book says it all without being the least bit long-winded. Pick up a copy today. It'll be your wisest investment ever!"

— Jim Beggs, VA

"Eric Tyson is doing something important — namely, helping people at all income levels to take control of their financial futures. This book is a natural outgrowth of Tyson's vision that he has nurtured for years. Like Henry Ford, he wants to make something that was previously accessible only to the wealthy accessible to middle-income Americans."

— James C. Collins, coauthor of the national bestsellers *Built to Last* and *Good to Great*

"Among my favorite financial guides are . . . Eric Tyson's *Personal Finance For Dummies.*"

— Jonathan Clements, the *Wall Street Journal*

"In *Investing For Dummies*, Tyson handily dispatches both the basics . . . and the more complicated."

— Lisa M. Sodders, *The Capital-Journal*

"Smart advice for dummies . . . skip the tomes . . . and buy *Personal Finance For Dummies*, which rewards your candor with advice and comfort."

— Temma Ehrenfeld, *Newsweek*

"Eric Tyson . . . seems the perfect writer for a . . . *For Dummies* book. He doesn't tell you what to do or consider doing without explaining the why's and how's — and the booby traps to avoid — in plain English. . . . It will lead you through the thickets of your own finances as painlessly as I can imagine."

— Clarence Peterson, *Chicago Tribune*

"*Personal Finance For Dummies* is the perfect book for people who feel guilty about inadequately managing their money but are intimidated by all of the publications out there. It's a painless way to learn how to take control."

— Karen Tofte, producer, National Public Radio's *Sound Money*

More Best-Selling For Dummies Titles by Eric Tyson

Personal Finance in Your 20s & 30s For Dummies

This hands-on, friendly guide provides you with the targeted financial advice you need to establish firm financial footing in your 20s and 30s and to secure your finances for years to come. When it comes to protecting your financial future, starting sooner rather than later is the smartest thing you can do. Also check out *Personal Finance For Dummies*.

Mutual Funds For Dummies

This best-selling guide is now updated to include current fund and portfolio recommendations. Using the practical tips and techniques, you'll design a mutual fund investment plan suited for your income, lifestyle, and risk preferences.

Home Buying Kit For Dummies

America's No. 1 real estate book includes coverage of online resources in addition to sound financial advice from Eric Tyson and front-line real estate insights from industry veteran Ray Brown. Also available from America's best-selling real estate team of Tyson and Brown — *Selling Your House For Dummies* and *Mortgages For Dummies* (Tyson co-authored with Robert Griswold).

Real Estate Investing For Dummies

Real estate is a proven wealth-building investment, but many people don't know how to go about making and managing rental property investments. Real estate and property management expert Robert Griswold and Eric Tyson cover the gamut of property investment options, strategies, and techniques.

Small Business For Dummies

Take control of your future, and make the leap from employee to entrepreneur with this enterprising guide. From drafting a business plan to managing costs, you'll profit from expert advice and real-world examples that cover every aspect of building your own business. Also check out Tyson's *Small Business Taxes For Dummies*.

Investing in Your 20s & 30s

A Wiley Brand

Investing in Your 20s & 30s

3rd Edition

by Eric Tyson, MBA
Author of *Personal Finance in Your 20s & 30s For Dummies*
and *Mutual Funds For Dummies*

Investing in Your 20s & 30s For Dummies®, 3rd Edition

Published by:
John Wiley & Sons, Inc.
111 River Street
Hoboken, NJ 07030-5774
www.wiley.com

Copyright © 2021 by Eric Tyson

Published by John Wiley & Sons, Inc., Hoboken, New Jersey

Published simultaneously in Canada

For general information on our other products and services, please contact our Customer Care Department within the U.S. at 877-762-2974, outside the U.S. at 317-572-3993, or fax 317-572-4002. For technical support, please visit https://hub.wiley.com/community/support/dummies.

Wiley publishes in a variety of print and electronic formats and by print-on-demand. Some material included with standard print versions of this book may not be included in e-books or in print-on-demand. If this book refers to media such as a CD or DVD that is not included in the version you purchased, you may download this material at http://booksupport.wiley.com. For more information about Wiley products, visit www.wiley.com.

Library of Congress Control Number: 2021937745

ISBN 978-1-119-80540-3 (pbk); ISBN 978-1-119-80541-0 (ebk); ISBN 978-1-119-80542-7 (ebk)

Manufactured in the United States of America

SKY10026814_050621

Contents at a Glance

Table of Contents

Introduction

nvesting offers so many possibilities and so many choices. Your young-adult years, which at least for the purposes of this book I define as your 20s and 30s, are filled with so much promise and potential. Your career, your interests, your personal life, and your family and friends all compete for your time and attention.

Most folks work upward of 2,000 hours per year earning a living. Managing the money that passes through their hands is an important task, one most people aren't trained to do.

Earning money generally takes a lot of work. Managing your personal finances and saving money take discipline and sacrifice. When you have money to invest, you want to do the best you can so you earn a decent return without ending up in failed investments.

About This Book

I designed and wrote this book to help you with the important and challenging task of investing. Your young adult years are a crucial and ideal time to lay the best foundation for investing wisely. After all, some of the investments you make now and in the near future will have decades to grow and multiply.

I talk some simple numbers here to get you excited and motivated. Stocks in the United States historically have returned an average of about 9 percent per year. At that rate of return, you will double your money every 8 years. So, in 16 years, your money will be up four times, in 24 years, your money will be up eight times and in 32 years, you money will be up 16 times. Wow! This means for every $1,000 you can invest in your 20s, you could have about 16 times that amount by your 50s and be on the road to financial independence. The more you can save and intelligently invest in your younger adult years, the quicker you will reach the land of financial independence.

I've worked with and taught people from widely varying financial situations, so I know the investing concerns and questions of real folks just like you. I've seen how important having healthy and strong personal finances and investments is.

I first became interested in money matters as a middle-school student when my father was laid off from his employer and received some retirement money. I worked with my dad to make investing decisions with the money. A couple of years later, I won my high school's science fair with a project on what influences the stock market.

During my younger adult years, I worked hard to keep my living expenses low and to save and invest money so I could leave my job and pursue my entrepreneurial ideas. I accomplished that goal in my late 20s. I hope to give you some tools to help you make the most of your money and investments so you too can meet your goals and dreams.

This book is basic enough to help a novice get their arms around thorny investing issues. But advanced readers will be challenged as well to think about their investments and finances in a new way and identify areas for improvement. Check out the table of contents for a chapter-by-chapter rundown of what this book offers. You can also look up a specific topic in the index. Or you can turn a few pages and start at the beginning: Chapter 1.

Foolish Assumptions

No matter what your current situation is — whether you're entering the job market right after high school, graduating college with substantial student loan debt, feeling pretty well established in your career, and so on — I thought of you as I wrote this book and made some assumptions about you:

» You want expert advice about important investing topics such as getting a preinvesting financial checkup, understanding the range of investments available, and assembling a killer investment portfolio. And you want that advice quickly.

» You want a crash course in investing and are looking for a book you can read cover to cover to help solidify major concepts and get you thinking about your investments in a more comprehensive way.

» You're tired of feeling overwhelmed by your investing choices and stressed out by the ever-changing economic and investing landscape, and you want to get more comfortable with your investment selections.

Icons Used in This Book

The icons in this book help you find particular kinds of information that may be of use to you:

TIP

This light bulb marks strategy recommendations for making the most of your investments.

REMEMBER

This icon points out information that you'll definitely want to remember.

WARNING

This icon marks things to avoid and points out common mistakes people make when making and managing their investments.

INVESTIGATE

This icon tells you when you should consider doing some additional research. Don't worry — I explain what to look for and what to look out for.

Beyond the Book

In addition to the material in the print or e-book you're reading right now, this product comes with a free access-anywhere Cheat Sheet that helps you get started with investing. To view this Cheat Sheet, simply go to www.dummies.com and enter "Investing in Your 20s & 30s For Dummies Cheat Sheet" in the Search box.

Where to Go from Here

This book is organized so you can go wherever you want to find complete information. You can use the table of contents to find broad categories of information or the index to look up more specific topics.

If you're not sure where you want to go, you may want to start with Part 1. It gives you all the basic info you need to assess your financial and investing situation and points to places where you can find more detailed information for improving it.

1

Getting Started with Investing

Chapter **1**

Making Sense of Your Investing Options

So many subject areas and disciplines are packed full of jargon. Some of this is the result of "progress" and advances, and some of it is caused by workers in the field not going out of their way to explain and define things.

In this chapter, I give you the lay of the land regarding the enormous numbers of investment choices and foreign-sounding terminology that await you in the world of investing. I also explain the types of companies that offer investments and their strengths and weaknesses. And should you want to hire some investing help, I detail the various professionals pitching their services to you and the common credentials they hawk to convince you of their expertise.

Growing Your Money in Ownership Investments

The most exciting thing about investing during your younger adult years is that you can be more aggressive with money that you've earmarked to help you accomplish long-term goals. To achieve typical longer-term financial goals, such as being financially independent (also known as retiring), the money that you save and invest generally needs to grow at a rate much faster than the rate of inflation. If you put your money in a bank account that pays little or no interest, for example, you're more likely to fall short of your goals.

Ownership investments are investments like stocks, where you own a piece of a company, real estate, or a small business that has the capability to generate revenue and profits. Over the long term, consider ownership investments if you want your money to grow much faster than the rate of inflation and don't mind more volatility in your investments' values.

The downside to such investments is that they can fall more significantly in value than *non-ownership investments* (for example, bank accounts, bonds, and so on), especially in the short term. So don't put money into ownership investments that you may need to tap in the short term for rent money or your next vacation. To reduce the risk of ownership investments, *diversify* — that is, hold different types of ownership investments that don't move in tandem.

I highlight three major ownership investments in the following sections: stocks, real estate, and small business.

Sharing in corporate growth and profits: Stocks

If you want the potential to share in the growth and profits of companies, you can gain it through buying shares of their stock. Stocks are shares of ownership in a company. You can buy stock directly in individual companies through a brokerage account, or you can buy a collection of stocks via a mutual fund or exchange-traded fund (see Chapter 10).

If you've followed the financial markets at all over some time or have friends or family who have spoken to you about this, you may have heard of companies/stocks like Amazon, Apple, Chipotle, McDonald's, Microsoft, Netflix, Ross Stores, Tesla, Ulta Beauty, and so on. Those who bought and held stocks like these made big returns over the past decade. Remember, though, that we're saying and seeing this now with the benefit of hindsight — looking in the rearview mirror. And, I'm sure you know that the future will be different than the past, so running out and buying these stocks now is far less likely to make you a mint going forward.

Now, what if I told you I've invested in and made good money in all of these stocks over the past decade? The fact is I have, but I never personally chose any of these particular stocks. I've owned these stocks and numerous other good companies and their stocks through mutual funds I've invested in. Of course, it's impossible for any fund manager to only have a portfolio of the best winners or winners in general. Some of their stock picks will be mediocre and others worse.

REMEMBER

You don't need to be a business genius to make money in stocks. Stocks in the United States, for example, have returned an average of 9 percent per year over the past two-plus centuries. That may not sound like a high return but at that rate of return, your money will double every eight years! Simply make regular and systematic investments, and invest in proven companies and funds while minimizing your investment expenses and taxes. Of course, there's no guarantee that every stock or stock fund that you buy will increase in value. In Chapter 8, I explain proven and time-tested methods for making money in stocks.

Profiting from real estate

You don't need to be a big shot to make money investing in real estate. Owning and managing real estate is like running a small business: You need to satisfy customers (tenants), manage your costs, keep an eye on the competition, and so on. Some methods of real estate investing require more time than others, but many are proven ways to build wealth. Historically, investment real estate has produced annual returns comparable to investing in stocks.

Among the key attributes of private real estate investment are the following:

>> You build wealth through your rental income exceeding your expenses and through property-value appreciation.

>> You can leverage your investment by borrowing money.

>> You must be comfortable dealing with property management, which includes finding and retaining tenants and keeping up (and possibly improving) your property.

This last point is super important. Buying and managing investment real estate is time intensive. Those whom I've seen succeed investing in real estate actually enjoy the challenge and work involved. And, over time, you can hire people to help you with managing properties if you don't want to spend so much time personally at it.

See Chapter 12 for the details on investing in real estate.

Succeeding in small business

I know people who have hit investing home runs by owning or buying businesses. Most people work full-time at running their businesses, increasing their chances of doing something big financially with them. Investing in the stock market, by contrast, tends to be more part-time in nature.

In addition to the financial rewards, however, small-business owners can enjoy seeing the impact of their work and knowing that it makes a difference. I can speak from firsthand experience (as can other small-business owners) in saying that emotionally and financially, entrepreneurship is a roller coaster.

Besides starting your own company, you can share in the economic rewards of the entrepreneurial world through buying an existing business or investing in someone else's budding enterprise. See Chapter 14 for more details.

Making "riskier" choices: Options, cryptocurrencies, and so on

I know from my many interactions with younger adults these days that there are some more exciting and enticing vehicles such as call options and cryptocurrencies. It's easy to get drawn into such things when you hear a story or two about someone hitting it big.

I'm certainly open to you taking sensible risks, and the fact of the matter is that the highest returning investment vehicles I discuss in this book do indeed carry notable risks. But options and cryptocurrencies carry enormous risks and actually far less upside than what many people believe or realize.

Rest assured that at relevant places in this book, I cover these other types of vehicles (especially in Chapter 15), but please know that these are generally vehicles you should stay away from.

Keeping Money in Lending Investments

In the first section of this chapter, "Growing Your Money in Ownership Investments," I outline how you can make your dough grow much faster than the cost of living by using stocks, real estate, and small business. However, you may want or need to play it safer when investing money for shorter-term purposes, so you should then consider lending investments. Many people use such investments through local banks, such as in a checking account, savings account, or certificate of deposit. In all these cases with a bank, you're lending your money to the bank.

Another lending investment is bonds. When you purchase a bond that has been issued by the government or a company, you agree to lend your money for a predetermined period of time and receive a particular rate of interest. A corporate bond may pay you 4 percent interest annually over the next ten years, for example.

An investor's return from lending investments is typically limited to the original investment plus interest payments. If you lend your money to a company through one of its bonds that matures in, say, five years, and the firm doubles its revenue and profits over that period, you won't share in its growth. The company's stockholders are likely to reap the rewards of the company's success, but as a bondholder, you don't. You simply get interest and the face value of the bond back at maturity.

Similar to bank savings accounts, money market mutual funds are another type of lending investment. Money market mutual funds generally invest in ultra-safe things such as short-term bank certificates of deposit, U.S. government–issued Treasury bills, and commercial paper (short-term bonds) that the most creditworthy corporations issue.

WARNING

Many people keep too much of their money in lending investments, thus allowing others to enjoy the rewards of economic growth. Although lending investments appear safer because you know in advance what return you'll receive, they aren't that safe. The long-term risk of these seemingly safe money investments is that your money will grow too slowly (perhaps not even keeping you ahead of or even with the rate of inflation) to enable you to accomplish your personal financial goals. In the worst cases, the company or other institution to which you're lending money can go under and fail to repay your loan.

Understanding Risks and Returns

Who among us wants to lose money? Of course you don't! You put your money into an investment in the hope and expectation that you will get back more in total than you put in. And you'd rather your chosen investments not fluctuate too widely in value. When it comes to investing, no concepts are more important to grasp than *risk* and *return*, which I explain in this section.

Realizing risks

The investments that you expect to produce higher returns (such as stocks) fluctuate more in value, particularly in the short term. However, if you attempt to avoid all the risks involved in investing, you probably won't succeed, and you likely won't be happy with your investment results and lifestyle. In the investment world, some people don't go near stocks or real estate that they perceive to be volatile, for example. As a result, such investors often end up with lousy long-term returns and expose themselves to some high risks that they overlooked, such as the risk of inflation and taxes eroding the purchasing power of their money.

You can't live without taking risks. Risk-free activities or ways of living don't exist. You can sensibly minimize risks, but you can never eliminate them. Some methods of risk reduction aren't palatable because they reduce your quality of life.

Risks are also composed of several factors. Following are the major types of investment risks and a few of the methods you can use to reduce these risks while not missing out on the upside that investments offer:

>> **Market-value risk:** Although stocks can help you build wealth, they can also drop 20 percent or more in a relatively short period of time. Entering 2020, who was thinking about how a pandemic and the government's response might impact stock prices? Then, in a few weeks, stocks slid more than 30 percent due to government-mandated economic shutdowns. Although real estate, like stocks, has been a rewarding long-term investment, various real estate markets get clobbered from time to time.

>> **Individual-investment risk:** A down market can put an entire investment market on a roller-coaster ride, but healthy markets also have their share of individual losers. Just as individual stock prices can plummet, so can individual real estate property prices.

WARNING

With lending investments, you have a claim on a specific amount of a currency. Occasionally, currencies falter. Most folks ignore this low frequency but very high impact risk when thinking about lending investments.

>> **Purchasing-power risk:** *Inflation* — which is an increase in the cost of living — can erode the value of your money and its *purchasing power* (what you can buy with that money). I often see skittish investors keep their money in bonds and money market accounts, thinking that they're playing it safe. The risk in this strategy is that your money won't grow enough over the years for you to accomplish your financial goals. In other words, the lower the return you earn, the more you need to save to reach a financial goal. As a younger investor with so many years and decades of investing in your future, you need to pay the most attention to the risk of generating low returns.

>> **Liquidity risk:** Some investments are more *liquid* (how quickly an investment can be converted to cash) than others and more readily sold at fair market value on short notice. Bank savings accounts have no real liquidity risk. A real estate investment, by contrast, takes time and money to sell, and if you must sell most real estate quickly, you'll likely get a fair amount less than its current full market value.

>> **Career risk:** In your 20s and 30s, your ability to earn money is probably your biggest asset. Education is a lifelong process. If you don't periodically invest in your education, you risk losing your competitive edge. Your skills and perspectives can become dated and obsolete. Although that doesn't mean you should work 80 hours a week and never do anything fun, it does mean that part of your "work" time should involve upgrading your skills.

Managing risks

Throughout this book as I discuss various investments, I explain how to get the most out of each one. Because I've introduced the important issue of risk in this chapter, I would be remiss if I also didn't give you some early ideas about how to minimize those risks. Here are some simple steps you can take to lower the risk of investments that can upset the achievement of your goals:

>> **Do your homework.** When you purchase real estate, various inspections, for example, can save you from buying a money pit. With stocks, you can examine some measures of value and the company's financial condition and business strategy to reduce your chances of buying into an overpriced company or one on the verge of major problems.

>> **Diversify.** Placing significant amounts of your capital in one or a handful of securities is risky, particularly if the stocks are in the same industry or closely related industries. To reduce this risk, purchase stocks in a variety of industries and companies within each industry. Even better is buying diversified mutual funds and exchange-traded funds. Diversifying your investments can involve more than just your stock portfolio. You can also hold some real estate investments to diversify your investment portfolio.

TIP

If you worry about the health of the U.S. economy, the government, and the dollar, you can reduce your overall investment risk by also investing overseas so that you have a globally diversified portfolio of stocks. Most large U.S. companies do business overseas, so when you invest in larger U.S. company stocks, you get some international investment exposure. You can also invest in international company stocks, ideally through funds.

>> **Minimize holdings in costly markets.** Although I don't believe that most investors can time the markets — buy low, sell high — spotting a greatly overpriced market isn't too difficult. You should avoid overpriced investments because when they fall, they usually fall farther and faster than more fairly priced investments. Also, you should be able to find other investments that offer higher potential returns. Throughout this book, I explain some simple yet powerful methods you can use to measure whether a particular investment market is of fair value, of good value, or overpriced.

>> **View market declines in a different light.** Instead of seeing declines and market corrections as horrible things, view them as potential opportunities or "sales." If you pass up the stock and real estate markets simply because of the potential market-value risk, you miss out on a historic, time-tested method of building substantial wealth. Try not to give in to the human emotions that often scare people away from buying something that others seem to be shunning.

Making sense of returns

Each investment has its own mix of associated risks that you take when you part with your investment dollar and, likewise, offers a different potential rate of return. When you make investments, you have the potential to make money in a variety of ways.

To determine how much money you've made or lost on your investment, you calculate the total return. To come up with this figure, you determine how much money you originally invested and then factor in the other components, such as interest, dividends, and appreciation or depreciation.

If you've ever had money in a bank account that pays interest, you know that the bank pays you a small amount of interest in exchange for your allowing the bank to keep your money. The bank then turns around and lends your money to some other person or organization at a much higher rate of interest. The rate of interest is also known as the *yield*. So if a bank tells you that its savings account pays 1.5 percent interest, the bank may also say that the account yields 1.5 percent. Banks usually quote interest rates or yields on an annual basis. Interest that you receive is one component of the return you receive on your investment.

If a bank pays monthly interest, the bank also likely quotes a compounded effective annual yield. After the first month's interest is credited to your account, that interest starts earning interest as well. So the bank may say that the account pays 1.5 percent, which compounds to an effective annual yield of 1.53 percent.

When you lend your money directly to a company — which is what you do when you invest in a bond that a corporation issues — you also receive interest. Bonds, as well as stocks (which are shares of ownership in a company), fluctuate in market value after they're issued.

When you invest in a company's stock, you hope that the stock increases (appreciates) in value. Of course, a stock can also decline, or depreciate, in value. This change in market value is part of your return from a stock or bond investment.

Stocks can also pay dividends, which are the company's way of sharing some of its profits with you as a stockholder and thus are part of your return. Some companies, particularly those that are small or growing rapidly, choose to reinvest all their profits back into the company.

REMEMBER

Unless you held your investments in a tax-sheltered retirement account, you owe taxes on your return. Specifically, the dividends and investment appreciation that you realize upon selling are taxed, although often at relatively low rates. The tax rates on so-called long-term capital gains and stock dividends are currently and historically lower than the tax rates on other income. I discuss the different tax rates that affect your investments and explain how to make tax-wise investment decisions that fit with your overall personal financial situation and goals in Chapter 4.

Where to Invest and Get Advice

Discussing the companies through which you can invest and where to get investing advice may seem out of place to you if you started reading this book from the beginning. But I'm doing this because I strongly believe that you should begin to think about and understand the lay of the land in these important areas so you can make the best choices.

Selecting the firm or firms through which to do your investing is a hugely important decision. So is the decision about from whom to get or pay for investing advice. In this section, I address both of these topics.

Finding the best fund companies and brokers

Insurance companies, banks, investment brokerage firms, mutual funds — the list of companies that stand ready to help you invest your money is nearly endless. Most people stumble into a relationship with an investment firm. They may choose a company because their employer uses it for company retirement plans or they've read about or been referred to a particular company. Maybe one of your parents or another relative recommended or got you started with a particular investment company.

When you invest in certain securities — such as stocks and bonds and exchange-traded funds (ETFs) — and when you want to hold mutual funds from different companies in a single account, you need brokerage services. Brokers execute your trades to buy or sell stocks, bonds, and other securities and enable you to centralize your holdings of mutual funds, ETFs, and other investments. Your broker can also assist you with other services that may interest you.

Deciding which investment company is best for you depends on your needs and wants. In addition to fees, consider how important having a local branch office is to you. If you want to invest in mutual funds, you'll want to choose a firm that offers access to good funds, including money market funds in which you can deposit money awaiting investment or proceeds from a sale.

TIP

For the lowest trading commissions, you generally must place your trades online. But you should be careful. A low brokerage fee of, say, $7 or $10 per trade doesn't really save you money if you trade a lot and rack up significant total commissions. (As you may know, some brokers are offering free online trading for stocks and certain other securities, but of course, they have to make this up elsewhere with fees for other needed services and by paying you little to nothing on your cash balances.) Also you pay more in taxes when you trade more frequently and realize shorter-term (one year or less) profits.

WARNING

Trading online is an easy way to act impulsively and emotionally when making important investment decisions. If you're prone to such actions, or if you find yourself tracking and trading investments too closely, stay away from this form of trading and use the internet only to check account information and gather factual information. Increasing numbers of brokers offer account information and trading capabilities via apps, which, of course, can also promote addictive investment behaviors.

Please see Chapter 9 for more details on selecting the best investment brokerage firms and my top investment firm selections that offer mutual funds and ETFs and/or brokerage services.

Finding an acceptable advisor

I would always counsel folks who took personal finance courses I taught or who contacted me seeking advice to get educated before engaging the services of any financial advisor. How can you possibly evaluate the competence of someone you may hire if you yourself are financially clueless? You've got this book, so read it before you consider hiring someone for financial advice.

By taking the themes and major concepts of this book to heart, you greatly minimize your chances of making significant investment blunders, including hiring an incompetent or unethical advisor. You may be tempted, for example, to retain the services of an advisor who claims that he and his firm can predict the future economic environment and position your portfolio to take advantage. But you find in reading this book that financial advisors don't have crystal balls and that you should steer clear of folks who purport to be able to jump into and out of investments based upon their forecasts.

WARNING

Finding a competent and objective financial advisor isn't easy. Historically, most financial consultants work on commission, and the promise of that commission can cloud their judgment. Among the minority of fee-based advisors, almost all manage money, which creates other conflicts of interest. The more money you give them to invest and manage, the more money these advisors make. That's why I generally prefer seeking financial (and tax) advice from advisors who sell their time (on an hourly basis) and don't sell anything else.

Because investment decisions are a critical part of financial planning, take note of the fact that the most common designations of educational training among professional money managers are MBA (master of business administration) and CFA (chartered financial analyst). Financial planners often have the CFP (certified financial planner) credential, and some tax advisors who work on an hourly basis have the PFS (personal financial specialist) credential.

INVESTIGATE

Advisors who provide investment advice and oversee at least $100 million must register with the U.S. Securities and Exchange Commission (SEC); otherwise, they generally register with the state that they make their principal place of business. They must file Form ADV, otherwise known as the Uniform Application for Investment Adviser Registration. This lengthy document asks investment advisors to provide in a uniform format such details as a breakdown of where their income comes from, their education and employment history, the types of securities the advisory firm recommends, and the advisor's fee schedule.

You can ask the advisor to send you a copy of his Form ADV. You can also find out whether the advisor is registered and whether he has a track record of problems by calling the SEC at 800-732-0330 or by visiting its website at www.adviserinfo.sec.gov. Many states require the registration of financial advisors, so you should also contact the department that oversees advisors in your state. Visit the North American Securities Administrators Association's website (www.nasaa.org), and click the Contact Your Regulator link on the home page.

Chapter **2**

Using Investments to Accomplish Your Goals

S aving and investing money can make you feel good and in control. Ultimately, most folks are investing money to accomplish particular goals. Saving and investing for a car purchase, expenses for higher education, a home purchase, new furniture, or a vacation are typical short-term goals. You can also invest toward longer-term goals, such as your financial independence or retirement decades in the future.

In this chapter, I discuss how you can use investments to accomplish common shorter- and longer-term goals.

Setting and Prioritizing Your Shorter-Term Goals

Unless you earn really big bucks or expect to have a large family inheritance to tap, your personal and financial desires will probably outstrip your resources. Thus, you must prioritize your goals.

One of the biggest mistakes I see people make is rushing into a financial decision without considering what's really important to them. Because many people get caught up in the responsibilities of their daily lives, they often don't take time for reflection often because they feel that they lack the time. Take that time, because people who identify their goals and then work toward them, which often requires changing some habits, are far more likely to accomplish something significant.

In this section, I discuss common "shorter-term" financial goals — such as establishing an emergency reserve, making major purchases, owning a home, and starting a small business — and how to work toward them. Accomplishing such goals almost always requires saving money.

Accumulating a rainy-day fund

The future is unpredictable. Take the uncertainty simply surrounding your job: You could lose your job, or you may want to leave it.

Consider what happened in 2020 with the COVID-19 pandemic and the unexpected and lengthy government-mandated shutdowns in some parts of the country, which led to large layoffs in particular industries like restaurants, retail, and travel-related businesses. While the 2020 recession was unusual in many respects, recessions aren't unusual and even when the overall economy is growing, some employers let employees go. Suppose an elderly relative, for example, needs some assistance for a period of time? Look, I'm not trying to be a pessimist or negative, but problems happen, and sometimes there are financially downsides that can come with them.

Because you don't know what the future holds, preparing for the unexpected is financially wise. Enter the emergency or rainy-day fund.

The size of your emergency fund depends on your personal situation. Begin by considering how much you spend in a typical month. Here are some benchmarks for how many months' worth of living expenses you should have:

>> **Three months' living expenses:** When you're starting out, this minimalist approach makes sense if your only current source of emergency funds is a high-interest credit card. Longer-term, you could make do with three months' living expenses if you have other accounts, such as a 401(k), or family members and close friends whom you can tap for a short-term loan.

>> **Six months' living expenses:** If you don't have other places to turn for a loan, or if you have some instability in your employment situation or source of income, you need more of a cushion.

> **>> Twelve months' living expenses:** Consider this large a stash if your income fluctuates greatly or if your occupation involves a high risk of job loss, finding another job could take you a long time, or you don't have other places to turn for a loan.

Saving for large purchases

Most people want things — such as furniture, a vacation, or a car — that they don't have cash on hand to pay for. I strongly advise saving for your larger consumer purchases to avoid paying for them over time with high-interest consumer credit. Don't take out credit card or auto loans — otherwise known as *consumer credit* — to make large purchases.

And, don't be duped by a seemingly low interest rate on, for example, a car loan. You could get the car at a lower price if you don't opt for such a loan.

TIP

Paying for high-interest consumer debt can undermine your ability to save toward your goals and your ability to make major purchases in the future. Don't deny yourself gratification if it's something you really need and want and can afford given your overall financial situation; just figure out how to delay it. When contemplating the purchase of a consumer item on credit, add up the total interest you'd end up paying on your debt, and call it the price of instant gratification.

Investing for a small business or home

In your early years of saving and investing, deciding whether to save money to buy a home or to put money into a retirement account (for the tax benefits and to work toward the goal of future financial independence) presents a dilemma. In the long run, owning your own home is usually a wise financial move. On the other hand, saving sooner for retirement makes achieving your goals easier and reduces your income tax bill.

Presuming that both goals are important to you, you can save toward both goals: buying a home and retiring. If you're eager to own a home, you can throw all your savings toward achieving that goal and temporarily put your retirement savings on hold.

TIP

You can make penalty-free withdrawals of up to $10,000 from Individual Retirement Accounts (IRAs) toward a first-time home purchase. You may also be able to have the best of both worlds if you work for an employer that allows borrowing against retirement account balances. You can save money in the retirement account and then borrow against it for the down payment on a home. Consider this option with great care, though, because retirement account loans generally must be repaid within a few years or when you quit or lose your job (ask your employer for the details).

When saving money for starting or buying a business, most people encounter the same dilemma they face when deciding to save to buy a house: If you fund your retirement accounts to the exclusion of earmarking money for your small-business dreams, your entrepreneurial aspirations may never become reality. Generally, I advocate hedging your bets by saving money in your tax-sheltered retirement accounts as well as toward your business venture. An investment in your own small business can produce great rewards, so you may feel comfortable focusing your savings on your own business.

Saving for kids' higher educational costs

Do you have little ones or plan to have them in your future? You probably know that rearing a child (or two or more) costs really big bucks. But the biggest potential expense awaits when they reach young adulthood and consider heading off to college, so your instincts may be to try to save money to accomplish and afford that goal.

WARNING

The college financial-aid system effectively penalizes you for saving money outside tax-sheltered retirement accounts and penalizes you even more if the money is invested in the child's name. Wanting to provide for your children's future is perfectly natural, but doing so before you've saved adequately toward your own goals can be a major financial mistake.

This concept may sound selfish, but the reality is that you need to take care of *your* future first. Take advantage of saving through your tax-sheltered retirement accounts before you set aside money in custodial savings accounts for your kids.

TIP

There are numerous higher education options besides costly four-year colleges and universities. I'm a big fan of alternatives to the traditional college path, which isn't right for everyone. Consider alternatives to traditional college (and whether they are right for your child). While college is a traditional path that many high school seniors follow, there are increasing numbers of attractive, low-cost, and faster alternatives to consider. For example:

>> **Last-mile boot camps:** Last-mile programs teach students technical skills and clear the pathways to jobs in growing industries like technology, biotech, fintech, and healthcare.

>> **College minimum viable products (MVPs):** These programs combine the technical skill training and placement of traditional last-mile programs with significant cognitive and noncognitive skill development that students get from a good college.

>> **Apprenticeships:** Emerging apprenticeships provide pathways for jobs in the manufacturing, healthcare, pharmacy, IT, insurance, financial services, and software development industries.

>> **Staffing firms:** These companies hire workers and staff them out to clients. For example, Revature, an IT staffing company, hires experienced software developers. Also, Avenica places students from many colleges and offers last-mile training across many industries.

>> **Vocational and trade schools:** Also known as career and technical education (CTE), these schools provide gateways to a wide range of jobs in the automotive industry, culinary arts, emergency services, healthcare, and more.

Investing short-term money

So where should you invest money earmarked for a shorter-term goal? A money market account or short-term bond fund is a good place to store your short-term savings. See Chapters 7 and 9 for more information on these options. The best bank or credit union accounts (covered in Chapter 6) may be worth considering as well.

Investing in Retirement Accounts

During your younger adult years, you may not be thinking much about retirement because it seems to be well off in the distance. But if you'd like to scale back on your work schedule someday, partly or completely, you're best off saving toward that goal as soon as you start drawing a regular paycheck.

TIP

Maybe the problem with thinking about this goal stems in part with the term *retirement.* Perhaps thinking about it in terms of saving and investing to achieve *financial independence* is better.

In this section, I explain the benefits and possible concerns of investing through so-called retirement accounts. I also lay out the retirement account options you may access.

Understanding retirement account perks

Where possible, try to save and invest in accounts that offer you a tax advantage, which is precisely what retirement accounts offer you. These accounts — known by such enlightening acronyms and names as 401(k), 403(b), SEP-IRA, and so on — offer tax breaks to people of all economic means. Consider the following advantages to investing in retirement accounts:

>> **Contributions often provide upfront tax breaks.** By investing through a retirement account, you not only plan wisely for your future but also get an immediate financial reward: lower taxes, which mean more money available for saving and investing. Retirement account contributions generally aren't taxed at either the federal or state income tax level until withdrawal (but they're still subject to Social Security and Medicare taxes when earned). If you're paying, say, 30 percent between federal and state taxes (see Chapter 4 to determine your tax bracket), a $4,000 contribution to a retirement account lowers your income taxes by $1,200.

Modest income earners also may get an additional government tax credit known as the Retirement Savings Contributions Credit. A maximum credit of 50 percent applies to the first $2,000 contributed for single taxpayers with an adjusted gross income (AGI) of no more than $19,750 and married couples filing jointly with an AGI of $39,500 or less. Singles with an AGI of between $19,750 and $21,500 and married couples with an AGI between $39,500 and $43,000 are eligible for a 20 percent tax credit. Single taxpayers with an AGI of more than $21,500 but no more than $33,000, as well as married couples with an AGI between $43,000 and $66,000, can get a 10 percent tax credit.

>> **Your employer may match some of your contributions.** This cash is free money from your employer, and it's use it or lose it, so don't miss out!

>> **Investment returns compound tax-free.** After you put money into a retirement account, you get to defer taxes on all the accumulating gains and profits (including interest and dividends) until you withdraw the money down the road. Thus, more money is working for you over a longer period of time. (One exception: Roth IRAs offer no upfront tax breaks but permit tax-free withdrawal of investment earnings in retirement.)

Grappling with retirement account concerns

There are legitimate concerns about putting money into a retirement account. First and foremost is the fact that once you place such money inside a retirement account, you can't generally access it before age 59½ without paying current income taxes and a penalty — 10 percent of the withdrawn amount in federal tax, plus whatever your state charges.

This poses some potential problems. First, money placed inside retirement accounts is typically not available for other uses, such as buying a car or starting a small business. Second, if an emergency arises and you need to tap the money, you'll get hit with paying current income taxes and penalties on amounts withdrawn.

TIP

You can use the following ways to avoid the early-withdrawal penalties that the tax authorities normally apply:

>> You can make penalty-free withdrawals of up to $10,000 from IRAs for a first-time home purchase or higher educational expenses for you, your spouse, or your children (and even grandchildren).

>> Some company retirement plans allow you to borrow against your balance. You're essentially loaning money to yourself, with the interest payments going back into your account.

>> If you have major medical expenses (exceeding 10 percent of your income) or a disability, you may be exempt from the penalties under certain conditions. (You will still owe ordinary income tax on withdrawals.)

>> You may withdraw money before age 59½ if you do so in equal, annual installments based on your life expectancy. You generally must make such distributions for at least five years or until age 59½, whichever is later.

REMEMBER

If you lose your job and withdraw retirement account money simply because you need it to live on, the penalties do apply. If you're not working, however, and you're earning so little income that you need to access your retirement account, you would likely be in a relatively low tax bracket. The lower income taxes you pay (compared with the taxes you would have paid on that money had you not sheltered it in a retirement account in the first place) should make up for most, if not all, of the penalty.

But what about simply wanting to save money for nearer-term goals and to be able to tap that money? If you're saving and investing money for a down payment on a home or to start a business, for example, you'll probably need to save that money outside a retirement account to avoid those early-withdrawal penalties.

If you're like most young adults and have limited financial resources, you need to prioritize your goals. Before funding retirement accounts and gaining those tax breaks, be sure to contemplate and prioritize your other goals (see the section "Setting and Prioritizing Your Shorter-Term Goals" earlier in this chapter).

Taking advantage of retirement accounts

REMEMBER

To take advantage of retirement savings plans and the tax savings that accompany them, you must spend less than you earn. Only then can you afford to contribute to these retirement savings plans, unless you already happen to have a stash of cash from previous savings or an inheritance.

The common mistake that many younger adults make is neglecting to take advantage of retirement accounts because of their enthusiasm for spending or investing in nonretirement accounts. Not investing in tax-sheltered retirement accounts can cost you hundreds, perhaps thousands, of dollars per year in lost tax savings. Add that loss up over the many years that you work and save, and not taking advantage of these tax reduction accounts can easily cost you tens of thousands to hundreds of thousands of dollars in the long term.

The sooner you start to save, the less painful it is each year to save enough to reach your goals, because your contributions have more years to compound. Each decade you delay saving approximately doubles the percentage of your earnings that you need to save to meet your goals. If saving 5 percent per year in your early 20s gets you to your retirement goal, waiting until your 30s to start may mean socking away approximately 10 percent to reach that same goal; waiting until your 40s means saving 20 percent. Start saving and investing now!

Surveying retirement account choices

If you earn employment income (or receive alimony), you have options for putting money away in a retirement account that compounds without taxation until you withdraw the money. In most cases, your contributions to these retirement accounts are tax-deductible. This section reviews your options.

Company-based retirement plans

Larger for-profit companies generally offer their employees a *401(k)* plan, which typically allows saving up to $19,500 per year (for tax year 2021). Many nonprofit organizations offer their employees similar plans, known as *403(b)* plans. Contributions to both traditional 401(k) and 403(b) plans are deductible on both your federal and state taxes in the year that you make them. Employees of nonprofit organizations can generally contribute up to 20 percent or $19,500 of their salaries, whichever is less.

There's a benefit in addition to the upfront and ongoing tax benefits of these retirement savings plans: Some employers match your contributions. (If you're an employee in a small business, you can establish your own SEP-IRA.) Of course, the challenge for many people is to reduce their spending enough to be able to sock away these kinds of contributions.

Some employers are offering a Roth 401(k) account, which, like a Roth IRA (discussed in the next section), offers employees the ability to contribute on an after-tax basis. Withdrawals from such accounts generally aren't taxed in retirement.

FIGURING HOW MUCH TO SAVE FOR RETIREMENT

Numerous mass market website tools exist and focus on retirement planning. Many investment firms offer these to lure you to their websites. Some require you to register whereas others can be accessed as a "guest." Such tools walk you through the calculations needed to figure how much you should be saving to reach your retirement goal.

The assumptions that you plug into these calculators are really important, so here's a review of the key ones:

- **Asset allocation:** Enter your current *allocation* (the portion invested in stocks versus bonds) and you'll also typically select an allocation for after you're retired. Most such calculators don't include real estate as a possible asset. If you own real estate as an investment, you should treat those assets as a stock-like investment, since they have similar long-term risk and return characteristics. (Calculate your equity in investment real estate, which is the difference between a property's current market value and mortgage debt on that property.)

- **Age of retirement:** Plug in your preferred age of retirement, within reason, of course. There's no point plugging in a dream number like "I'd like to retire by age 45, but I know the only way I can do that is to win the lottery!" Depending on how the analysis works out, you can always go back and plug in a different age. Sometimes folks are pleasantly surprised that their combined accumulated resources provide them with a decent enough standard of living that they can consider retiring sooner than they thought.

- **Include Social Security:** Some calculators ask whether you want to include expected Social Security benefits. I'd rather that they didn't pose this question at all, because you definitely should include your Social Security benefits in the calculations. Don't buy into the nonsense that the Social Security program will vaporize and you'll get little to nothing from it. For the vast majority of people, Social Security benefits are an important component of their retirement income, so do include it. Based on your current income, the calculator will automatically plug in your estimated benefits. So long as your income hasn't changed or won't change dramatically, using the calculator's estimated number should be fine. Alternatively, you can use your personal information that you can access on the Social Security website at www.ssa.gov.

Many calculators allow you to make adjustments such as to your desired age of retirement, rate of savings, and to what age you'd like your savings to last. So, for example, if the analysis shows that you have much more than enough to retire by age 65, try plugging in, say, age 62 and voilà, the calculator quickly shows you how the numbers change.

If you're self-employed, you can establish your own retirement savings plans for yourself and any employees you have. *Simplified Employee Pension-Individual Retirement Accounts* (SEP-IRA) allow you to put away up to 20 percent of your self-employment income up to an annual maximum of $58,000 (for tax year 2021).

Individual Retirement Accounts

If you work for a company that doesn't offer a retirement savings plan, or if you've exhausted contributions to your company's plan, consider an *Individual Retirement Account* (IRA). Anyone who earns employment income or receives alimony may contribute up to $6,000 annually to an IRA (or the amount of your employment income or alimony income, if it's less than $6,000 in a year). A nonworking spouse may contribute up to $6,000 annually to a spousal IRA.

Your contributions to an IRA may or may not be tax-deductible. For tax year 2021, if you're single and your adjusted gross income is $66,000 or less for the year, you can deduct your full IRA contribution. If you're married and you file your taxes jointly, you're entitled to a full IRA deduction if your AGI is $105,000 per year or less.

TIP

If you can't deduct your contribution to a standard IRA account, consider making a contribution to a nondeductible IRA account called the *Roth IRA.* Single taxpayers with an AGI less than $125,000 and joint filers with an AGI less than $198,000 can contribute up to $6,000 per year to a Roth IRA. Although the contribution isn't deductible, earnings inside the account are shielded from taxes, and unlike withdrawals from a standard IRA, qualified withdrawals from a Roth IRA account are free from income tax.

TIP

Should you be earning a high enough income that you can't fund a Roth IRA, there's an indirect "backdoor" way to fund a Roth IRA. First, you contribute to a regular IRA as a nondeductible contribution. Then, you can convert your regular IRA contribution into a Roth IRA. Please note that this so-called backdoor method generally only makes sense if you don't have other money already invested in a regular IRA because in that case, you can't simply withdraw your most recent contribution and not owe any tax.

Annuities: Maxing out your retirement savings

What if you have so much cash sitting around that after maxing out your contributions to retirement accounts, including your IRA, you still want to sock more away into a tax-advantaged account? Enter the annuity. *Annuities* are contracts that insurance companies back. If you, the investor (annuity holder), should die during the so-called accumulation phase (that is, before receiving payments from the annuity), your designated beneficiary is guaranteed reimbursement of the amount of your original investment.

Annuities, like IRAs, allow your capital to grow and compound tax-deferred. You defer taxes until you withdraw the money. Unlike an IRA, which has an annual contribution limit of a few thousand dollars, an annuity allows you to deposit as much as you want in any year — even millions of dollars, if you've got millions! As with a Roth IRA, however, you get no upfront tax deduction for your contributions.

WARNING

Because annuity contributions aren't tax-deductible, and because annuities carry higher annual operating fees to pay for the small amount of insurance that comes with them, don't consider contributing to one until you've fully exhausted your other retirement account investing options. Because of their higher annual expenses, annuities generally make sense only if you won't need the money for 15 or more years.

Selecting retirement account investments

When you establish a retirement account, you may not realize that the retirement account is simply a shell or shield that keeps the federal, state, and local governments from taxing your investment earnings each year. You choose what investments you want to hold inside your retirement account shell.

You may invest the money in your IRA or self-employed plan retirement account (SEP-IRAs and so on) in stocks, bonds, mutual funds, and some other common investments, including bank accounts. Mutual funds (offered in most employer-based plans) and exchange-traded funds (ETFs) are ideal choices because they offer diversification and professional management. See Chapter 10 for more on mutual funds and ETFs.

Assessing Your Risk-Taking Desires

With money that you're investing for shorter-term goals, you have a more limited menu of investments to choose among. For your emergency/rainy-day fund, for example, you should consider only a money market fund or bank/credit union savings account. Down-payment money for a home purchase that you expect to make in a few years should be kept in short-term bonds.

When you're younger and have more years until you plan to use your money, you should keep larger amounts of your long-term investment money in growth (ownership) investments, such as stocks, real estate, and small business. The attraction of these types of investments is their potential to really grow your money, but the risk is that the value of such investments can fall significantly.

The younger you are, the more time your investments have to recover from a bad fall. A long-held guiding principle says to subtract your age from 110 and invest the resulting number as a percentage of money to place in growth (ownership) investments. So if you're 30 years old, 110 – 30 = 80 percent in growth investments

Should you want to be more conservative, subtract your age from 100: 100 – 30 = 70 percent in growth investments.

Want to be even more aggressive? Subtract your age from 120: 120 – 30 = 90 percent in growth investments.

REMEMBER

These guidelines are general ones that apply to money that you invest for the long term (ideally, for ten years or more). In your younger adult years, you can consider investing all of your money in retirement accounts in stocks and stock funds given the long time frame you have with such accounts.

Chapter **3**

Setting Your Return Expectations

We invest to earn returns. In my experience as a former financial advisor and as a writer interacting with many folks, I still find it noteworthy how many people have unrealistic and inaccurate return expectations for particular investments.

Where do these silly numbers come from? There are numerous sources, most of which have a vested interest in convincing you that you can earn really high returns if you simply buy what they're selling. Examples include newsletter publishers and writers, some financial advisors, and various financial publishing outlets.

Interestingly, and not surprisingly, less experienced groups of investors (for example, young investors just beginning to invest) tend to have higher and more unrealistic return expectations. In this chapter, I reveal and discuss the actual returns you can reasonably expect from common investments. I also illustrate the power of compounding those returns over the years and decades ahead, and I show you why you won't need superhuman returns to accomplish your personal and financial goals.

Estimating Your Investments' Returns

When examining expected investment returns, you have to be careful because you're largely using historic returns as a guide. Using history to predict the future, especially the near future, is dangerous. History may repeat itself, but not always in exactly the same fashion and not necessarily when you expect it to.

REMEMBER

Historical returns should be used only as a guide, not viewed as a guarantee. Please keep that in mind as I discuss the returns on money market funds and savings accounts, bonds, stocks, real estate, and small-business investments in this section.

Money market funds and savings account returns

Be sure to keep your extra cash that awaits investment (or an emergency) in a safe place, preferably one that doesn't get hammered by the sea of changes in the financial markets. By default, and for convenience, many people keep their extra cash in a bank savings account, which tends to pay relatively low rates of interest. Banks accounts come with Federal Deposit Insurance Corporation (FDIC) backing, which costs the bank some money.

Another place to keep your liquid savings is a money market mutual fund. These funds are the safest types of mutual funds around and, for all intents and purposes, comparable to a bank savings account's safety. Technically, money market mutual funds don't carry FDIC insurance. To date, however, only one money market fund has lost money for retail shareholders (and in that case, it amounted to less than 1 percent). Bank account depositors have lost money, by the way, when they had more than the insured amount (currently $250,000) in a bank that failed. When a bank fails, it's typically merged into a financially healthy bank and those who had more than the insured limit at the failed bank generally take a haircut.

TIP

The best money market funds generally pay higher yields than most bank savings accounts (although this has been less true in recent years, with low overall interest rates). When shopping for a money fund, be sure to pay close attention to the fund's expense ratio, because lower expenses generally translate into higher yields. If you're in a higher income tax bracket, you should also consider tax-free money market funds. (See Chapter 7 for all the details on money market funds.)

If you don't need immediate access to your money, consider using Treasury bills (T-bills) or bank certificates of deposit (CDs), which are usually issued by banks for terms such as 3, 6, or 12 months. The drawback to T-bills and bank certificates of deposit is that you generally incur a transaction fee (with T-bills) or a penalty (with CDs) if you withdraw your investment before the T-bill matures or the CD's term expires. If you can let your money sit for the full term, you can generally earn more in CDs and T-bills than in a bank savings account. Rates vary by bank, however, so be sure to shop around.

Bond returns

When you purchase a bond, you should earn a higher yield than you can with a money market or savings account. You're taking more risk because some bond issuers (such as corporations) aren't always able to fully pay back all that they borrow.

By investing in a bond (at least when it's originally issued), you're effectively lending your money to the issuer of that bond (borrower), which is generally the federal government or a corporation, for a specific period of time. Companies can and do go bankrupt, in which case you may lose some or all of your investment. Government debt can go into default as well. You should get paid in the form of a higher yield for taking on more risk when you buy bonds that have a lower credit rating. (See Chapter 9 for more information on bonds, including how to invest in a diversified portfolio of relatively safe bonds.)

Jeremy Siegel, who is a professor of finance at the Wharton School at the University of Pennsylvania, has tracked the performance of bonds (and stocks) for more than two centuries! His research has found that bond investors generally earn about 4 to 5 percent per year on average, which works out to about 2 to 3 percent per year above the rate of inflation.

REMEMBER

Returns, of course, fluctuate from year to year and are influenced by *inflation* (increases in the cost of living). Generally speaking, increases in the rate of inflation, especially when those increases weren't expected, erode bond returns.

Consider a government bond that was issued at an interest rate of 4 percent when inflation was running at just 2 percent. Thus, an investor in that bond was able to enjoy a 2 percent return after inflation, or what's known as the *real return* — *real* meaning after inflation is subtracted. Now, if inflation jumps to, say, 6 percent per year, why would folks want to buy your crummy 4 percent bond? They wouldn't unless the price drops enough to raise the effective yield higher.

Longer-term bonds generally yield more than shorter-term bonds because they're considered to be riskier due to the longer period until they pay back their principal. What are the risks of holding a bond for more years? There's more time for the credit quality of the bond to deteriorate (and for the bond to default), and there's also more time for inflation to come back and erode the purchasing power of the bond.

Stock returns

The long-term returns from stocks that investors have enjoyed, and continue to enjoy, have been remarkably constant from one generation to the next. Since 1802, the U.S. stock market has returned an annual average of about 9+ percent per year, or in other words about 6 to 7 percent per year above the rate of inflation. That's a remarkable track record, but don't forget that it's an annual *average* return.

Now some people think that a 9 percent annual average return doesn't sound like much. But at that rate of return, an investment will double in value every eight years.

Stocks have significant downdrafts and can easily drop 10, 20, or 30 or more percent in relatively short periods of time. Stocks can also rise dramatically in value over short periods. The keys to making money in stocks are to be diversified, to invest consistently, and to own stocks over the long run.

Stocks exist worldwide, of course, not just in the United States. When investing in stocks, go global for diversification purposes. Diversified portfolios of international stocks have produced annual returns comparable to those generated by U.S. stocks.

International (non-U.S.) stocks don't always move in tandem with U.S. stocks. As a result, overseas stocks help diversify your portfolio. Thus, in addition to enabling U.S. investors to diversify, investing overseas has proven to be profitable over the years and decades.

WARNING

Now, some folks make stock investing riskier than need be by doing some foolish things:

>> **Chasing after specific stocks or sectors that have recently been hot:** Yes, what a rich genius you'd have been if you'd invested in Apple stock (or Chipotle, Google, McDonald's, Amazon, Ulta Beauty, or Facebook) when it went public. With the benefit of hindsight, it's easy to spot the "best" stock investments (companies or sectors) over specific periods. It's quite another thing to put your money on the line now and to hope and expect that you have the ability to pick the best-performing stocks of the future.

>> **Excessive trading and market timing:** Another type of wishful thinking occurs when folks would like to believe that they can jump into and out of the market at the right times to participate in moves higher and to sidestep downturns.

IS HIGHER ECONOMIC GROWTH BETTER FOR STOCK PRICES?

Stocks for the Long Run (McGraw-Hill) author Jeremy Siegel makes a surprising statement in his book: ". . . economic growth has nowhere near as big an impact on stock returns as most investors believe." Siegel presents a long-term analysis going back to 1900, which shows that a country's real GDP growth (that is, growth above the rate of inflation) is negatively correlated with stock market returns.

This surprising finding means that those economies experiencing higher rates of growth actually tend to produce lower long-term stock market returns. Siegel's analysis shows that this fact is even more pronounced in developing countries. China is a recent example of a country that has enjoyed high rates of growth but relatively low stock market returns.

In explaining how this reality could possibly be, Siegel points out that the primary determinants of stock prices are earnings per share and dividends per share. Economic growth doesn't necessarily boost earnings and dividends per share because growth requires higher capital expenditures, and as Siegel points out, this capital does not come freely. "The added interest costs in the case of debt financing and the dilution of earnings in the case of equity financing reduce the growth of earnings per share," says Siegel.

Chapter 8 goes into detail on stocks, explaining how to invest in them successfully and not lose your shirt.

Real estate returns

Just before, during, and for some time after the financial crisis of 2008 and associated severe recession, most types of real estate in most parts of the country declined in value. Thus, you may think that real estate isn't a good investment, but you'd be incorrect.

Real estate is a solid long-term investment. Real estate, as an investment, has produced returns comparable to those of investing in the stock market. Both stocks and real estate have down periods but have historically produced attractive long-term returns. Overall, real estate prices in most parts of the United States now have bounced back to record high levels.

Real estate does well in the long run because of growth in the economy, in jobs, and in population. Real estate prices in and near major metropolises and suburbs generally appreciate the most because people and businesses tend to cluster in those areas.

WARNING

I'd like to make an important caution here about viewing a home in which you live solely as an investment. As I discuss in Chapter 12, your primary reason to buy and own a home should not be high expected investment returns, because you won't be earning rental income if you live in your own home. That's why you should thoroughly understand the effect that owning a home will have on your monthly spending and budget. (Investment real estate examples include a small apartment building and retail or office space.)

Small-business returns

When we think of the "American dream," one image that comes to the minds of many folks is owning their own business and possibly making it big by doing so.

You have numerous choices for tapping into the rewards of the small-business world. If you have the drive and determination, you can start your own small business. Or perhaps you have what it takes to buy an existing small business. If you obtain the necessary capital and skills to assess opportunities and risk, you can invest in someone else's small business. None of these avenues is easy. In fact, all these routes require drive, determination, and some skills and money (more on this in Chapter 14).

By starting a small business and retaining a major ownership stake, you can potentially earn high effective returns. Unlike with the stock market, for which plenty of historic rate-of-return data exists, no specific data exists on the returns that small-time investors have had from investing in small private companies. (We do know that successful venture capital firms, which invest in small businesses with large potential, earn generous returns for the general partners.)

While the financial rewards can be attractive, there are other rewards from investing in small businesses. In my small-business ventures, for example, I've enjoyed designing and running businesses that provide useful and valued services. I also enjoy having flexible work hours and not feeling like I'm punching a time clock to satisfy a boss.

Compounding Your Returns

If you've read this chapter up to this point, you see that I've discussed the historic investment returns on common investments. To summarize: During the past century, stocks and investment real estate returned around 9 percent per year, bonds around 5 percent, and savings accounts about 3 percent.

In case you're curious about some alternative investments like gold and currencies, here are those numbers. Gold has just kept investors up with inflation with a tiny bit to spare — returning an average of about 0.5 percent per year after inflation. Currencies like the U.S. dollar have depreciated about 1.5 percent per year adjusting for inflation. (There's no reason to think that cryptocurrencies as a group will fair any better over time. See Chapter 15 for more information.)

This section illustrates how compounding seemingly modest investment returns can help you accumulate a substantial sum of money to help you accomplish your personal and financial goals.

The value of getting a few extra percent

As I discuss in Chapter 1, investing in the stock market (and real estate) can be risky, which logically raises the question of whether investing in stocks and real estate is worth the anxiety and potential losses. Why bother for a few extra percent per year?

Here's a good answer to that sensible question: Over many years, a few extra percent per year will increase your nest egg dramatically. The more years you have to invest, the greater the difference a few percent makes in your returns (see Table 3-1).

TABLE 3-1 **How Compounding Grows Your Investment Dollars**

For Every $1,000 Invested at This Return	In 25 Years	In 40 Years
1%	$1,282	$1,489
2%	$1,641	$2,208
3%	$2,094	$3,262
4%	$2,666	$4,801
5%	$3,386	$7,040
6%	$4,292	$10,286
7%	$5,427	$14,974
8%	$6,848	$21,725
9%	$8,623	$31,409

These numbers are simply amazing! Start first with the 25-year column in Table 3-1. For every $1,000 invested over 25 years, you'll have $1,282 at a 1 percent annual return. At a 9 percent return, you'll have $8,623, or nearly seven times as much!

Now look at what happens over 40 years. At a 9 percent investment return, you'll have more than 21 times as much money versus what you'd have with a 1 percent annual investment return.

Here's a practical example to show you what a dramatic difference earning a few extra percent can make in accomplishing your financial goals. Consider a 30-year-old investor who's saving toward financial independence/retirement on his $60,000 annual salary. Suppose that his goal is to retire by age 67 with about $45,000 per year to live on (in today's dollars), which would be about 75 percent of his working salary.

If he begins saving at age 30, he needs to save about $690 per month if you assume that he earns about 5 percent per year average return on his investments. That's a big chunk to save each year (about $8,300) — amounting to about 14 percent of his gross (pretax) salary.

But what if this investor can earn just a few percent more per year on average from his investments — 8 percent instead of just 5 percent? In that case, he could accomplish the same goal by saving just half as much: $345 per month (or $4,150 per year)!

Considering your goals

How much do you need or want to earn on your investments?

You have to balance your goals with how you feel about risk. Some people can't handle higher-risk investments. Although investing in stocks, real estate, or small business can produce high long-term returns, investing in these vehicles comes with greater risk, especially over the short term.

Others are at a time in their lives when they can't afford to take great risk. If you're still in school, if you've lost your job, or if you're starting a family, your portfolio and nerves may not be able to wait a decade for your riskier investments to recover after a major stumble.

If you work for a living, odds are that you need and want to make your investments grow at a healthy clip. Should your investments grow slowly, you may fall short of your goals of owning a home or retiring or changing careers.

INVESTIGATE

All this is to say that you should take the time to contemplate and prioritize your personal and financial goals. If you haven't already sorted them out, see Chapter 2 to get started.

Chapter **4**

Minimizing Your Taxes When Investing

You should pay attention to tax issues when making investing decisions. Actually, let me rephrase that. Like plenty of other folks, you could ignore or pay half attention to taxes on your investments. Unless you enjoy paying more taxes, however, you should understand and consider tax ramifications when choosing and managing your investments over the years.

Tax considerations alone shouldn't dictate how and where you invest your money. You should also weigh investment choices, your desire and the necessity to take risk, personal likes and dislikes, and the number of years you plan to hold the investment.

In this chapter, I explain how the different components of investment returns are taxed. I also present proven, up-to-date strategies to minimize your investment taxes and maximize your returns. Finally, I discuss tax considerations when selling an investment.

Understanding Investment Taxes

When you invest outside tax-sheltered retirement accounts, the profits and distributions on your money are subject to taxation. (Distributions are taxed in the year that they are paid out; appreciation is taxed only when you sell an investment at a profit.) So the nonretirement-account investments that make sense for you depend (at least partly) on your tax situation.

Tracking taxation of investment distributions

The distributions that various investments pay out and the profits that you may make are often taxable, but in some cases, they're not. It's important to remember that it's not what you make before taxes (pretax) on an investment that matters, but what you get to keep after taxes.

REMEMBER

Interest you receive from bank accounts and corporate bonds is generally taxable. U.S. Treasury bonds, which are issued by the U.S. federal government, pay interest that's state-tax-free but federally taxable.

Municipal bonds, which state and local governments issue, pay interest that's federally tax-free and also state-tax-free to residents in the state where the bond is issued. (For more on bonds, see Chapter 9.)

Taxation on your *capital gains*, which is the profit (sales price minus purchase price) on an investment, is computed under a unique federal taxation system. Investments held and then sold in less than one year at a profit generate what is called short-term capital gains, which are taxed at your normal marginal income tax rate (which I explain in the next section).

Profits from investments that you hold longer than 12 months and then sell at a profit generate what are called long-term capital gains. Under current tax law, these long-term gains are taxed at a maximum 20 percent rate, except for most folks in the two lowest income tax brackets: 10 percent and 12 percent. For these folks, the long-term capital gains tax rate is 0 percent (as in nothing). Dividends paid out on stock are also taxed at the same favorable long-term capital gains tax rates under current tax law.

The Patient Protection and Affordable Care Act (informally referred to as Obamacare) increased the tax rate on the net investment income for taxpayers with adjusted gross income above $200,000 (single return) or $250,000 (joint return). Net investment income includes interest, dividends, and capital gains. The increased tax rate is 3.8 percent.

Determining your tax bracket

Many folks don't realize it, but the federal government (like most state governments) charges you different income tax rates for different parts of your annual income. You effectively pay less tax on the first dollars of your earnings and more tax on the last dollars of your earnings. As a wage earner receiving a paycheck, you won't actually notice or see your actual tax rate rising during the year. The reason: Taxes are withheld at a constant rate from your paycheck based upon estimating your expected income for the year and your total expected tax bill for the year.

Your *federal marginal income tax rate* is the rate of tax that you pay on your last, or so-called highest, dollars of income (see Table 4-1). Your taxable income is the income that is left after taking allowed deductions on your return.

TABLE 4-1   **2021 Federal Income Tax Rates for Single and Married Households Filing Jointly**

Federal Income Tax Rate	Singles Taxable Income	Married Filing Jointly Taxable Income
10%	Up to $9,950	Up to $19,900
12%	$9,951 to $40,525	$19,901 to $81,050
22%	$40,526 to $86,375	$81,051 to $172,750
24%	$86,376 to $164,925	$172,751 to $329,850
32%	$164,926 to $209,425	$329,851 to $418,850
35%	$209,426 to $523,600	$418,851 to $628,300
37%	Over $523,600	Over $628,300

Your actual marginal tax rate includes state income taxes if your state levies an income tax. Though this chapter focuses upon the federal income tax system and strategies to reduce those taxes, most of what is discussed also helps you reduce your state income taxes, which the vast majority of states levy. Each state income tax system is unique, so covering them all here is impossible. All but eight states — Alaska, Florida, Nevada, South Dakota, Tennessee, Texas, Washington, and Wyoming — impose a state income tax. (New Hampshire has only a state income tax on dividend and interest investment income.)

REMEMBER

There's value in knowing your marginal tax rate. This knowledge allows you to determine the following (among other things):

>> How much you could reduce your taxes if you contribute more money to retirement accounts

>> How much you would pay in additional taxes on extra income you could earn from working more

>> How much you could reduce your taxable income if you use investments that produce tax-free income (which may make sense only if you're in a higher tax bracket — more on this later in the chapter)

Highlighting the Tax Cuts and Jobs Act bill

The Tax Cuts and Jobs Act bill took effect in 2018, and most people and small businesses enjoyed lower federal income taxes as a result. Most federal income tax bracket rates were reduced by 2 to 3 percent.

Here are some of the other major changes in the tax bill:

>> **Increased Child Tax Credit:** The child tax credit, which previously stood at $1,000 per child under the age of 17, was increased to $2,000 per child, and up to $1,400 of that will be refundable for taxpayers not otherwise owing federal income tax. Also, the incomes at which this credit starts phasing out rises from $110,000 for married couples to $400,000, and from $75,000 for non-married filers to $200,000.

>> **State and local taxes deduction capped at $10,000:** This also includes property taxes on your home. For homeowners in high cost of living areas with high state income taxes (for example, metro areas such as San Francisco, Los Angeles, New York, Washington D.C.), this cap poses a modest or even significant negative change. Because state and local taxes are itemized deductions, only being able to take up to $10,000 (previously unlimited) for them may cause some taxpayers to no longer be able to itemize. Also, by reducing the tax benefits of home ownership (see also the next item), this change effectively raises the cost of home ownership, especially in high-cost and highly taxed areas.

>> **Mortgage-interest deduction for both primary and second homes capped at $750,000 borrowed:** This represents a modest reduction from the previous $1,000,000 limit on mortgage indebtedness deductibility.

The Tax Cuts and Jobs Act slashed the corporate income tax rate to 21 percent, which represented a 40 percent reduction. At 35 percent, the U.S. previously had one of the highest corporate income tax rates in the world before 2018.

Another change simplified the corporate tax rules and deductions, including the elimination of the corporate alternative minimum tax, and some loopholes closed. The U.S. also moved to a "territorial" tax structure, whereby U.S. companies no longer pay a penalty to bring their overseas profits back home. The immediate impact of this change was to enable U.S. corporations to bring back to the U.S. more than $2 trillion being kept overseas to avoid excessive taxation.

REMEMBER

Changes to small business tax rules were also established. First, it's important to note that the vast majority of small businesses are not operated as traditional so-called C-corps (more on those in a moment). Most small business owners operate as sole proprietorships (filing Schedule C), LLCs, partnerships, or S-corporations. In those cases, the business owner's profits from the business generally flow or pass through to the owner's personal income tax return and that income is taxed at personal income tax rates.

You will note that at higher levels of income, the individual income tax rates begin to exceed the 21 percent corporate tax rate. Seeing this can help you to better understand the next point as to why pass-through entities are being granted a special tax deduction on their profits.

In redesigning the tax code, Congress rightfully realized that the many small businesses that operate as so-called pass-through entities would be subjected to higher federal income tax rates compared with the newer 21 percent corporate income tax rate. To address this concern, Congress provided a 20 percent deduction for those businesses. So, for example, if your sole proprietorship netted you $70,000 in 2021 as a single taxpayer, that would push you into the 22 percent federal income tax bracket. But you get to deduct 20 percent of that $70,000 of income (or $14,000), so you would only owe federal income tax on the remaining $56,000 ($70,000 − $14,000).

Another way to look at this is that the business would only pay taxes on 80 percent of their profits and would be in the 22 percent federal income tax bracket. This deduction effectively reduces the 22 percent tax bracket to 17.6 percent.

This is a major change, which not surprisingly, has made small business owners exceedingly optimistic about being able to grow their businesses. In fact, in a 2018 survey of small business owners conducted by the nonprofit National Federation of Independent Business just after the tax bill was passed and signed into law, a record percentage of those surveyed (covering the survey's 45-year history) expressed optimism about it being a good time to expand their businesses.

This 20 percent pass-through deduction gets phased out for service business owners (such as lawyers, doctors, real estate agents, consultants, and so forth) at single taxpayer incomes above $157,500 (up to $207,500) and for married couples filing jointly incomes over $315,000 (up to $415,000). For other types of businesses above these income thresholds, this deduction may be limited, so consult with a tax advisor.

At the time this book is being published, the new administration in Washington is proposing tax changes, including some potential tax increases. For the latest on important changes to federal income tax rates and rules, please visit my website at www.erictyson.com.

Devising tax-reduction strategies

Use these strategies to reduce the taxes you pay on investments that are exposed to taxation:

» **Make use of retirement accounts and health savings accounts.** Most contributions to retirement accounts gain you an immediate tax break, and once they're inside the account, investment returns are sheltered from taxation, generally until withdrawal. Think of these as tax reduction accounts that can help you work toward achieving financial independence. See Chapter 2 for details on using retirement accounts when investing.

Similar to retirement accounts are health savings accounts (HSAs). With HSAs, you get a tax break on your contributions upfront; investment earnings compound without taxation over time; and there's no tax on withdrawal so long as the money is used to pay for health-related expenses (which enjoy a fairly broad list as delineated by the IRS).

» **Consider tax-free money market funds and tax-free bond funds.** Tax-free investments yield less than comparable investments that produce taxable earnings, but because of the tax differences, the earnings from tax-free investments can end up being greater than what taxable investments leave you with. If you're in a high-enough tax bracket, you may find that you come out ahead with tax-free investments.

TIP

For a proper comparison, subtract what you'll pay in federal and state income taxes from the taxable investment income to see which investment nets you more.

» **Invest in tax-friendly stock funds.** Mutual funds and exchange-traded funds that tend to trade less tend to produce lower capital gains distributions. For funds held outside tax-sheltered retirement accounts, this reduced trading effectively increases an investor's total rate of return. *Index funds* invest in a relatively static portfolio of securities, such as stocks and bonds. They don't attempt to beat the market; rather, they invest in the securities to mirror or match the performance of an underlying index. Although index funds can't beat the market, the typical actively managed fund usually doesn't, either, and index funds have several advantages over actively managed funds. See Chapter 10 to find out more about tax-friendly stock mutual funds, including some non-index funds and exchange-traded funds.

>> **Invest in small business and real estate.** The growth in value of business and real estate assets isn't taxed until you sell the asset. Even then, with investment real estate, you often can roll over the gain into another property as long as you comply with tax laws. Increases in value in small businesses can qualify for the more favorable longer-term capital gains tax rate and potentially for other tax breaks. However, the current income that small business and real estate assets produce is taxed as ordinary income.

Short-term capital gains (investments held one year or less) are taxed at your ordinary income tax rate. This fact is another reason why you shouldn't trade your investments quickly (within 12 months).

Reducing Your Taxes When Selling Investments

I advocate doing your homework so you can purchase and hold on to good investments for many years and even decades. That said, each year, folks sell and trade lots of investments.

My experience in helping people get a handle on their investments suggests that too many investors sell for the wrong reasons (while other investors hold on to investments for far too long and should sell them).

In this section, I highlight important tax and other issues to consider when you contemplate selling your investments, but I start with the nontax, bigger-picture considerations.

Weighing nontax issues

Although the focus of this chapter is on tax issues to consider when making, managing, and selling your investments, I'd be remiss not to raise bigger-picture considerations:

>> **Meeting your goals and preferences:** If your life has changed (or if you've inherited investments) since the last time you took a good look at your investment portfolio, you may discover that your current holdings no longer make sense for you. To avoid wasting time and money on investments that aren't good for you, be sure to review your investments at least annually.

WARNING

Don't make quick decisions about selling. Instead, take your time, and be sure you understand tax and other ramifications before you sell.

>> **Keeping the right portfolio mix:** A good reason to sell an investment is to allow yourself to better diversify your portfolio. Suppose that through your job, you've accumulated such a sizeable chunk of stock in your employer that this stock now overwhelms the rest of your investments. Or perhaps you've simply kept your extra money in a bank account or inherited stock from a dear relative. Conservative investors often keep too much of their money in bank accounts, Treasury bills, and the like. If your situation is like these, it's time for you to diversify. Sell some of the holdings of which you have too much, and invest the proceeds in some of the solid investments that I recommend in this book.

INVESTIGATE

If you think your employer's stock is going to be a superior investment, holding a big chunk is your gamble. At minimum, review Chapter 8 to see how to evaluate a particular stock. Remember to consider the consequences if you're wrong about your employer's stock. Develop an overall investment strategy that fits your personal financial situation (see Chapter 5). A problem with holding a large amount of stock in your employer is that both the stock and your job are compromised if the company has a significant downturn.

>> **Deciding which investments are keepers:** Often, people are tempted to sell an investment for the wrong reasons. One natural tendency is to want to sell investments that have declined in value. Some people fear a further fall, and they don't want to be affiliated with a loser, especially when money is involved. Instead, step back, take some deep breaths, and examine the merits of the investment you're considering selling. If an investment is otherwise still sound per the guidelines I discuss in this book, why bail out when prices are down and a sale is going on? What are you going to do with the money? If anything, you should be contemplating buying more of such an investment.

Also, don't make a decision to sell based on your current emotional response, especially to recent news events. If bad news has hit recently, it's already old news. Don't base your investment holdings on such transitory events. Use the criteria in this book for finding good investments to evaluate the worthiness of your current holdings. If an investment is fundamentally sound, don't sell it.

Tuning in to tax considerations

When you sell investments that you hold outside a tax-sheltered retirement account, such as in an IRA or a 401(k), taxes should be one factor in your decision. If the investments are inside retirement accounts, taxes aren't an issue because the accounts are sheltered from taxation until you withdraw funds from them.

Just because you pay tax on a profit from selling a nonretirement-account investment doesn't mean you should avoid selling. With real estate that you buy directly, as opposed to publicly held securities like real estate investment trusts (REITs), you can often avoid paying taxes on the profit you make. (See Chapter 12 for more information.)

With stocks and mutual funds, you can specify which shares you want to sell. This option makes selling decisions more complicated, but you may want to consider specifying what shares you're selling because you may be able to save taxes. (Read the next section for more information on this option.) If you sell all your shares of a particular security that you own, you don't need to concern yourself with specifying which shares you're selling.

Determining the cost basis of your shares

When you sell a portion of the shares of a security (such as a stock, bond, or mutual fund) that you own, specifying which shares you're selling may benefit you taxwise. Here's an example to show you why you may want to specify selling certain shares — especially those shares that cost you more to buy — so you can save on your taxes.

Suppose you own 300 shares of a stock, and you want to sell 100 shares. You bought 100 of these shares a long, long time ago at $10 per share, 100 shares two years ago at $16 per share, and the last 100 shares one year ago at $14 per share. Today, the stock is at $20 per share. Although you didn't get rich, you're grateful that you haven't lost your shirt the way some of your stock-picking pals have.

The Internal Revenue Service allows you to choose which shares you want to sell. Electing to sell the 100 shares that you purchased at the highest price — those you bought for $16 per share two years ago — saves you in taxes now. To comply with the tax laws, you must identify the shares that you want the broker to sell by the original date of purchase and/or the cost when you sell the shares. The brokerage firm through which you sell the stock should include this information on the confirmation that you receive for the sale.

The other method of accounting for which shares are sold is the method that the IRS forces you to use if you don't specify before the sale which shares you want to sell — the *first-in-first-out (FIFO) method*. FIFO means that the first shares that you sell are simply the first shares that you bought. Not surprisingly, because most stocks appreciate over time, the FIFO method usually leads to your paying more tax sooner. The FIFO accounting procedure leads to the conclusion that the 100 shares you sell are the 100 that you bought long, long ago at $10 per share. Thus, you owe a larger amount of taxes than if you'd sold the higher-cost shares under the specification method.

Although you save taxes today if you specify selling the shares that you bought more recently at a higher price, when you finally sell the other shares, you'll owe taxes on the larger profit. The longer you expect to hold these other shares, the greater the value you'll likely derive from postponing, realizing the larger gains and paying more in taxes.

When you sell shares in a mutual fund, the IRS has yet another accounting method, known as the *average cost method*, for figuring your taxable profit or loss. This method comes in handy if you bought shares in chunks over time or reinvested the fund payouts in purchasing more shares of the fund. As the name suggests, the average cost method allows you to take an average cost for all the mutual fund shares you bought over time.

Selling large-profit investments

No one likes to pay taxes, of course, but if an investment you own has appreciated in value, someday you'll have to pay taxes on it when you sell. (There is an exception: You hold the investment until your death and will it to your heirs. The IRS wipes out the capital gains tax on appreciated assets at your death.)

Capital gains tax applies when you sell an investment at a higher price than you paid for it. As I explain earlier in this chapter, your capital gains tax rate is different from the tax rate that you pay on ordinary income (such as from employment earnings or interest on bank savings accounts).

Odds are that the longer you've held securities such as stocks, the greater the capital gains you'll have, because stocks tend to appreciate over time. If all your assets have appreciated significantly, you may resist selling to avoid taxes. If you need money for a major purchase, however, sell what you need and pay the tax. Even if you have to pay state as well as federal taxes totaling some 35 percent of the profit, you'll have lots left. (For "longer-term" profits from investments held more than one year, your federal and state capital gains taxes probably would total somewhat less.)

Before you sell, do some rough figuring to make sure you'll have enough money left to accomplish what you want. If you seek to sell one investment and reinvest in another, you'll owe tax on the profit unless you're selling and rebuying real estate (see Chapter 12).

If you hold several assets, to diversify and meet your other financial goals, give preference to selling your largest holdings with the smallest capital gains. If you have some securities that have profits and some with losses, you can sell some of each to offset the profits with the losses.

Handling losers in your portfolio

Perhaps you have some losers in your portfolio. If you need to raise cash for some particular reason, you may consider selling select securities at a loss. You can use losses to offset gains as long as you hold both offsetting securities for more than one year (long term) or hold both for no more than one year (short term). The IRS makes this delineation because it taxes long-term gains and losses on a different rate schedule from short-term gains and losses.

If you sell securities at a loss, you can claim up to $3,000 in net losses for the year on your federal income tax return. If you sell securities with net losses totaling more than $3,000 in a year, you must carry the losses over to future tax years.

WARNING

Some tax advisors advocate doing year-end tax-loss selling with stocks, bonds, and mutual funds. The logic goes that if you hold a security at a loss, you should sell it, take the tax write-off, and then buy it (or something similar) back. When selling investments for tax-loss purposes, be careful of the so-called wash sale rules. The IRS doesn't allow the deduction of a loss for a security sale if you buy that same security back within 30 days. As long as you wait 31 or more days, you won't encounter any problems.

TIP

If you're selling a mutual fund or exchange-traded fund, you can purchase a fund similar to the one you're selling to easily sidestep this rule.

Selling investments when you don't know their original cost

Sometimes, you may not know what an investment originally cost you, or you received some investments from another person, and you're not sure what they paid for them.

If you don't have the original statement, start by calling the firm where the investment was purchased. Whether it's a brokerage firm or mutual fund company, the company should be able to send you copies of old account statements, although you may have to pay a small fee for this service.

Also, increasing numbers of investment firms, especially mutual fund companies, can tell you upon the sale of an investment what its original cost was. The cost calculated is usually the average cost for the shares you purchased.

2

Preparing Your Investing Foundation

IN THIS PART . . .

Identify what should be included in your personal financial plan.

Understand bank and credit union accounts, as well as what they are and aren't good for.

Make sense of money market funds and how to find the best one for your situation.

IN THIS CHAPTER

» Knowing what you should do before
investing

» Understanding how your financial
plan translates into your
investing plan

Chapter **5**

Laying Out Your Financial Plans

Most folks love to pick an investment, put their money into it, and then enjoy seeing it increase in value. And though I try to simplify and clearly explain investing, it isn't that easy. You can do your homework and make a good decision but then see your well-chosen investment fall in value and test your nerves and commitment.

But that's putting the cart before the horse. Before you make any great, wealth-building investments, you should get your financial house in order. Understanding and implementing some simple personal financial management concepts can pay off big for you in the decades ahead.

In this chapter, I explain what financial housekeeping you should do before you invest, as well as how to translate your overall personal and financial plans into an investment plan.

First Priorities: Paying Off High-Cost Debt and Building a Safety Reserve

Plenty of younger adults have debts to pay and lack an emergency reserve of money for unexpected expenses. High-cost debts, such as on a credit card, can be a major impediment to investing, in particular, and accomplishing your future personal and financial goals, in a broader sense. A high interest rate keeps the debt growing and can cause your debt to spiral out of control, which is why I discuss dealing with such consumer debt as your first priority, just before establishing an emergency reserve.

Paying off high-cost consumer debt

Paying down debts isn't nearly as exciting as investing, but it can make your investment decisions less difficult. Rather than spending your time investigating specific investments, paying off your debts with money you've saved may indeed be your best investment.

Consumer debt includes borrowing on credit cards, auto loans, and the like, which are often costly ways to borrow. Banks and other lenders charge higher interest rates for consumer debt than for debt for investments, such as real estate and business, because consumer loans are the riskiest type of loans for a lender. Risk means the chance of the borrower's defaulting and being unable to pay back all that they borrowed.

Many folks have credit card debt that costs 18 percent or more per year in interest. Some credit cards levy interest rates well above 20 percent if you make a late payment or two. Reducing and eventually eliminating this debt with your savings is like putting your money in an investment with a guaranteed tax-free return equal to the rate that you pay on your debt.

For example, if you have outstanding credit card debt at 18 percent interest, paying off that debt is the same as putting your money to work in an investment with a guaranteed 18 percent tax-free annual return. Because the interest on consumer debt isn't tax-deductible, you would need to earn more than 18 percent by investing your money elsewhere to net 18 percent after paying taxes. Earning such high investing returns is highly unlikely, and to earn those returns, you'd be forced to take great risk.

REMEMBER

Consumer debt is hazardous to your long-term financial health (not to mention damaging to your credit score and future ability to borrow for a home or general ability to save and invest) because it encourages you to borrow against your future earnings. I often hear people say such things as "I can't afford to buy a new car for cash, given how expensive new cars are." Well, okay. New cars are expensive, so you need to set your sights lower and buy a good used car that you can afford. You can then invest the money that you'd otherwise spend on your auto loan.

TIP

Now, I do recommend one exception to my guideline of not borrowing through a credit card: Tapping credit card debt may make sense if you're financing a business. If you don't have home equity, personal loans (through a credit card or auto loan) may actually be your lowest-cost source of small-business financing (see Chapter 14 for more information).

Establishing an emergency reserve

You never know what life will bring, so having an accessible reserve of cash to meet unexpected expenses makes good financial sense. If you have generous parents or dear relatives, you can certainly consider using them as your emergency reserve. Just be sure you ask them in advance how they feel about that before you count on receiving funding from them. If you don't have a financially flush family member, the onus is on you to establish a reserve.

TIP

I generally recommend that you have at least three months' worth of living expenses to as much as six months' worth of living expenses as an emergency reserve. Invest this personal-safety-net money in a money market fund (see Chapter 7). You may also be able to borrow against your employer-based retirement account or against your home's equity, should you find yourself in a bind, but these options are much less desirable.

If you don't have a financial safety net, you may be forced, under duress, to sell an investment (at a relatively low price) that you've worked hard for. And selling some investments, such as real estate, can take time and cost significant money (transaction costs, taxes, and so on).

REMEMBER

Riskier investments like stocks aren't a suitable place to keep your emergency money invested. While stocks historically have returned about 9 percent per year (see Chapter 3), about one-third of the time, stocks decline in value in a given year, sometimes substantially. Stocks can drop and have dropped 20, 30, or 50 percent or more over relatively short periods of time. Suppose that such a decline coincides with an emergency, such as the loss of your job or a health problem that creates major medical bills. During the 2020 government-mandated economic shutdowns due to the COVID-19 pandemic, remember how (U.S. and most international) stocks dropped more than 30 percent in just a few weeks while millions of people lost their jobs? Your situation may force you to sell at a loss, perhaps a substantial one. As I discuss in Chapter 8, stocks are intended to be a longer-term investment, not an investment that you expect (or need) to sell in the near future.

What about Paying Down Other Debts?

Getting out from under 18 percent interest rate credit-card debt is clearly a priority and a bit of a no-brainer. But what should you do about other debts that carry a more reasonable interest rate? This section talks you through some common examples: student loans and mortgage debt.

Assessing student loans

If you're one of many young adults with lingering student loan debt, you're probably wondering whether you should focus your efforts on paying down that debt or instead invest the extra cash you have.

The best choice hinges on the interest rate on this debt (after factoring in any tax breaks) and how that compares with the expected return from investing. Of course, you must be reasonable and not pie-in-the-sky about the rate of return you expect from your investments.

While the government has paused student loan payments and interest due to the government-mandated economic shutdowns during the COVID-19 pandemic, you should probably stop any payments on your student loans. I would make an exception, though, if you're likely to spend/waste the extra money that would have been going to debt repayment.

Under current tax laws, with student loans, you can deduct up to $2,500 in student loan interest annually on your federal 1040 income tax return. So this deduction can lower the effective interest rate you're paying on your student loans. This deduction is available to single taxpayers with adjusted gross incomes (before subtracting the student loan interest) of $70,000 or less and married couples filing jointly with such incomes of $140,000 or less. Partial deductions are allowed for incomes up to $85,000 for singles and $170,000 for married couples filing jointly. Another requirement for taking this deduction is that you and your spouse, if filing jointly, cannot be claimed as dependents on someone else's income tax return.

If you can deduct student loan interest on your tax return, to determine the value of that deduction, please see Chapter 4 to understand what tax bracket you're in (what your marginal tax rate is). For most moderate income earners, 25 percent is a reasonable number to work with.

Suppose you have student loans outstanding at the attractive interest rate of just 3.5 percent. Assume that you're able to deduct all this interest and that your income tax bracket is 25 percent. So, after taxes, the effective interest rate on your student loan is 3.5 percent – (0.25 × 3.5 percent) = 2.63 percent.

Now, the question to consider is this: Can you reasonably expect to earn an average annual rate of return from your investments of more than this 2.63 percent? If you invest your money in a sleepy bank account, the answer will surely be no. If you instead invest in things like stocks and bonds, over the long term, you should come out with a higher return.

If you have student loans at a higher interest rate — say, 6 percent — it may make more sense to pay those loans down faster with your extra cash than to invest that money elsewhere. To get a higher return than that from investments, you need to take a fair amount of risk, and of course there's no guarantee that you'll actually make a high enough return to make it worth your while.

When deciding whether you should pay down student loans faster, there are some factors to consider besides the cost of your student loans and comparing this cost to the expected return on your investments. Other good reasons not to pay off your student loans any quicker than necessary include the following:

>> **Paying off your student loan faster has no tax benefit.** Instead, you could contribute to your retirement (also known as tax reduction) accounts, such as a 401(k), an IRA, or a SEP-IRA plan (especially if your employer offers matching money). Putting additional money in a retirement plan can immediately reduce your federal and state income tax bills. The more years you have until retirement, the greater the benefit you receive if you invest in your retirement accounts. Thanks to the compounding of your retirement account investments without the drain of taxes, you can actually earn a lower rate of return on your investments than you pay on your student loans and still come out ahead.

>> **You're willing to invest in growth-oriented investments, such as stocks and real estate.** To have a reasonable chance of earning more on your investments than it costs you to borrow on your student loans, you must be aggressive with your investments. As I discuss in Chapter 3, stocks and real estate have produced annual average rates of return of about 9 percent. You may be able to earn even more in your own small business or by investing in others' businesses.

Keep in mind that you have no guarantee, especially in the short term, of earning high returns from growth-type investments, which can easily drop 20 percent or more in value over a year or two.

REMEMBER

>> **Paying down your student loans depletes your emergency reserves.** Psychologically, some people feel uncomfortable paying off debt more quickly if it diminishes their savings and investments. You probably don't want to pay down your debt if doing so depletes your financial safety cushion. Make sure you have access — through a money market fund or other sources (a family member, for example) — to at least three months' worth of living expenses (as I explain in "Establishing an emergency reserve" earlier in this chapter).

Considering paying down mortgage debt

Paying off your mortgage more quickly is an "investment" for your spare cash that may make sense for your financial situation. However, the wisdom of making this financial move isn't as clear as is paying off high-interest consumer debt; mortgage interest rates are generally lower, and the interest is typically tax-deductible.

As with the decision to pay off a student loan faster (look to the previous section), when evaluating whether to pay down your mortgage quicker than necessary, compare your mortgage interest rate with your investments' rates of return. Suppose you have a fixed-rate mortgage with an interest rate of 5 percent. If you decide to make investments instead of paying down your mortgage more quickly, your investments need to produce an average annual rate of return, before taxes, of more than 5 percent for you to come out ahead financially.

TIP

Don't get hung up on mortgage tax deductions. Although it's true that mortgage interest is usually tax-deductible, you must also pay taxes on investment profits generated outside retirement accounts. You can purchase tax-free investments like municipal bonds, but over the long haul, such bonds and other types of lending investments (bank savings accounts, CDs, and other bonds) are unlikely to earn a rate of return that's higher than the cost of your mortgage.

Sorting Out Your Financial Plans

TIP

I recommend establishing your financial goals before you begin investing. Otherwise, you won't know how much to save or how much risk you need to take or are comfortable taking.

You may want to invest money for several goals, or you may have just one purpose. When I was in my 20s, I put some money away toward retirement, but my bigger priority at that time was to save money so I could hit the eject button from my management consulting job. I knew that I wanted to start my own business and that in the early years of my entrepreneurial endeavors, I couldn't count on an income as stable or as large as the one I had in consulting.

I invested these two chunks of money quite differently. I kept the money I saved for the start-up of my small business, which was a shorter-term goal, safely invested in a money market fund that had a decent yield but didn't fluctuate in value. By contrast, my retirement was a longer-term goal, so I invested the bulk of my retirement money in stock funds. If these funds fluctuated and declined in value, that was okay in the short term, because I wouldn't be tapping that money.

Considering your investment options and desires

Numerous good investing choices exist: You can invest in real estate, the stock market, mutual funds, exchange-traded funds, or your own business or someone else's. Or you can pay down debts such as student loans, credit cards, an auto loan, or mortgage debt more quickly.

What makes the most sense for you depends on your goals as well as your personal preferences. If you detest risk-taking and volatile investments, paying down some debts, as recommended earlier in this chapter, may make better sense than investing in the stock market.

To determine your general investment desires, think about how you would deal with an investment that plunges 20 percent or 40 percent, over a short period of time. Some aggressive investments can fall fast. You shouldn't go into the stock market, real estate, or small-business investment arena if such a drop is likely to cause you to sell or make you a miserable wreck. If you haven't tried riskier investments yet, you may want to experiment a bit to see how you feel with your money invested in them.

TIP

A simple way to mask the risk of volatile investments is to diversify your portfolio — that is, put your money into different investments. Not watching prices too closely helps, too; that's one of the reasons why real estate investors are less likely to bail out when the market declines. Unfortunately (from my perspective), stock market investors can get minute-by-minute price updates. Add that fact to the quick click of your computer mouse or tap on your smartphone that it takes to dump a stock or fund in a flash, and you have all the ingredients for shortsighted investing — and potential financial disaster.

Making investing decisions and determining your likes and dislikes is challenging when you consider just your own concerns. When you have to also consider someone else, dealing with these issues becomes doubly hard, given the typically different money personalities and emotions that come into play. In most couples with whom I've worked as a financial counselor, usually one person takes primary responsibility for managing the household finances, including investments. In my observation, the couples who do the best job with their investments are those who communicate well, plan ahead, and compromise.

TIP

In my work as a financial counselor, one of the most valuable and difficult things I did for couples stuck in unproductive patterns of behavior was help them get the issue out on the table. For these couples, the biggest step was making the time to discuss their financial management, whether as a couple or working with an advisor or counselor. The key to success is taking the time for each person to explain their different point of view and then offer compromises. So be sure to make time to discuss your points of view or hire a financial advisor or psychologist/marriage counselor to help you deal with these issues and differences.

Assessing your savings rate

To accomplish your financial goals, you need to save money, and you also should know your savings rate. Your savings rate is the percentage of your past year's income that you saved and didn't spend.

Part of being a smart investor involves figuring out how much you need to save to reach your goals. Not knowing what you want to do a decade or more from now is perfectly normal; after all, your goals, wants, and needs evolve over the years. But that doesn't mean you should just throw your hands in the air and not make an effort to see where you stand today and think about where you want to be in the future.

An important benefit of knowing your savings rate is that you can better assess how much risk you need to take to accomplish your goals. Seeing the amount that you need to save to achieve your dreams may encourage you to take more risk with your investments.

REMEMBER

During your working years, if you consistently save about 10 percent of your annual income, you're probably saving enough to meet your goals (unless you want to retire at a relatively young age). On average, most people need about 75 percent of their preretirement income throughout retirement to maintain their standard of living.

If you're one of the many people who don't save enough, it's time do some homework. To save more, you need to reduce your spending, increase your income, or both. For most people, reducing spending is the more feasible way to save.

To reduce your spending, first figure out where your money goes. You may have some general idea, but to make changes, you need to have the data and facts. Examine your bill-paying records and review your credit card bills and any other documentation that shows your spending history. Tally up how much you spend on getting food out, operating your car(s), paying your taxes, and everything else. After you have this information, you can begin to prioritize and make the necessary trade-offs to reduce your spending and increase your savings rate. Earning more income may help boost your savings rate as well. Perhaps you can get a higher-paying job or increase the number of hours you work. But if you already work a lot, reining in your spending is usually better for your emotional and economic well-being.

If you don't know how to evaluate and reduce your spending or haven't thought about your retirement goals, looked into what you can expect from Social Security, or calculated how much you should save for retirement, now's the time to do so. Pick up my companion book *Personal Finance in Your 20s & 30s For Dummies* (Wiley) to find out all the necessary details for retirement planning and much more.

Investing regularly with dollar cost averaging

Regularly investing money at set time intervals, such as monthly or quarterly, in volatile investments such as stocks, stock mutual funds, or exchange-traded funds is called *dollar cost averaging* (DCA). If you've ever had money regularly deducted from your paycheck and contributed to a retirement savings plan investment account, you've done DCA.

TIP

Most folks invest a portion of their employment compensation as they earn it, but if you have extra cash sitting around, you can choose to invest that money in one fell swoop or to invest it gradually via DCA. The biggest appeal of gradually feeding money into the market via DCA is that you don't dump all your money into a potentially overheated investment just before a major drop. No one has a crystal ball and can predict which direction investments will move next in the short term. DCA helps shy investors psychologically ease into riskier investments.

REMEMBER

DCA is made to order for skittish investors with larger lump sums of money sitting in safe investments like bank accounts. It also makes sense for investors with a large chunk of their net worth in cash who want to minimize the risk of transferring that cash to riskier investments, such as stocks.

As with any risk-reducing investment strategy, DCA has its drawbacks. If growth investments appreciate (as they're supposed to over time), a DCA investor misses out on earning higher returns on his money awaiting investment. Studying U.S. stock market data over seven decades, finance professors Richard E. Williams and Peter W. Bacon found that approximately two-thirds of the time, a lump-sum stock market investor earned higher first-year returns than an investor who fed the money in monthly over the first year.

However, knowing that you'll probably be ahead most of the time if you dump a lump sum into the stock market is little consolation if you happen to invest just before a major drop in prices. For example, from late 2007 to early 2009, global stocks shed about half of their value. And how about those who invested in stocks in late 2019 and early 2020 only to see stocks slide by more than one-third in just a matter of weeks in March of 2020 due to the government-mandated economic shutdowns resulting from the COVID-19 pandemic?

If you use DCA too quickly, you may not give the market sufficient time for a correction to unfold, during and after which some of the DCA purchases may take place. If you practice DCA over too long a period of time, you may miss a major upswing in stock prices. I suggest using DCA over one to two years to strike a balance. Alternatively, if you're comfortable with the risk, get your money invested and get on with your life!

TIP

When you use DCA, establish an automatic investment plan so you're less likely to wimp out of your strategy. Your money that awaits investment in DCA should have a suitable parking place. I recommend a money market fund that's appropriate for your tax situation.

Knowing the Impact of Investing for College Costs

Many well-intentioned parents want to save for their children's future educational expenses. The mistake that they often make, however, is putting money in accounts in the child's name (in so-called custodial accounts) or saving outside retirement accounts in general. The more money you accumulate outside tax-sheltered retirement accounts, the more you will generally end up paying for college costs.

REMEMBER

Under the current financial needs analysis used by most colleges and universities in awarding "financial aid" (that is, how much of their very high sticker price they will charge you), the value of your retirement plan is not considered to be an asset. Money that you save outside retirement accounts, including money in the child's name, is counted as an asset and reduces eligibility for financial aid.

Also, be aware that your family's assets, for purposes of financial aid determination, generally include equity in real estate and businesses you own. Although the federal financial aid analysis no longer counts equity in your home as an asset, many private (independent) schools continue to ask parents for this information when they make their own financial aid determinations. Thus, paying down your home mortgage more quickly instead of funding retirement accounts can harm you financially. You may end up paying more for college costs and pay more in taxes.

TIP

Make it a priority to contribute to your retirement savings plan(s). If you instead save money in a nonretirement account for your children's college expenses, you will pay higher taxes both on your current income and on the interest and growth of this money. In addition to paying higher taxes, you'll be expected to pay a higher price for your child's educational expenses.

Paying for college

If the way in which the financial aid system works effectively encourages you to save in your own retirement accounts, how will you pay for your kid's education expenses? Here are some ideas and resources:

>> **Home equity:** You can borrow against your home at a relatively low interest rate, and the interest is generally tax-deductible.

>> **Company retirement plans:** Some 401(k)s allow borrowing for educational costs.

>> **Student loans:** Several financial aid programs allow you to borrow at reasonable interest rates. The Unsubsidized Stafford Loans and Parent Loans for Undergraduate Students (PLUS), for example, are available, even when your family isn't deemed financially needy.

>> **Grants and scholarships:** Grant programs are available through schools and the government, as well as through independent sources. Complete the Free Application for Federal Student Aid (FAFSA) application to apply for the federal government programs. Grants available through state government programs may require a separate application. Specific colleges and other private organizations — including employers, banks, credit unions, and community groups — also offer grants and scholarships.

>> **Work and save:** Your child can work and save money during high school and college. In fact, if your child qualifies for financial aid, they're generally expected to contribute a certain amount to education costs from employment (both during the school year and summer breaks) and from savings. Besides giving your gangly teen a stake in their own future, this training encourages sound personal financial management down the road.

No one enjoys filling out financial aid forms. It's difficult, intimidating, invasive, and stressful. Yet it's a necessary step many families must take in order to make college more affordable. First, let's clear up a major misconception: Receiving financial aid doesn't actually mean you receive money for college. Rather it means they charge different customers widely differing prices based upon the college's assessment of your ability to pay. Your goal is to position your finances to receive more favorable pricing. And doing that is not as hard as it may seem. Here are some tips:

>> **Assume that you qualify for financial aid.** Financial aid consultants agree that you should assume you're eligible. Don't rule yourself out because of income or academics. And don't rule out a college because you think it's too expensive. The higher the cost, the more aid you may receive.

>> **Use colleges' "net price calculator" to estimate your expected costs.** No matter where you are in the planning process, there is a simple method you can use now to get a general idea as to what price you may pay at a given college or university (and therefore how much financial aid or discount you will receive from those institutions). Colleges are required to have a net price calculator (NPC) on their websites. I've seen situations for a given family where the pricing among private colleges can differ by tens of thousands of dollars among schools driven by factors like how much equity a family has in their home.

>> **Fill out the FAFSA form online.** The Free Application for Federal Student Aid — also known as the FAFSA form — is the starting point in applying for financial aid. You can complete the FAFSA form online (fafsa.ed.gov).

>> **Don't wait around to be accepted to a college to apply for aid.** The coffers may be empty by spring, so get application forms completed as soon as possible. You'll need the latest version of the federal FAFSA form. You may also need to complete the College Board's CSS Profile application (cssprofile. collegeboard.org), state aid forms, and/or forms provided by the colleges. The FAFSA form and Profile become available for the next academic year on October 1 of the current year (meaning the soonest you can apply for financial aid for your first year of college is October 1 of senior year of high school).

Parents, keep in mind that the questions presume that the student is applying for aid (even though parents fill out the form!). Be aware that questions like name, address, social security number, date of birth, and so on in the beginning part of the form refer to the student. Parent information is collected later in the form. Entering parent information in a student section is a common mistake, and it can cause problems for your financial aid application.

TIP

As I discuss in Chapter 2, there are increasing numbers of faster and cheaper alternatives to traditional four-year colleges which lead to interesting and rewarding jobs and careers. For more information, please pick up a copy of my book, *Paying For College For Dummies* (Wiley).

Considering educational savings account options

You'll hear about various accounts you can use to invest money for your kid's future college costs. Tread carefully with these, especially because they can affect future financial aid.

The most popular of these accounts are qualified state tuition plans, also known as Section 529 plans. These plans offer a tax-advantaged way to save and invest more than $100,000 per child toward college costs. (Some states allow upward of $300,000 per student.) After you contribute to one of these state-based accounts, the invested funds grow without taxation. Withdrawals are also tax-free provided the funds are used to pay for qualifying higher-education costs (which include college, graduate school, and certain additional expenses of special-needs students) as well as up to $10,000 per year toward K-12 school expenses. (The schools need not be in the same state as the state administering the Section 529 plan.)

Section 529 plan balances can harm your child's financial aid chances. Thus, such accounts make the most sense for affluent families who are sure they won't qualify for any type of financial aid. If you do opt for a 529 plan and intend to apply for financial aid, you should be the owner of the accounts (not your child) to maximize qualifying for financial aid.

Investing money earmarked for college

Diversified mutual funds and exchange-traded funds — which invest in stocks in the United States and internationally, as well as bonds — are ideal vehicles to use when you invest money earmarked for college. Be sure to choose funds that fit your tax situation if you invest your funds in nonretirement accounts. (See Chapter 10 for more information.)

When your child is young (preschool age), consider investing up to 80 percent of your investment money in stocks (diversified worldwide) with the remainder in bonds. Doing so can maximize the money's growth potential without taking extraordinary risk. As your child makes his way through the later years of elementary school, you need to begin to make the mix more conservative. Scale back the stock percentage to 50 or 60 percent. Finally, in the years just before the child enters college, reduce the stock portion to no more than 20 percent or so.

Some 529s offer target-date-type funds that reduce the stock exposure as target college dates approach so you don't have to make the adjustments yourself.

Securing Proper Insurance

As a financial counselor, I've seen that although many people lack particular types of insurance, others possess unnecessary policies. Many people also keep very low deductibles. Remember to insure against potential losses that would be financially catastrophic for you; don't waste your money to protect against smaller losses.

You may be at risk of making a catastrophic investing mistake by not protecting your assets properly. Decisions regarding what amount of insurance you need to carry are, to some extent, a matter of your desire and ability to accept financial risk. But some risks aren't worth taking. Don't overestimate your ability to predict what accidents and other bad luck may befall you.

Here's what insurance I recommend that you have to protect yourself, your loved ones, and your assets:

>> **Major medical health insurance:** You need a policy that pays for all types of major illnesses and major medical expenditures. If your financial situation allows, consider taking a health plan with a high deductible, which can minimize your premiums. Also consider channeling extra money into a health savings account (HSA), which provides tremendous tax breaks. As with a retirement account, contributions provide an upfront tax break, and money can grow over the years in an HSA without taxation. You can also tap HSA funds without penalty or taxation for a wide range of current health expenses.

>> **Adequate liability insurance on your home and car to guard your assets against lawsuits:** You should have at least enough liability insurance to protect your net worth (assets minus your liabilities/debts) or, ideally, twice your net worth. If you run your own business, get insurance for your business assets if they're substantial. Also consider professional liability insurance to protect against a lawsuit. You may also want to consider incorporating your business. (See Chapter 14 for more on small-business issues.)

>> **Long-term disability insurance:** Even if you don't have dependents, odds are that you're dependent on your employment income. What would you (and your family) do to replace your income if a major disability prevented you from working? Most large employers offer group plans that have good benefits and are much less expensive than coverage you'd buy on your own. Also check with your professional association for a competitive group plan.

>> **Life insurance, if others are dependent on your income:** If you're single or your loved ones can live without your income, skip life insurance. If you need coverage, buy term insurance that, like your auto and home insurance, is pure insurance protection. The amount of term insurance you need to buy largely depends on how much of your income you want to replace.

>> **Estate planning:** Most folks need a simple will to delineate to whom they would like to leave all their worldly possessions. If you hold significant assets outside retirement accounts, you may also benefit from establishing a living trust, which keeps your money from filtering through the hands of probate lawyers. Living wills and medical powers of attorney are useful to have in case you're ever in a medically incapacitated situation. If you have substantial assets, doing more involved estate planning is wise to minimize estate taxes and ensure the orderly passing of your assets to your heirs.

For all the details on the best and most effective ways to buy insurance, what to look for in policies, and where to get good policies, see my book *Personal Finance in Your 20s & 30s For Dummies* (Wiley), and visit my website at www.erictyson.com.

Chapter **6**

Starting Out with Bank and Credit Union Accounts

C ustomer visits to stand-alone bank branches with a lobby and tellers are going the way of the big-city newspaper business. Both are in decline and in industries that are being disrupted by the internet.

Who needs retail banks, with their costly-to-maintain branches, when you can do your banking online? You can conduct most transactions quicker online, and it saves the bank money, which enables it to offer you better account terms. And there's no need to rush out at lunchtime to be sure you make it to your bank during its limited open hours. Online banking is generally available 24/7.

But I have even bigger questions for you to consider: Do you even need a bank account? What are your best alternatives? That's what this chapter explores.

Everyone needs an account or two from which to conduct transactions, including paying bills and storing newly earned money. Such foundational accounts are essential to get in order before proceeding with investing that has the potential to produce higher returns.

Understanding FDIC Bank Insurance

What makes keeping your money in a U.S. bank unique is the Federal Deposit Insurance Corporation (FDIC) insurance that protects bank deposits. If your bank fails (and as history shows, some banks do fail), and if your bank participates in the FDIC system, your bank account is insured by the U.S. government up to $250,000. The stamp of FDIC backing, and insurance is soothing to some folks who worry about all the risks and dangers in the investment world.

While the FDIC insurance is worth something, banks have to pay for this protection. That cost is effectively passed along to you in the form of lower interest rates on your deposits.

WARNING

Just because the federal government stands behind the banking FDIC system doesn't mean your money is 100 percent safe in the event of a bank failure. Although you're insured for $250,000 in a bank, if the bank fails, you may wait quite a while to get your money back — and you may get less interest than you thought you would. Banks fail and will continue to fail. During the 1980s and early 1990s, and again in the late 2000s, hundreds of insured banks and savings and loans failed. (Between the early 1990s and mid-2000s — a relatively strong economic period — only a handful of banks failed annually.)

REMEMBER

Any investment that involves lending your money to someone else or to some organization, including putting your money in a bank or buying a Treasury bond that the federal government issues, carries risk. Although I'm not a doomsayer, any student of history knows that governments and civilizations fail.

FDIC backing is hardly a unique protection. Every Treasury bond is issued and backed by the federal government, the same debt-laden organization that stands behind the FDIC. Plenty of other nearly equivalent safe lending investments yield higher returns than bank accounts. Highly rated corporate bonds are good examples (see Chapter 9). That's not to say that you shouldn't consider keeping some of your money in a bank. But first, you should be aware of the realities and costs of FDIC insurance.

Investing in Banking Account and Savings Vehicles

While traditional banks with walk-in branch locations are shrinking in number due to closures, bank mergers, and failures, online banks are growing — and for good reason. Some of the biggest expenses of operating a traditional retail bank are the cost of the real estate and the related costs of the branch. An online bank eliminates much of those costs; thus, these banks are able, for example, to pay their customers higher interest rates on their account balances. And online banks can offer better terms on checking accounts and loans.

The internet is lowering costs for many industries, and the banking industry is one of those. This doesn't mean, however, that you should rush to become a customer of an online bank, because other financial companies, like mutual funds and brokerage firms, offer attractive investment accounts and options as well. (See the section "Exploring Alternatives to Bank Accounts" later in this chapter.)

Bank checking accounts and debit cards

Whether it's paying monthly bills or having something in your wallet to make purchases with at restaurants and retail stores, we all need the ability to conduct transactions and access our money. I'm not a fan of credit cards for most people, because the credit feature enables you to spend money you don't have and carry a debt balance month to month. Notwithstanding the lower short-term interest rates some cards charge to lure new customers, the reality is that borrowing on credit cards is expensive — usually, to the tune of more than 18 percent for most young adults.

Paying a credit card bill in full each month is the smart way to use such a card and avoid these high interest charges. But about half of all credit-card holders use the high-interest-rate credit feature on their cards. And, even if you pay your bill in full each month, it's worth considering whether charging purchases on your credit card encourages you to spend more.

Debit cards are useful transaction vehicles and a better alternative for folks who are prone to borrow via their credit cards. A debit card connects to your checking account, thus eliminating the need for you to carry around excess cash. Unlike a credit card, a debit card has no credit feature, so you can't spend money you don't have. (Some checking accounts offer prearranged lines of credit for overdrafts.) And as with a credit card, you can dispute debit card transactions if the product or service isn't what the seller claimed it would be and fails to stand behind it.

TIP

During periods of relatively low interest rates like those of the last several years, the fees levied on a transaction account, like a checking account, should be of greater concern to you than the interest paid on account balances. After all, you shouldn't be keeping lots of extra cash in a checking account; you've got better options for that, which I discuss in the rest of this chapter.

One reason why bank customers have gotten worse terms on their accounts is that they gravitate toward larger banks and their extensive ATM networks so they can easily get cash when they need it. These ATM networks (and the often-associated bank branches) are costly for banks to maintain. So you generally pay higher fees and get lower yields when you're the customer of a bank with a large ATM network, especially a bank that does tons of advertising.

By using a debit card that carries a Visa or Mastercard logo, you won't need to access and carry around much cash. Debit cards are widely accepted by merchants and are connected to your checking account. These cards can be used for purchases and for obtaining cash from your checking account.

Savings accounts and certificates of deposit

Banks generally pay higher interest rates on savings account balances than they do on checking account balances. But they have often lagged behind the best money market funds, offered by mutual fund companies and brokerage firms (see Chapter 7). Online banking is changing that dynamic, however, and now the best banks offer competitive rates on savings accounts.

The virtue of most savings accounts is that you can earn some interest yet have penalty-free access to your money. The investment won't fluctuate in value the way that a bond will, and you don't have early-withdrawal penalties, as you do with a certificate of deposit (CD).

The yield on bank savings accounts is generally pretty crummy. That's why your friendly neighborhood banker will be quick to suggest a CD as a higher-yielding investment alternative to a bank savings account. They may tout the fact that unlike a bond (discussed in Chapter 9), a CD doesn't have fluctuating principal value. CDs also give you the peace of mind afforded by the government's FDIC insurance program.

CDs pay higher interest rates than savings accounts because you commit to tie up your money for a period of time, such as 6 or 12 months, or 3 or 5 years. The bank pays you, say, 2 percent and then turns around and lends your money to others through credit cards, auto loans, and so on. The bank often charges those borrowers an interest rate of 10 percent or more. Not a bad business!

I'm generally not a fan of CDs. I've found that some investors (typically older ones who are worried about risk) use CDs by default without researching their pros and cons. Here are some drawbacks that your banker may neglect to mention:

>> **Early-withdrawal penalties:** When you tie up your money in a CD and later decide you want it back before the CD matures, a hefty penalty (typically, about six months' interest) is usually shaved from your return. With other

lending investments, such as bonds and bond mutual funds, you can access your money without penalty and generally at little or no cost.

>> **Mediocre yields:** In addition to carrying penalties for early withdrawal, a CD yields less than a high-quality bond with a comparable maturity (such as two, five, or ten years). Often, the yield difference is 1 percent or more, especially if you don't shop around and simply buy CDs from the local bank where you keep your checking account.

>> **Only one tax flavor:** High-tax-bracket investors who purchase CDs outside their retirement accounts should be aware of a final and perhaps fatal flaw of CDs: The interest on CDs is fully taxable at the federal and state levels. Bonds, by contrast, are available in tax-free (federal and/or state) versions, if you desire.

TIP

You can earn higher returns and have better access to your money when it's in bonds and bond funds than you can when it's in CDs. Bonds make especially good sense when you're in a higher tax bracket and would benefit from tax-free income in a nonretirement account. CDs may make sense when you know, for example, that you can invest your money for, say, two years, after which time you need the money for some purchase that you expect to make. Just make sure you shop around to get the best interest rate from an FDIC-insured bank. If having that U.S. government insurance gives you peace of mind, consider investing in Treasury bonds, which tend to pay more interest than many CDs (see Chapter 9).

Negotiating with Bankers

Especially at traditional brick-and-mortar banks in your local community, you may be able to get better terms and deals if you ask. Let me give you a common example.

Suppose that for several years, you've had a checking account at your local bank and have not had any real issues or problems. Then one month, you end up bouncing several check payments (say, four at $30 each) because a deposit into your account didn't clear in time. You may very well be able to get some or even all of these fees waived by pleading your case to the local branch manager. Explain how long you've been a good customer and why this was a one-time case of bad luck, something beyond your control, and so on. The worst that can happen is that the manager will turn down your request, and you'll have wasted a few minutes of your day. More likely, however, is that you may save yourself $90 to $120 for a small amount of your time.

Deposit account terms and loan terms are harder to negotiate, but I've seen folks have some success even in those arenas. Your regular bank may offer better mortgage terms if it knows it needs to match or beat a more competitive offer from another bank you've shopped, for example.

Feeling Secure with Your Bank

Putting your money in a bank may make you feel safe for a variety of reasons. For your parents and your grandparents, the first investing experience was likely at the neighborhood bank where they established checking and savings accounts.

Part of your comfort in keeping your money in a bank may stem from the fact that the bank is where your well-intentioned mom and dad may have first steered you financially. Also, at a local branch, often within a short distance of your home or office, you find vaults and security-monitoring cameras to protect your deposits.

Bank branches cost a lot of money to operate. Guess where that money comes from? From bank depositors and the customers of the banks' various services, of course! These operating costs are one of the reasons why the interest rates that banks pay often pale in comparison to some of the similarly secure alternatives discussed elsewhere in this book (such as in Chapter 7, where I discuss money market funds in detail as alternatives to bank savings accounts). This also explains why an online bank may be your best choice if you want to keep some of your money in a bank.

Evaluating any bank

Most folks know to look for a bank that participates in the U.S.-government-operated FDIC program. Otherwise, if the bank fails, your money on deposit isn't protected. FDIC covers your deposits up to a cool $250,000.

WARNING

Some online banks are able to offer higher interest rates because they are based overseas and, therefore, are not participating in the FDIC program. (Banks must pay insurance premiums into the FDIC fund, which adds, of course, to a bank's costs.) Another risk for you is that noncovered banks may take excessive risks with their business to be able to pay depositors higher interest rates.

When considering doing business with an online bank or a smaller bank you've not heard of, you should be especially careful to ensure that the bank is covered under FDIC. Don't simply accept the bank's word for it or the display of the FDIC logo in its offices or on its website.

INVESTIGATE

Check the FDIC's website database of FDIC-insured institutions to see whether the bank you're considering doing business with is covered. Search by going to the FDIC's Bank Find page (banks.data.fdic.gov/bankfind-suite/bankfind). You can search by the name, city, state, or zip code of the bank. For insured banks, you can see the date when it became insured, its insurance certificate number, the main office location for the bank (and branches), its primary government regulator, and other links to detailed information about the bank. In the event that your bank doesn't appear on the FDIC list, yet the bank claims FDIC coverage, contact the FDIC at (877) 275-3342.

In addition to ensuring that a bank is covered by the FDIC, investigate the following:

>> **What is the bank's reputation for its services?** This may not be easy to discern, but at a minimum, you should conduct an internet search of the bank's name along with the word "complaints" or "problems" and examine the results.

>> **How accessible are customer-service people at the bank?** Is a phone number provided on the bank's website? How hard is it to reach a live person, the local branch, and its personnel (including the manager)? Are the customer-service representatives you reach knowledgeable and service-oriented?

>> **What are the process and options for getting your money out?** This issue is a good one to discuss with the bank's customer-service people.

>> **What fees are charged for particular services?** This information should be posted on the bank's website in a section called something like Account Terms or Disclosures. Also, request and inspect the bank's Truth in Savings Disclosure, which answers relevant account questions in a standardized format. Figure 6-1 is an example of an online bank's disclosure for savings accounts.

Protecting yourself when banking online

The attractions of banking online are pretty obvious. For starters, it can be enormously convenient, as you bank when you want on your computer or smartphone. You don't have to find a local bank branch during their limited open hours. And thanks to their lower overhead, the best online banks are able to offer competitive interest rates and account terms to their customers.

You probably know from experience that conducting any type of transaction online is safe as long as you use some common sense and know who you're doing business with before you go forward. That said, others who've gone before you have gotten ripped off, and you do need to protect yourself.

Truth in Savings Disclosure: Savings Account

Minimum balance to open the account — You must deposit $50.00 to open this account.

Rate information — Your interest rate is variable, and the annual percentage yield may be changed at any time at our discretion.

Compounding and crediting frequency — Interest will be compounded every quarter. Interest will be credited to your account every quarter.

Daily balance computation method — We use the daily balance method to calculate the interest on your account. This method applies a daily periodic rate to the principal in the account each day of the statement cycle.

Accrual of interest on noncash deposits — Interest begins to accrue on the first business day after the banking day you deposit noncash items (for example, checks).

Minimum balance to obtain the annual percentage yield disclosed — You must maintain a minimum balance of $15.00 in the account each day of the quarter to obtain the disclosed annual percentage yield.

Transaction limitations — Transfers from an Advantage Savings account to another account or to third parties by preauthorized, automatic, or telephone transfer are limited to six per month, with no transfers by check, draft, debit card, or similar order to third parties.

Minimum balance to avoid imposition of fees — You must maintain a minimum balance of $200.00 each day of the month to avoid monthly maintenance fees.

Fees — A monthly maintenance fee of $3.00 will be imposed if your account balance falls below the daily minimum balance requirement on any day during the month.

May be subject to additional fees for overdrafts or items returned for nonsufficient funds (NSF returned item fee).

© *John Wiley & Sons, Inc.*

FIGURE 6-1:
A sample Truth in Savings Disclosure statement from an online bank.

Take the following steps to protect yourself and your identity when conducting business online:

>> Never access your bank accounts from a shared computer or on a shared network, such as the free access networks offered in hotel rooms and in other public or business facilities.

>> Use two-factor authentication to minimize the chances that anyone other than you can access your account(s).

>> Be aware of missed statements, which could indicate that your account has been taken over.

>> Report unauthorized transactions to your bank or credit-card company as soon as possible; otherwise, your bank may not stand behind the loss of funds.

>> Use a complicated and unique password (including letters and numbers) for your online bank account.

>> Log out immediately after completing your transactions on financial websites.

Exploring Alternatives to Bank Accounts

If you've been with me since the beginning of this chapter, you know that the best banks that are focused online should have a cost advantage over their peers that have branch locations. Well, there are other financial companies that have similar, and in some cases even better, cost advantages (which translates into better deals for you): credit unions, discount and online brokerage firms, and mutual fund companies.

Credit union accounts and benefits

Credit unions are unique creatures (I guess I should say a unique species) within the financial-services–firm universe. Credit unions are similar to banks in the products and services that they offer (although private banks tend to offer a deeper array).

However, unlike banks, which are run as private businesses seeking profits, credit unions operate as nonprofit entities and are technically owned by their members (customers). If they're efficiently operated, the best credit unions offer their customers better terms on deposits, including checking and savings accounts (higher interest rates and lower fees) and some loans (lower rates and fees).

REMEMBER

Don't assume that credit unions necessarily or always offer better products and services than traditional banks, because they don't. The profit motive of private businesses isn't evil; quite to the contrary, the profit motive spurs businesses to keep getting better at and improving on what they do.

Credit unions have insurance coverage up to $250,000 per customer through the National Credit Union Administration (NCUA), similar to the FDIC protection that banks offer their customers. As when checking out a bank, be sure that any credit union you may deposit money into has NCUA insurance coverage.

The trick to getting access to a credit union is that by law, each individual credit union may offer its services only to a defined membership. Examples of the types of credit union memberships available include

>> Alumni

>> College and university

>> Community

>> Employer

>> Place of worship

There can be some overlap between these groups. To access a credit union, you also may be able to use your family ties.

To find credit unions in your local area, visit the Credit Union National Association consumer's website at www.asmarterchoice.org/.

Brokerage cash management accounts

A type of account worth checking out at brokerage firms is generally known as an asset management account. When these types of accounts first came into existence decades ago, they really were only for affluent investors. That is no longer the case, although the best deals on such accounts at some firms are available to higher-balance investors.

Brokerage firms enable you to buy and sell stocks, bonds, and other securities. Among the larger brokerage firms or investment companies with substantial brokerage operations you may have read or heard about are Charles Schwab, ETrade, Fidelity, and T.D. Ameritrade. Vanguard has a solid brokerage offering but discontinued their cash management account and is exploring whether to offer another again.

Now, some of these firms have fairly extensive branch office networks, and others don't. But those that have a reasonable number of branch offices have been able to keep a competitive position because of their extensive customer and asset base and because they aren't burdened by banking regulations (they aren't banks) and the costs associated with operating as a bank.

The best of brokerage firm asset management accounts typically enable you to

>> Invest in various investments, such as stocks, bonds, mutual funds, and exchange-traded funds, and hold those investments in a single account.

>> Write checks against a money market balance that pays competitive yields.

>> Use a Visa or Mastercard debit card for transactions.

Money market mutual funds

Because bank savings accounts historically have paid pretty crummy interest rates, you need to think long and hard about keeping your spare cash in the bank during normal times for interest rates and the economy. Instead of relying on the bank, try keeping your extra savings in a money market fund, which is a type of mutual fund. (Other funds focus on bonds or stocks.) Money market funds historically have offered a higher-yielding alternative to bank savings and bank money market deposit accounts. I use a money market fund that offers unlimited check writing at a mutual fund company. I also don't keep my extra savings in the bank.

During recent periods of ultra-low interest rates, you may find slightly better interest rates on some of the best online bank savings accounts and at some credit unions.

A money market fund is similar to a bank savings account except that it is offered by a mutual fund company and therefore lacks FDIC coverage. Historically, this hasn't been a problem because retail money market funds have lost shareholder principal in only one case for retail investors (the Reserve Primary fund lost less than 1 percent of assets during the 2008 financial crisis).

The attraction of money market funds has been that the best ones pay higher yields than bank savings accounts and also come in tax-free versions, which is good for higher-tax-bracket investors. I explain money market funds in greater detail in Chapter 7.

Chapter **7**

Managing Money Market Funds

For many years, folks kept their spare cash in a local bank, and for good reason. The local bank was convenient, offered safety and peace of mind with the government backing for money on deposit, and generally paid some interest on the money.

In the 1970s, however, the investment landscape changed for smaller investors. Interest rates and inflation increased, yet banks were limited by regulations in the interest rates they could pay depositors. Thus, was born, before you were born, the money market fund.

In this chapter, I discuss the risks and rewards of money funds, uses for funds, and how to pick the best ones to help you meet your investing goals.

Defining Money Market Mutual Funds

Money market mutual funds began in 1971. They invested in the higher-yielding financial instruments that were accessible only to larger institutional investors with large sums to invest. Money market funds "democratized" these investments by selling shares to investors with relatively small amounts to invest.

By pooling the money of thousands of investors, and after charging a reasonable fee to cover their operational expenses and make a profit, money market funds were able to offer investors a better yield than typical bank accounts.

Money market funds are unique among mutual fund company offerings because they don't fluctuate in value and maintain a fixed $1-per-share price. (An exception: During the 2008 financial crisis, the Reserve Primary fund had a small portion of its investments go bad, and some shareholders lost just under 1 percent of their invested principal.) As with a bank savings account, your principal investment in a money market fund doesn't change in value.

With a money market fund, your investment earns dividends. Dividends are much like the interest you receive from a bank savings account.

Making sense of the appeal of money market funds

During times of normal interest rates, the best money market mutual funds offer the following benefits over bank savings accounts:

» **Higher yields:** Money market mutual funds generally yield more because they don't have the higher costs that banks do from having branch offices all over. Banks can get away with paying lower yields because they know that many depositors believe that the Federal Deposit Insurance Corporation (FDIC) insurance that comes with a bank savings account makes it safer than a money market mutual fund. (For more on the safety of money funds compared with banks, see the next section, "Understanding the drawback of money market funds.") Also, the FDIC insurance is an expense that banks ultimately pass on to their customers. (See Chapter 6 for more on banks and banking options.)

» **Tax-free flavors:** If you're in a high tax bracket, tax-free money market funds offer you something that bank accounts don't. Bank accounts only pay interest that is fully taxable at both the federal and state levels. Money market funds can be state and federal tax-free (for folks in high tax brackets), just federal tax-free (for folks in a high federal tax bracket), or fully taxable.

» **Check writing:** Another useful feature of money market mutual funds is the ability they provide you to write checks, free of charge, against your account. Most mutual fund companies require that the checks that you write be for larger amounts — typically $250 minimum. Some brokerage cash management accounts that include money funds (at firms like Charles Schwab, Fidelity, and T.D. Ameritrade) allow you to write checks for any amount. With these types of money market fund accounts, you can ditch your bank completely because such accounts often come with debit cards that you can use at bank ATMs for a nominal fee. (Some brokerage firms levy service fees if you don't have enough assets with them or don't have regular monthly electronic transfers, such as direct deposit of your paycheck.)

Understanding the drawback of money market funds

During periods of normal interest rates, the best money market mutual funds have higher yields, tax-free alternatives, and check writing — features not offered by bank savings accounts. But you need to know about one difference between bank accounts and money market mutual funds: Money funds aren't insured (except for a one-year period during the 2008–2009 financial crisis).

Bank accounts come with FDIC insurance that protects your deposited money up to $250,000 (see Chapter 6). So if a bank fails because it lends too much money to people and companies that go bankrupt or abscond with the funds, you should get your money back from the FDIC.

REMEMBER

The lack of FDIC insurance on a money fund shouldn't trouble you, however. Mutual fund companies can't fail because they have a dollar invested in securities for every dollar that you deposit in their money funds. By contrast, banks are required to have available just a portion — about 10 cents for every dollar that you hand over to them.

Cases have occurred in which money market funds bought some investments that declined in value. However, in all but one case (and where the fund lost just under 1 percent of shareholder money) involving funds taking in money from retail investors like you and me, the money funds kept their $1-per-share price.

TIP

If you're concerned about the lack of FDIC insurance on a money market fund, stick with money market funds from the bigger mutual fund companies. They have the financial wherewithal and the biggest incentive to save a foundering money fund. Fortunately, the bigger fund companies typically have the best money funds anyway.

Looking at Money Market Fund Holdings

Money market funds are a safe, higher-yielding alternative to bank accounts. Under Securities and Exchange Commission regulations, money market funds can invest only in the highest-credit-rated securities, and their investments must have an average maturity of less than 60 days. The short-term nature of these securities effectively eliminates the risk of money market funds being sensitive to changes in interest rates (a concern with bonds, which are covered in Chapter 9).

The securities that money market funds buy and hold are extremely safe. General-purpose money market funds invest in government-backed securities, bank certificates of deposit, and short-term corporate debt that the largest and most creditworthy companies and the U.S. government issue.

You may not know (or care) what these holdings are. However, here's a short explanation of the most common money fund holdings to aid your understanding and comfort level:

>> **Commercial paper:** Larger corporations often need to borrow money to help make their businesses grow and prosper. In the past, most companies needing a short-term loan had to borrow money from a bank. In recent decades, issuing short-term debt known as *commercial paper* directly to interested investors has become easier. Money market funds buy high-quality commercial paper issued by large companies, banks, and foreign governments.

>> **Certificates of deposit:** When you put your money in a certificate of deposit (CD) at your local bank, what you're doing is making a specific-term loan (3 months, 6 months, 2 years) to your bank. Money market funds can buy CDs as well. When they do, however, they usually invest millions of dollars in bank CDs. Thus, they can command a higher interest rate than you can get on your own. Money funds buy CDs that mature within a couple of months. The money fund is insured only up to $250,000 per bank CD (so they may use multiple banks), just like the bank insurance that customers receive. As with other money fund investments, the money fund does research to determine the credit quality of banks and other institutions that it invests in. Remember that money funds' other investments aren't insured.

>> **Government debt:** The U.S. federal government has trillions of dollars in debt outstanding in the form of Treasury securities. In addition to investing in Treasuries soon to mature, money funds invest in short-term debt issued by government-affiliated agencies. Some money market funds specialize in certain types of government securities that distribute tax-free income to their investors. Treasury money market funds, for example, buy Treasuries and pay dividends that are state-tax-free but federally taxable. State-specific municipal money market funds invest in debt issued by state and local governments in one state. The dividends on state money funds are federal-tax-free and state-tax-free, if you're a resident of that state.

Protecting and Accessing Your Money in Money Funds

A potential psychological impediment to some folks, especially those from your parents' generation, of using money funds is that they must deal with money funds online, by phone, and through the mail. That creates some worries, like one of your checks getting lost or stolen and how accessible your money is, but protecting and accessing your money isn't as challenging as it may seem. And increasing numbers of fund companies allow you to do nearly everything sans paper.

Protecting your money

Checks received and sent from a money market fund are just as safe as those received and sent from any other type of account. No one can legally cash a check made payable to you. Don't mistakenly think that going to your local bank in person is safer. Bank robberies happen all the time, totaling in the thousands annually.

Increasing numbers of money market funds offer mobile apps that enable you to take a picture of and deposit checks with your smartphone, all from the comfort of your home or wherever you happen to be. If your fund company doesn't offer a mobile check deposit app and you're really concerned about sending a check in the mail, use a fund company or discount broker with branch offices reasonably close to your home or office. I don't recommend spending the extra money and time required to send your check by way of registered or certified mail. You know if your check got there when you get the transaction entry from the fund company processing the deposit.

In those rare cases where a check does get lost, remember that checks can be reissued. And when you're depositing a check made payable to you, be sure to endorse the check with the notation "For deposit only" along with your account number under your signature.

Accessing your money

With most money market mutual funds, you will likely be sending your money to a company out of state, so it may seem to you that you won't be able to easily access these funds if you need to. However, you can efficiently tap your money market fund in a variety of ways. You can use the following methods at most fund companies:

>> **Check writing:** The simplest way to access your money market fund is to write a check. Suppose you have an unexpectedly large expense that you can't afford to pay out of your bank checking account. Just write a check on your

money market mutual fund. Alternatively, you can simply charge such an expense on your credit card and pay off that bill when due through check writing or the bill payment feature if you have that on your cash management type account.

>> **Electronic fund transfers:** Another handy way to access your money is to have your money sent electronically from your money market fund to your bank account, or vice versa. Such transactions can also usually be done on fund companies' websites or through your smartphone and typically take one business day to complete. Or you can have the fund company mail you a check for your desired amount from your money fund (although that obviously isn't a "quick" way to get needed money). If you need money regularly sent from your money market fund to, say, your local bank checking account, you can set up an automatic withdrawal plan. On a designated day of the month, your money market fund electronically sends money to your checking account.

>> **Debit cards:** Brokerage account money funds that offer debit cards allow access to your money through bank ATMs. Just find out first what fees you may have to pay for using particular ATM networks.

>> **Wiring:** If you need cash in a flash (for example, same day), many money market funds offer the option of wiring money to and from your bank. Banks usually assess a charge for this service, especially when you're wiring money out from your bank. Most companies can also send you money via an overnight express carrier, although you'll likely have to foot that bill.

REMEMBER

Unlike when you visit a bank, you can't simply drop by the branch office of a mutual fund company (even if it happens to be nearby) and withdraw funds from your account. Money market fund companies don't keep money in branch offices because they're not banks. However, you can establish the preceding account features, if you didn't set them up when you originally set up your account, by completing online forms at the fund company's website, by mailing in a form, or by visiting the fund's branch office.

Using Money Market Funds in Your Investment Plan

The best money market funds enable you to substitute for a bank savings account while offering comparable safety to a bank, but with a better yield during times of normal interest rates. Money market funds are well suited for some of the following purposes:

>> **Rainy-day/emergency reserve:** Because you don't know what the future holds, you're wise to prepare for the unexpected, such as job loss, the desire to take some extra time when changing jobs, unexpected healthcare bills, or a leaky roof on your home. Three to six months' worth of living expenses is a good emergency reserve target for most people. (If you spend $2,500 in an average month, for example, keep $7,500 to $15,000 in reserve.) Three months' living expenses may do if you have other accounts, such as a 401(k), or family that you could tap for a loan. Keep up to one year's expenses if your income fluctuates greatly. If your profession involves a high risk of job loss, and if finding another job could take a long time, you also need a significant cash safety net.

>> **Short-term savings goals:** If you're saving money for a big-ticket item that you hope to purchase within the next couple of years — whether it's a vacation, a car, or a down payment on a home — a money market fund is a sensible place to save the money. With a short time horizon, you can't afford to expose your money to the gyrations of stocks or longer-term bonds. A money market fund offers a safe haven for your principal and some positive return.

>> **A parking spot for money awaiting investment:** Suppose you have a significant chunk of money that you want to invest for longer-term purposes, but you don't want to invest it all at once, for fear that you may buy into stocks and bonds just before a big drop. A money market fund can be a friendly home to the money awaiting investment as you gradually move it into your chosen investment. (I explain this technique, known as dollar cost averaging, in Chapter 5.)

>> **Personal checking accounts:** You can use money market funds with no restrictions on check writing for household checking purposes. Some discount brokerage services that offer accounts with a check-writing option downplay the fact that an investor is allowed to write an unlimited number of checks in any amounts on their account. You can leave your bank altogether; some money funds even come with bill payment features and debit cards that you can use at bank ATMs for a nominal fee.

>> **Business accounts:** You can also open a money market fund for your business. You can use this account for depositing checks received from customers and holding excess funds, as well as for paying bills by means of the check-writing feature. Some money funds allow checks to be written for any amount, and such accounts can completely replace a bank checking account.

Shopping for the Best Money Funds

If you're interested in putting some of your money into a money market mutual fund, in this section, I name names. Before getting to that, however, allow me to explain what I look for when selecting a money market fund.

Discovering traits of leading money funds

When looking for an outstanding money market fund, look for these attributes:

>> **Low expenses:** Select a money market fund that does a good job of controlling its expenses. The operating expenses that the fund deducts before payment of dividends are the biggest determinant of yield. All other things being equal (which they usually are with different money market funds), lower operating expenses translate into higher yields for you. Within a given category of money market funds (general, Treasury, municipal, and so on), fund managers invest in the same basic securities. The market for these securities is pretty darn efficient, so "superstar" money market fund managers may eke out an extra 0.1 percent per year in yield, but not much more. Lower expenses don't mean that a fund company cuts corners or provides poor service. By attracting more money to manage, efficiently managed larger funds are able to manage money for a lower expense percentage.

>> **Tax appropriate for your situation:** With money market funds, all your return comes from dividends. What you actually get to keep of these returns is what's left over after the federal and state governments take their cut of your investment income. If you invest money that's held outside a retirement account, and you're in a high tax bracket, you may come out ahead if you invest in tax-free money market funds. (*Tax-free* refers to the taxability of the dividends that the fund pays. You don't get a tax deduction for money that you put into the fund, as you do with certain retirement accounts.) If you're in a high-tax state, a state money market fund — if a good one exists for your state — may be a sound move.

>> **Other attractive fund offerings:** Consider what other investing you plan to do at the fund company where you establish a money market fund. Suppose you decide to make mutual fund investments in stocks and bonds at a specific fund company. In that case, keeping a money market fund at a different firm that offers a slightly higher yield may not be worth the time and administrative hassle, especially if you don't plan on holding much cash in your money market fund.

>> **Associated services:** Good money market funds offer other useful services included with their accounts, such as check writing, telephone exchange and redemptions, and automated electronic exchange services with your bank account.

Most mutual fund companies don't have many local branch offices. Generally, this fact helps fund companies keep their expenses low so they can pay you greater money market fund yields.

You may open and maintain your mutual fund account via the fund's company's website and toll-free phone lines. You don't really get much benefit from selecting a fund company with an office in your area (although you may feel some peace of mind).

Naming good money funds

Using the criteria in the preceding section, in this section, I recommend good money market funds — that is, those that offer competitive yields, check writing, access to other excellent mutual funds, and other commonly needed money market services.

Money market funds that pay taxable dividends may be appropriate for retirement account funds that await investment as well as nonretirement-account money when you're not in a high federal tax bracket and aren't in a high state tax bracket (less than 5 percent).

Here are the best taxable money market funds to consider:

>> Fidelity Cash Reserves

>> T. Rowe Price Cash Reserves

>> Vanguard's Federal Money Market

Consider U.S. Treasury money market funds if you prefer a money market fund that invests in U.S. Treasuries, which maintain the safety of government backing, or if you're not in a high federal tax bracket but are in a high state tax bracket (5 percent or higher).

Here are the U.S. Treasury funds that I recommend:

>> Fidelity's Government Cash Reserves

>> USAA's Treasury Money Market

>> Vanguard Treasury Money Market

Municipal (also known as *muni*) money market funds invest in short-term debt that state and local governments issue. A municipal money market fund, which pays you federally tax-free dividends, invests in munis issued by state and local governments throughout the country.

A state-specific municipal fund invests in state and local government-issued munis for one state, such as New York. So, if you live in New York and buy a New York municipal fund, the dividends on that fund are federal and New York state tax-free.

So how do you decide whether to buy a nationwide or state-specific municipal money market fund? Federal tax-free-only money market funds may be appropriate when you're in a high federal tax bracket but not in a high state bracket (less than 5 percent). State tax-free municipal money market funds are worth considering when you're in a high federal and a high state tax bracket (5 percent or higher).

If you're in a higher state tax bracket, your state may not have good (or any) state tax-free municipal money market funds available. If you live in any of those states, you're likely best off with one of the following national municipal money market funds:

>> USAA Tax-Exempt Money Market

>> Vanguard Tax-Exempt Money Market

Fidelity, USAA, and Vanguard have good funds for several states. If you can't find a good state-specific fund for your state, or you're in a high federal tax bracket only, use one of these nationwide muni money markets.

Alternatives to Money Market Mutual Funds

Banks have an account that is similar to a money market mutual fund, which they typically call a money market deposit account (MMDA). Banks set the interest rate on MMDAs, and historically, those rates have been a bit lower than what you can get from one of the better money market mutual funds (although this has been less true during the extended period of recent low interest rates). Check writing on MMDAs, if it's available, may be restricted to a few checks monthly.

As latecomers to the mutual fund business, some banks now offer real money market mutual funds, including tax-free money funds. Again, the better money market mutual funds from mutual fund companies are generally superior to those offered by banks. The reason: Most bank money market funds have higher operating expenses and, hence, lower yields than the best money funds offered by mutual fund companies.

Although I advocate use of the best money market funds, I realize that a bank or credit union savings account is sometimes the most practical place to keep your money. Your local bank, for example, may appeal to you if you like being able to conduct business face to face. Perhaps you operate a business where some cash is processed; in this case, you probably can't beat the convenience and other services that a local bank offers.

If you have only $1,000 or $2,000 to invest, a bank savings account may be your better option; the best money market funds generally require a higher minimum initial investment.

TIP

For investing short-term excess cash, you may first want to consider keeping it in your checking account. This option may make financial sense if the extra money helps you avoid monthly service charges on your checking account because your balance occasionally dips below the minimum. In fact, keeping money in a separate savings account rather than in your checking account may not benefit you if service charges wipe out your interest earnings. This is especially true with interest rates at such relatively low levels.

Be sure to shop around for the best deals on your checking account because minimum balance requirements, service fees, and interest rates vary. Credit unions offer some of the best deals, although they usually don't offer extensive access to free ATMs (see Chapter 6). The largest banks with the most ATMs generally don't have the best terms on checking and savings accounts.

3

Investing in Stocks, Bonds, and Funds

IN THIS PART . . .

Discover how to make money with stocks.

See how bonds can bring stability to your investment portfolio.

Use mutual funds and exchange-traded funds to invest in stocks, bonds, and other common investments.

Find out how to select the right brokerage firm.

Chapter **8**

Getting Your Slice of Capitalism with Stocks

I
s it true that only the rich get richer and that to get ahead, you have to know the right people?

I've never been a fan of the class warfare that too often permeates partisan political discourse these days. One reason for my distaste is the simple truth that the facts are on the side of capitalism's being the best system to allow folks of all different means to better their lives and enjoy a good standard of living.

Consider the opportunity to share in the upside presented by owning a stake in successful businesses. That's exactly what you're doing when you buy shares of stock, either through funds or directly through a stock exchange.

You don't need big bucks or the right connections or inside information to earn handsome long-term returns in stocks. (Trading on true inside information can land you in legal hot water.) You simply need to read and digest the time-tested principles I present in this chapter.

I explain what stocks are, how you can make money with them, and the pros and cons of the various methods for purchasing them. I also detail how to time your purchases and sales and how to sidestep disasters and maximize your chances for success.

What Are Stocks?

Entrepreneurs start companies, and at some point in that process, perhaps even many years after the company was initially formed, company founders may sell a portion of their shares of ownership in the company known as *stock*. Some companies choose to issue stock to raise money, whereas others choose to issue bonds, which are simply loans that the company promises to repay (see Chapter 9).

When you and other members of the investing public buy stock, these outside investors continue to hold and trade it over time. From time to time, some companies may choose to buy back some of their own stock, usually because they think it's a good investment, but they're under no obligation to do so.

By issuing stock, company founders and employee-owners are able to sell some of their relatively illiquid private stock and reap the rewards of their successful company. Growing companies also generally favor stock offerings (over selling bonds to investors) because the company doesn't want the future cash drain that comes from paying loans (bonds) back.

Although many company owners like to take their companies public (issuing stock) to cash in on their stake in the company, not all owners want to go public, and not all who do go public are happy that they did. One of the numerous drawbacks of establishing your company as public includes the burdensome financial reporting requirements, such as publishing quarterly earnings statements and annual reports. Going public also can increase awareness and generate good press for the company, which can increase the company's value.

Regulatory required documents not only take lots of time and money to produce, but they can also reveal competitive secrets. Some companies also harm their long-term planning ability because of the pressure and focus on short-term corporate performance that comes with being a public company.

REMEMBER

From your perspective as a potential investor, you can usually make more money in stocks than bonds, but stocks are generally more volatile in the short term. You can also get burned when buying stock when a company is issuing new stock for the first time, through what is called an *initial public offering* (IPO).

Ultimately, companies seek to raise capital in the lowest-cost way they can, so they elect to sell stocks or bonds based on what the finance folks tell them is the best option. For example, if the stock market is booming and new stock can sell at a premium price, companies opt to sell more stock through an IPO. (Some have jokingly said that IPO may actually stand for "It's Probably Overpriced!") Some companies opt for selling stock because they don't like carrying debt.

You generally should avoid IPOs because newly issued stock more often than not declines or underperforms in price soon after the offering. Of course, there are exceptions to this, especially when growth stocks are in high demand. But such demand can quickly change, and prices quickly retreat.

When a company decides to issue stock, the company's management team typically works with investment bankers, who help companies decide when and at what price to sell stock. When a company issues stock, the price per share that the stock is sold for is somewhat arbitrary.

The amount that a prospective investor will pay for a particular portion of the company's stock should depend on the company's profits and future growth prospects. Companies that produce higher levels of profits and grow faster generally command a higher sales price for a given portion of the company.

REMEMBER

A stock's price per share by itself is meaningless in evaluating whether to buy a stock. Ultimately, the amount that investors will pay for a company's stock should depend greatly on the company's growth and profitability prospects, which I discuss in the next section.

How (and Why) You Can Make Money with Stocks

Understanding why stocks tend to appreciate over time and produce better returns than bonds and bank accounts isn't rocket science. It's really pretty simple. In this section, I explain how corporate profits drive stock prices and the different ways you can make money from stocks.

Understanding the importance of corporate profits

The goal of most companies is to make a profit, or earnings. *Earnings* result from the difference between what a company takes in (revenue) and what it spends (costs). I say *most companies* because some organizations' primary purpose is not to maximize profits.

Nonprofit organizations — such as the American Cancer Society, Goodwill, Red Cross, and numerous medical centers, colleges, and universities — are well-known examples. However, even nonprofits can't thrive and prosper over the long haul without a steady flow of money.

Companies that trade publicly on the stock exchanges seek to maximize their profit; that's what their shareholders want. Higher profits generally make stock prices increase. Most private companies seek to maximize their profits as well, but they retain much more latitude to pursue other goals.

Among the major ways that successful companies increase profits are

>> **Building (or buying) a brand name:** What comes to mind when you think of Amazon, Apple, Costco, CVS, eBay, McDonald's, Microsoft, Target, and UPS? These are all powerful brand names that have taken their respective companies many years and many dollars to build. Companies with recognizable and positive brand images enjoy more consumer traffic, sales, and profits.

>> **Containing costs:** Well-managed companies continually search for ways to control costs without compromising quality. Lowering the cost of manufacturing their products or providing their services allows companies to offer their products and services at lower prices. Managing costs may help boost a company's profits. The marketplace and a company's reputation (and the threat of lawsuits) keep companies from cutting corners and making their products and services dangerous in some way.

>> **Developing superior products or services:** Some companies develop or promote an invention or innovation that better meets customer needs. Smartphones, 3-D printers, home gutters that don't require cleaning, hybrid vehicles, numerous biotechnology offerings — the list goes on. This progress is what keeps the American economy resilient and strong, regardless of the parade of knuckleheads in Washington.

>> **Monitoring competitors:** Successful companies don't follow the herd, but they do keep an eye on what their competition is up to. If lots of competitors target one part of the market, some companies target a less-pursued segment that, if they can capture it, may produce higher profits thanks to reduced competition.

>> **Selling products and services in new markets:** Many successful U.S.-based companies, for example, have been expanding into foreign countries to sell their products. Although some product or service adaptation is generally required to sell overseas, selling a proven, developed product or service to new markets generally increases a company's chances for success.

Making sense of how you profit with stocks

Company stock prices tend to rise over time as the company's profits increase. So how do you make money investing in a company's stock? When you purchase a share of a company's stock, you can profit from your ownership in two ways:

>> **Price appreciation:** When the price per share of your stock rises to a higher price than you originally paid for it, you can make money. This profit, however, is only on paper until you sell the stock, at which time you realize a capital gain. Such gains realized over periods longer than one year are taxed at the lower long-term capital gains tax rate (see Chapter 4). Of course, the stock price per share can fall below what you originally paid, in which case you have a loss on paper unless you realize that loss by selling at a lower price than you paid for the stock.

>> **Dividends:** Most stocks pay dividends. Companies generally make some profits during the year. Some high-growth companies reinvest most or all of their profits right back into the business. Many companies, however, pay out some of their profits to shareholders in the form of dividends. Increasing numbers of companies use part of their profits to buy back stock, which is a tax-friendly way to provide benefits to current shareholders compared with paying out more in the form of taxable dividends.

Your total return from investing in a stock, then, comes from dividends and stock price appreciation. Stocks differ in the dimensions of these possible returns, particularly with respect to dividends. (See the sections on stock funds and exchange-traded funds in Chapter 10 for more information.)

Timing Your Stock Buying and Selling

One of the biggest temptations and one of the mistakes you're most likely to make investing in stocks is trying to jump into and out of stocks based on your shorter-term expectations of where a particular stock or the market as a whole may be heading.

In this section, I explain what the major market indexes mean and what value there may be in "following" any of them. I cover what measures may be useful in spotting when to buy and sell, and what problematic practices are likely to undermine your stock market investing success.

Following market indexes

You invest in stocks to share in the rewards of capitalistic economies. When you invest in stocks, you do so through the stock market. In the United States, when folks talk about "the market," they're usually referring to the Dow Jones Industrial Average (DJIA), a widely watched U.S. stock market index created by Charles Dow and Eddie Jones of the *Wall Street Journal.* The DJIA market index tracks the performance of 30 large companies that are headquartered in the United States, but it's not the only index.

Indexes serve the following purposes:

>> They can quickly give you an idea of how particular types of stocks are doing at the moment and over time.

>> They enable you to compare or benchmark the performance of your stock market investments. If you invest primarily in large-company U.S. stocks, for example, you should compare the overall return of the stocks in your portfolio to a comparable index — in this case, the S&P 500 (which I define later in this chapter).

You may also hear about some other types of more narrowly focused indexes, including those that track the performance of stocks in particular industries, such as airlines, energy, financials, healthcare, retail, semiconductors, technology, and utilities. Other indexes cover other stock markets, such as those in the United Kingdom, Germany, France, Canada, and Hong Kong.

WARNING

Focusing your investments on the stocks of just one or two industries, especially those that aren't major ones, or smaller countries is dangerous due to the lack of diversification and your lack of expertise in making the difficult decision about what to invest in and when. Thus, I suggest that you ignore these narrower indexes.

In addition to the DJIA, important market indexes and the types of stocks they track include

>> **Standard & Poor's (S&P) 500:** Like the DJIA, the S&P 500 tracks the price of 500 larger-company U.S. stocks. These 500 big companies account for about 75 percent of the total market value of the tens of thousands of stocks traded in the United States. Thus, the S&P 500 is a much broader and more representative index of the larger-company stocks in the United States than is the DJIA.

>> **Russell 2000:** This index tracks the market value of 2,000 smaller U.S. company stocks of various industries. Although small-company stocks tend to move in tandem with larger-company stocks over the longer term, it's not unusual for one to rise or fall more than the other or for one index to fall while the other rises in a given year.

>> **Wilshire 5000:** Despite its name, the Wilshire 5000 index actually tracks the prices of about 3,500 stocks of U.S. companies of all sizes — small, medium, and large. Thus, many people consider this index to be the broadest and most representative of the overall U.S. stock market.

>> **MSCI EAFE:** Stocks don't exist only in the United States. MSCI's EAFE (Europe, Australasia, and Far East) index tracks the prices of stocks in the other major developed countries of the world.

>> **MSCI Emerging Markets:** This index follows the value of stocks in less economically developed but emerging countries, such as South Korea, Brazil, China, Russia, Taiwan, India, South Africa, and Mexico. These stock markets tend to be more volatile than those in established economies. During good economic times, emerging markets usually reward investors with higher returns, but stocks can fall farther and faster than stocks in developed markets.

Using price/earnings ratios to value stocks

You can't compare different companies' stock prices and determine from that which one(s) may be a better investment. The level of a company's stock price relative to its earnings or profits per share helps you measure how expensively, cheaply, or fairly a stock price is valued.

Over the long term, stock prices and corporate profits tend to move in tandem. The *price/earnings (P/E) ratio* compares the level of stock prices to the level of corporate profits, giving you a good sense of the stock's value. Over shorter periods of time, investors' emotions as well as *fundamentals* (data that can affect the perceived value or price of a stock) move stocks, but over longer terms, fundamentals possess a far greater influence on stock prices.

P/E ratios can be calculated for individual stocks as well as entire stock indexes, portfolios, or funds. The P/E ratio of U.S. stocks has averaged around 15 over the past century. During times of low interest rates and inflation, the ratio has tended to be higher — in the high teens to low twenties.

Just because U.S. stocks have historically averaged P/E ratios of about 15 to 20 doesn't mean that every individual stock will trade at that P/E level. Faster-growing companies usually command higher P/E ratios.

TIP

Though a stock price or an entire stock market may appear to be at a high price level, that doesn't necessarily mean that the stock or market is overpriced. Compare the price of a stock to that company's profits per share or the overall market's price level to the overall corporate profits. The P/E ratio captures this comparison. Faster-growing and more-profitable companies generally have higher P/E ratios (meaning that they sell for a premium). Also remember that future expected earnings, which are difficult to predict, influence stock prices more than current earnings, which are old news.

Most of the time, the stock market is reasonably efficient. By that, I mean that a company's stock price normally reflects many smart people's assessments as to what is a fair price. Thus, it's not realistic for an investor to expect to discover a system for how to "buy low and sell high." A few investors may have some ability to spot good times to buy and sell particular stocks, but doing so consistently is enormously difficult.

TIP

The simplest and best way to make money in the stock market is to regularly feed new money into building a diversified and larger portfolio. If the market drops, you can use your new investment dollars to buy more shares. The danger of trying to time the market is that you may be out of the market when it appreciates greatly and in the market when it plummets.

Avoiding temptations and hype

Because the financial markets move on the financial realities of the economy and companies, as well as on people's expectations and emotions (particularly fear and greed), you shouldn't try to time the markets. Knowing when to buy and sell is much harder than you may think.

There are millions of investors around the world who follow stocks and companies closely, and they are well aware of all the news that you've likely been listening to and reading. What typically moves the stock market in the short term are surprises that few if any investors saw coming. Consider what happened, for example, in early 2020 with COVID-19 and how stocks got clobbered in a few weeks once it became clear that the government was going to mandate a widespread economic shutdown.

WARNING

As a young adult, you're in a position to take more risks because you're investing for the long haul. However, you should be careful that you don't get sucked into investing a lot of your money in aggressive investments that seem to be in a hyped state. Many people don't become aware of an investment until it receives lots of attention. By the time everyone else talks about an investment, it's often nearing or at its peak.

INVESTIGATE

Before you invest in any individual stock, no matter how great a company you think it is, you need to understand the company's line of business, strategies, competitors, financial statements, and P/E ratio versus the competition, among many other issues. Selecting and monitoring good companies take research, time, and discipline.

Also, remember that if a company taps into a product line or way of doing business that proves to be highly successful, that success invites competition. So you need to understand the barriers to entry that a leading company has erected and how difficult or easy it is for competitors to join the fray.

WARNING

Be wary of analysts' predictions about earnings and stock prices. Investment banking firm analysts, who are too optimistic (as shown in numerous independent studies), have a conflict of interest because the investment banks that they work for seek to cultivate the business (new stock and bond issues) of the companies that they purport to rate and analyze.

Simply buying today's rising and analyst-recommended stocks often leads to future disappointment. If the company's growth slows or the profits don't materialize as expected, the underlying stock price can nosedive.

Psychologically, it's easier for many folks to buy stocks after those stocks have had a huge increase in price. Just as you shouldn't attempt to drive your car looking solely through your rearview mirror, choosing investments solely on past performance usually leads novice investors into overpriced investments. If many people are talking about the stunning rise in the market, and new investors pile in based on the expectation of hefty profits, tread carefully.

I'm not saying that you need to sell your current stock holdings if you see an investment market getting frothy and speculative. As long as you diversify your stocks worldwide and hold other investments, such as real estate and bonds, the stocks that you hold in one market need to be only a portion of your total holdings.

REMEMBER

Timing the markets is difficult: You can never know how high is high and when it's time to sell, and then how low is low and when it's time to buy. And if you sell nonretirement-account investments at a profit, you end up sacrificing a lot of the profit to federal and state taxes.

Getting past the gloom

During the 2008 financial crisis, panic (and talk of another Great Depression) was in the air, and stock prices dropped sharply. Peak to trough, global stock prices plunged more than 50 percent. While some companies went under (and garnered lots of news headlines), those firms were few and were the exception rather than the norm. Many terrific companies weathered the storm, and their stock could be scooped up by investors with cash and courage at attractive prices and valuations.

When bad news and pessimism abound and the stock market has dropped, it's actually a much safer and better time to buy stocks. You may even consider shifting some of your money out of your safer investments, such as bonds, and invest more aggressively in stocks. During these times, investors often feel that prices can drop further, but if you buy and wait, you'll likely be amply rewarded.

Even when the economy is not obviously doing poorly, you can easily find concerns and reasons not to invest. Maybe you don't like the current political party in power or worry about the declining dollar, too much inflation or not enough, conflicts in various parts of the world, and so on. It's not hard, especially if you consume plenty of media, to find numerous reasons to not invest in stocks due to things others say you should worry about. It does take courage to invest in stocks and similar assets and to take risks. But history has repeatedly shown that those who take sensible risks are rewarded over the long term.

Sidestepping common investing minefields

Shares of stock, which represent fractional ownership in companies, offer a way for people of all economic means to invest in companies and build wealth. History shows that long-term investors can win in the stock market because it appreciates over the years. That said, some people who remain active in the market over many years manage to lose some money because of easily avoidable mistakes, which I can keep you from making in the future.

WARNING

You can greatly increase your chances of investing success and earning higher returns if you avoid the following common stock investing mistakes:

>> **Broker conflicts:** Some investors make the mistake of investing in individual stocks through a broker who earns commissions. The standard pitch of these firms and their brokers is that they maintain research departments that monitor and report on stocks. Their brokers use this research to tell you when to buy, sell, or hold. It sounds good in theory, but this system has significant problems. Many brokerage firms happen to be in another business that creates enormous conflicts of interest in producing objective company reviews. These investment firms also solicit companies to help them sell new stock and bond issues. To gain this business, the brokerage firms need to demonstrate enthusiasm and optimism for the company's future prospects. Studies of brokerage firms' stock ratings have shown that from a predictive perspective, their research generally has a poor predictive track record.

>> **Short-term trading:** Unfortunately (for themselves), some investors track their stock investments closely and believe that they need to sell after short holding periods — months, weeks, or even days. With the growth of internet and smart phone trading, such shortsightedness has taken a turn for the worse as more investors now engage in a foolish process known as *day trading,* in which they buy and sell a stock within the same day! Whether you hold a stock for only a few hours or a few months, you're not investing; you're gambling. Specifically, the numerous drawbacks that I see to short-term trading include more taxes and tax headaches, lower returns from being out

of the market when it moves up, and inordinate amounts of time spent researching and monitoring your investments. Even if you use a broker offering "free" trading, you pay an implicit price every time you buy and sell.

>> **Following gurus:** It's tempting to wish that you could consult a guru who could foresee an impending major decline and get you out of an investment before it tanks. Believe me when I say that plenty of these pundits are talking up such supposed prowess. From having researched many such claims (see the "Guru Watch" section of my website, www.erictyson.com), I can tell you that nearly all these folks significantly misrepresent their past predictions and recommendations. Also, the few who made some halfway-decent predictions in the recent short term had poor or unremarkable longer-term track records. As you develop your investment portfolio, take a level of risk and aggressiveness with which you're comfortable. No pundit has a working crystal ball that can tell you what's going to happen with the economy and financial markets in the future.

Highlighting How to Invest in Stocks

When you invest in stocks, you have lots of choices. In addition to the tens of thousands of stocks to choose from, you can invest in mutual funds, exchange-traded funds (ETFs), or hedge funds.

Investing in stock mutual funds and exchange-traded funds

Mutual funds take money invested by people like you and me and pool it into professionally managed investment portfolios in securities, such as stocks and bonds. *Stock mutual funds*, as the name suggests, invest primarily or exclusively in stocks. (Some stock funds sometimes invest a bit in other stuff, such as bonds.)

If you're busy and realize your lack of expertise analyzing and picking stocks, you'll love the best stock mutual funds. Investing in stocks through mutual funds can be as simple as dialing a toll-free phone number or logging on to a fund company's website, completing some application forms, and zapping off the money you want to invest.

Exchange-traded funds (ETFs) are newer versions of mutual funds. The best ETFs are in many ways similar to mutual funds except that they trade on a stock exchange. The chief attractions are those ETFs that offer investors the potential for even lower operating expenses than those of comparable mutual funds.

The best stock mutual funds and ETFs offer numerous advantages:

>> **Diversification:** Buying individual stocks on your own is relatively costly through most brokers unless you buy reasonable chunks (100 shares or so) of each stock. But to buy 100 shares each of, say, a dozen companies' stocks to ensure diversification, you may need about $60,000 if the stocks you buy average $50 per share.

>> **Professional management:** Even if you have big bucks to invest, funds offer something that you can't deliver: professional, full-time management. Mutual fund managers peruse a company's financial statements and otherwise track and analyze its business strategy and market position. The best managers put in long hours and possess lots of expertise and experience in the field.

>> **Low costs:** To convince you that mutual funds and ETFs aren't good ways for you to invest, those with a vested interest, such as stock-picking pundits, may point out the high fees that some funds charge. But high-cost funds aren't the only ones out there. Through a *no-load* (commission-free) mutual fund or ETF, you can hire a professional, full-time money manager to invest $10,000 for a mere $10 to $50 per year.

Mutual funds and ETFs, of course, have drawbacks:

>> **Less control:** If you like being in control, sending your investment dollars to a seemingly black-box process in which others decide when and in what to invest your money may unnerve you. However, you should be more concerned about the potential blunders that you may make investing in individual stocks of your own choosing or, even worse, those stocks pitched to you by a broker.

>> **Taxes:** Taxes are a concern when you invest in mutual funds and ETFs outside retirement accounts. Because the fund manager decides when to sell specific stock holdings, some funds may produce relatively high levels of taxable distributions. But you can use tax-friendly funds and ETFs if taxes concern you.

Picking your own stocks

Plenty of investing blogs, gurus, and books enthusiastically encourage people to do their own stock picking. However, the vast majority of investors are better off not picking their own stocks.

INVESTING THROUGH HEDGE FUNDS

Like mutual funds, hedge funds are managed investment vehicles — an investment management team researches and manages the funds' portfolio. However, hedge funds are oriented toward affluent investors and typically charge steep fees — a 1.0 percent to 1.5 percent annual management fee, plus a 20 percent cut of the annual fund returns. Those high hedge-fund fees depress their returns.

Notwithstanding the small number of hedge funds that have produced better long-term returns, too many affluent folks invest in hedge funds due to the funds' hyped marketing and the badge of exclusivity they offer.

I've long been an advocate of people educating themselves and taking responsibility for their own financial affairs, but taking responsibility for your own finances doesn't mean you should do everything yourself.

Some popular investing websites and books try to convince investors that they can do a better job than the professionals at picking their own stocks. Amateur investors, however, need to devote a lot of study to become proficient at stock selection. Many professional investors work 80 hours a week at investing, but you're unlikely to be willing or able to spend that much time on it.

Researching individual stocks

When investing in stocks, I think you're better off sticking to mutual funds and ETFs. In Chapter 10, I dive into far more detail about how to do just that. However, I realize that you may be interested in picking some stocks on your own.

You can spend hundreds of hours researching and reading information on one company alone. Therefore, unless you're financially independent and want to spend nearly all your productive time investing, you need to focus on where you can get the best bang for your buck and time:

>> **The *Value Line Investment Survey:*** Value Line is an investment research company. Value Line's securities analysts have been tracking and researching stocks since 1931. Its analysis and recommendation track record is quite good, and its analysts are beholden to no one. Many professional money managers use the *Value Line Investment Survey,* Value Line's weekly publication (and website subscription at www.valueline.com), as a reference because of its comprehensiveness. Value Line condenses the key information and statistics about a stock and the company behind the stock to a single page.

>> **Morningstar:** This firm (www.morningstar.com) is better known for its reports on funds, but it has decent research summaries for many individual stocks, especially those of larger and well-followed companies. The very basic information on companies is available without charge, but to get the more comprehensive information (including their research analysts' reviews), you must be a paid subscriber.

>> **Independent brokerage research:** If you're going to invest in individual stocks, you need a brokerage account. In addition to offering low trading fees, the best brokerage firms allow you to easily tap into useful research, especially through the firm's website, that you can use to assist with your investing decisions. Because discount brokers aren't in the investment-banking business of working with companies to sell new issues of stock, discount brokers have a level of objectivity in their research reports that traditional brokers (ones like Merrill Lynch, Morgan Stanley, and so on) often lack. Some discount brokers, such as Charles Schwab, produce their own highly regarded research reports, but most discount brokers simply provide reports from independent third parties.

>> **Successful money managers' stock picks:** To make money in stocks, you certainly don't need an original idea. In fact, it makes sense to examine what the best money managers are buying for their portfolios. Mutual fund managers, for example, are required to disclose at least twice a year what stocks they hold in their portfolios. You can call the best fund companies and ask them to send their most recent semiannual reports that detail their stock holdings, or you can view those reports on many fund companies' websites. Through its website, Morningstar allows you to see which mutual funds hold large portions of a given stock that you may be researching and what the success or lack thereof is of the funds that are buying a given stock. Finally, you can follow what Warren Buffett's and other successful investors' funds are buying by visiting the Securities and Exchange Commission website at www.sec.gov and looking up specific investment funds' holdings (via their so-called 13F filings).

>> **Financial publications and websites:** Many publications and websites cover the world of stocks. But you have to be careful: Just because certain columnists or publications advocate particular stocks or investing strategies doesn't mean that you'll achieve success by following their advice. Many publications, blogs, and websites are devoted to stock picking. (Visit my site at www.erictyson.com for more information.)

>> **Annual reports:** Publicly traded companies must file certain financial documents annually. Consider reviewing these documents to enhance your understanding of a company's businesses and strategies rather than for the predictive value that you may hope they provide. The annual report is a yearly report that provides standardized financial statements, as well as management's discussion of how the company has performed and how it plans to

improve future performance. While some companies have been sued for misleading shareholders with inflated forecasts or lack of disclosure of problems, know that responsible companies try to present a balanced — and, of course, hopeful — perspective in their annual reports.

>> **10-Ks:** 10-Ks are expanded versions of annual reports. Most investment professionals read the 10-K rather than the annual report because the 10-K contains additional data and information, especially for a company's various divisions and product lines. Also, 10-Ks contain little of the verbal hype that you find in most annual reports. In fact, the 10-K is probably one of the most objective reports that a company publishes. If you're not intimidated by annual reports or if you want more details, read the 10-Ks of the companies you want to check out. 10-Qs provide information similar to 10-Ks, but on a quarterly basis.

>> **Earnings calls:** Listen to a recent earnings call. Earnings calls allow you to hear from management, as well as listen to the questions that professional analysts ask. Replays are often available on companies' investor-relations websites.

Final thoughts on stock picking

Keep the amount that you dedicate to individual stock investments to a minimum — ideally, no more than 20 percent of your invested dollars. I encourage you to do such investing for the educational value and enjoyment that you derive from it, not because you smugly think you're as skilled as the best professional money managers. Unless you're extraordinarily lucky or unusually gifted at analyzing company and investor behavior, you won't earn above-average returns if you select your own stocks.

When investing in stocks, you should be doing it with the goal and expectation of holding on to the stocks over a number of years and perhaps even decades. After putting a good deal of time and effort into identifying stocks to buy, why would you want to turn around and sell your stocks after just a few days, weeks, or even months of holding?

TIP

Try to buy stock in good-size chunks. Otherwise, commissions at some brokers gobble a large percentage of the small dollar amount you invest. If you don't have enough money to build a diversified portfolio all at once, don't sweat it. Diversify over time. Purchase shares of one stock after you have enough money accumulated and then wait to buy the next stock until you've saved another chunk of money to invest.

Maximizing Your Stock Market Returns

Anybody, no matter what their educational background, IQ, occupation, income, or assets, can make solid returns investing in stocks.

To ensure your stock market investment success, remember the following:

» **Don't try to time the markets.** Anticipating where the stock market and specific stocks are heading is next to impossible, especially over the short term. Economic factors, which are influenced by thousands of elements as well as human emotions, determine stock market prices. Be a regular buyer of stocks with new savings. As I discuss earlier in this chapter, buy more stocks when prices are down and market pessimism is high.

» **Diversify your investments.** Invest in the stocks of different-size companies in varying industries around the world. When assessing your investments' performance, examine your whole portfolio at least once a year, and calculate your total return after expenses and trading fees.

» **Keep trading costs, management fees, and commissions to a minimum.** These costs represent a big drain on your returns. If you invest through an individual broker or a financial advisor who earns a living on commissions, odds are that you're paying more than you need to be, and you're likely receiving biased advice, too.

» **Pay attention to taxes.** Like commissions and fees, federal and state taxes are major investment expenses that you can minimize. Contribute most of your money to your tax-advantaged retirement accounts. You can invest your money outside retirement accounts, but keep an eye on taxes (see Chapter 4). Calculate your annual returns on an after-tax basis.

» **Don't overestimate your ability to pick the big-winning stocks.** One of the best ways to invest in stocks is through mutual funds and ETFs, which allow you to use an experienced, full-time money manager at a low cost to perform all the investing grunt work for you (see Chapter 10).

Chapter **9**

Securing Investment Income and Principal with Bonds

When you invest, it's fun and rewarding to see your investments grow over the years. Riskier investments like stocks and real estate can produce generous long-term returns, well in excess of the rate of inflation. But lending investments like bonds make sense for a portion of your money if

» **You expect to sell some of those investments within five years.** Stocks and other growth-oriented investments can fluctuate too much in value to ensure you're getting your principal back within five years.

» **Investment volatility makes you nervous, or you just want to cushion some of the volatility of your other, riskier investments.** High-quality and shorter-term bonds tend to provide investors a smoother ride.

» **You need more current income from your investments.** Bonds tend to produce more income in the short term. That said, you need to be aware that dividend-paying stocks may offer more income over the long term, as their dividends tend to increase over time.

>> **You don't need to make your money grow after inflation and taxes.** Perhaps you're one of those rare folks who has managed to amass a nice-size nest egg at a relatively young age, and you're less concerned with growing that money.

Mind you, all these conditions need not apply for you to put some of your money into bonds. And, in reality, it's really just the first two points listed that would be more typical reasons for a young adult to consider some bonds. Also, this list isn't meant to be an exhaustive list of reasons to invest some money in bonds.

In this chapter, I discuss how and why to use bonds in your investment portfolio, explain the different types of bonds as well as alternatives to bonds, and describe the best ways to invest in bonds.

Defining Bonds

Bonds are middle-ground investments. They generally offer higher yields than bank accounts and less volatility than the stock market. That's why bonds appeal to safety-minded investors as well as to otherwise-aggressive investors who seek diversification or investments for short-term financial goals.

Bonds differ from one another according to several factors: the entities that issue the bonds (which has important associated income tax implications), credit quality, and time to maturity. After you have a handle on these issues, you're ready to consider investing in bond mutual funds, exchange-traded bond funds, and perhaps even some individual bonds (although I caution you especially against jumping into individual bonds, which can be minefields for inexperienced investors).

Unfortunately, due to shady marketing practices by some investing companies and bond salespeople, you can have your work cut out for you while trying to get a handle on what many bonds really are and how they differ from their peers. I walk you through how bonds differ from one another in this section.

Understanding bond issuers

A major dimension in which bonds differ is the organizations that issued the bonds. The issuer of a bond is actually borrowing money from the folks who buy the bonds when they're originally sold.

REMEMBER

Who issues a bond is hugely important. First, it determines how likely the bond issuer is to be able to pay back the bonds' principal when the bonds mature. Second, the type of entity doing the bond issuance determines the federal and state income taxation of the bond's interest payments.

The following list covers the major options for who issues bonds (in order of popularity) and tells you when each option may make sense for you:

>> **Corporate bonds:** Companies such as CVS, Delta Air Lines, Disney, Microsoft, Tesla, and Visa issue corporate bonds. Corporate bonds pay interest that's fully taxable at the federal and state levels. Thus, such bonds make sense for investing inside retirement accounts. Lower-tax-bracket investors can consider investing in such bonds outside a tax-sheltered retirement account. (Higher-tax-bracket investors should consider municipal bonds, which appear later in this list.)

>> **Treasury bonds:** Treasuries are issued by the U.S. government. Treasuries pay interest that's state-tax-free but federally taxable. Thus, they make sense if you want to avoid a high state income tax bracket but not a high federal income tax bracket. However, most people in a high state income tax bracket also happen to be in a high federal income tax bracket. Such investors may be better off in municipal bonds (explained next), which are both free of federal and state income tax (in their state of issuance). The best use of Treasuries is in place of bank certificates of deposit (CDs), as both types of investments have government backing. Treasuries that mature in the same length of time as a CD may pay the same interest rate or a better one.

REMEMBER

Bank CD interest is fully taxable, whereas a Treasury's interest is state-tax-free.

>> **Municipal bonds:** Municipal bonds (muni bonds, for short) are issued by state or local governments. Muni bonds pay interest that's free of federal and state taxes to residents in the state of issue. For example, if you live in New York and buy a bond issued by a New York government agency, you probably won't owe New York state or federal income tax on the interest. The government organizations that issue municipal bonds know that the investors who buy these bonds don't have to pay most or any of the income tax that is normally assessed on other bonds' interest payments. Therefore, the issuing governments can pay a lower rate of interest. If you're in a high tax bracket and want to invest in bonds outside of your tax-sheltered retirement accounts, compare the yield on a given muni bond (or muni bond fund) to the after-tax yield on a comparable taxable bond (or bond fund).

>> **Convertible bonds:** Convertible bonds are bonds that you can convert under a specified circumstance into a preset number of shares of stock in the company that issued the bond. Although these bonds do pay taxable interest, their yield is lower than that of nonconvertible bonds because convertibles offer you the potential to make more money from the underlying stock.

>> **International bonds:** You can buy bonds issued in foreign countries. These international bonds, which can be issued by foreign companies and governments, are riskier because their interest payments can be offset by currency price changes. The prices of foreign bonds tend not to move in tandem with U.S. bonds. Foreign bond values benefit from, and thus protect against, a declining U.S. dollar; therefore, they offer some diversification value. Conversely, when the U.S. dollar appreciates versus most currencies (which happened during the early 1980s, from 1995 to 2002, and during the early 2010s), that lowers a U.S. investor's return on foreign bonds.

Foreign bonds aren't vital holdings for a diversified portfolio. They're generally more expensive to purchase and hold than comparable domestic bonds.

TREASURY INFLATION-PROTECTED SECURITIES (TIPS)

The U.S. government offers bonds called Treasury inflation-protected securities (TIPS). Compared with traditional Treasury bonds, TIPS usually carry a lower interest rate. The reason for this lower rate is that the other portion of your return with these inflation-indexed bonds comes from the annual inflation adjustment to the principal you invest. The inflation portion of the return gets added back into the principal yearly.

If you invest $10,000 in an inflation-indexed bond, and inflation is 3 percent the first year you hold the bond, your principal increases to $10,300 at the end of the first year.

What's potentially attractive about these bonds is that no matter what happens with the rate of inflation, investors who buy TIPS earn some return (the yield or interest rate paid) above and beyond the rate of inflation, especially when held to maturity. Thus, holders of inflation-indexed Treasuries can't have the purchasing power of their principal or interest eroded by high inflation.

Because inflation-indexed Treasuries protect investors from the ravages of inflation, they represent less-risky securities. But consider this little-known fact: If the economy experiences deflation (falling prices), your principal isn't adjusted down, so these bonds offer some deflation protection as well. Technically, the principal can't fall below the original par amount, but it can decline back to that level. So if you buy a TIPS that was issued a while ago and it has had the principal factored higher due to inflation, you could suffer a declining principal if deflation occurs.

Considering credit (default) risk

Closely tied to what organizations are actually issuing the bonds, bonds also differ in the creditworthiness of their issuers. Credit rating agencies such as Moody's, Standard & Poor's, and Fitch rate the credit quality and likelihood of default of bonds.

The credit rating of a bond depends on the issuer's ability to pay back its debt. Bond credit ratings are usually done on some sort of a letter-grade scale. AAA usually is the highest rating, and ratings descend through AA and A, followed by BBB, BB, B, CCC, CC, C, and so on.

>> **AAA- and AA-rated bonds** are considered to be high-grade or high-credit-quality bonds. Such bonds possess little chance of default (a fraction of 1 percent).

>> **BBB-rated bonds** are considered to be investment-grade or general-quality bonds.

>> **BB- or lower-rated bonds** are known as junk bonds (or as their marketed name, high-yield bonds). Junk bonds, also known as non-investment-grade bonds, are more likely to default; perhaps as many as 2 percent per year actually default but it can spike higher during downturns.

TIP

To minimize investing in bonds that default, purchase highly rated bonds. Now, you may ask why investors would knowingly buy a bond with a low credit rating. They may purchase one of these bonds because the issuer pays a higher interest rate on lower-quality bonds to attract investors. The lower a bond's credit rating and quality, the higher the yield you can and should expect from such a bond.

WARNING

Poorer-quality bonds aren't for the faint of heart because they're generally more volatile in value. I don't recommend buying individual high-yield/junk bonds; consider investing in these only through a well-run high-yield/junk-bond fund. (Keep in mind that the volatility profile for such a bond fund is closer to stocks than it is for high-grade corporate bonds.)

Making sense of bond maturities

Bonds are generally classified by the length of time until maturity. *Maturity* simply means the time at which the bond promises to pay back your principal if you hold the bond. Maturity could be next year, in 7 years, in 15 years, and so on.

Bonds classifications are as follows:

>> **Short-term bonds** mature in the next few years.

>> **Intermediate-term bonds** come due within three to ten years.

>> **Long-term bonds** mature in more than 10 years and generally up to 30 years.

WARNING

A small number of companies (such as Coca-Cola, Disney, Ford, and IBM) have issued 100-year bonds. I don't recommend buying such bonds, however, especially those issued during a period of low interest rates, because they get hammered if long-term interest rates spike higher. There's also a lot more time for the borrower to default — that's what happened with now failed retailer J.C. Penney's 100-year bonds issued in the late 1990s.

You should care how long a bond takes to mature because maturity gives you some sense of how volatile a bond may be if overall market interest rates change. If interest rates fall, bond prices rise; if interest rates rise, bond prices fall. Longer-term bonds generally drop more in price when the overall level of interest rates rises.

If you hold a bond until it matures, you get your principal back unless the issuer defaults. In the meantime, however, if interest rates rise, bond prices fall. The reason is simple: If the bond that you hold is issued at, say, 3 percent, and interest rates on similar bonds rise to 5 percent, no one (except someone who doesn't know any better) will want to purchase your 3 percent bond. The value of your bond has to decrease enough so it effectively yields 5 percent.

Most of the time, long-term bonds pay higher yields than short-term bonds do. You can look at a chart of the current yield of similar bonds plotted against when they mature — a chart known as a *yield curve*. At most times, this curve slopes upward. Investors generally demand a higher rate of interest for taking the risk of holding longer-term bonds.

Using Bonds in a Portfolio

Investing in bonds is a time-honored way to earn a better rate of return on money that you don't plan to use within the next couple of years or more but without the relatively high short-term volatility and larger downside risk of stocks. Like stocks, bonds can generally be sold any day that the financial markets are open.

In this section, I discuss how to use bonds as an investment and explain how bonds compare with other lending investments.

Finding uses for bonds

Because their value fluctuates, you're more likely to lose money if you're forced to sell your bonds sooner rather than later. In the short term, if the bond market happens to fall and you need to sell, you could lose money. In the long term, as is the case with stocks, you're far less likely to lose money.

Following are some common situations in which investing in bonds can make sense:

>> **You're looking to make a major purchase.** This purchase should be one that won't happen for at least two years. Examples include buying a car or a home. Short-term bonds may work for you as a higher-yielding and slightly riskier alternative to money market funds.

>> **You want to diversify your portfolio.** Bonds don't move in lockstep with the performance of other types of investments, such as stocks. In fact, in a poor economic environment (such as during the Great Depression of the 1930s or the 2008 financial crisis), bonds may appreciate in value while riskier investments such as stocks decline. Bonds increased in value while stocks initially plummeted in March 2020 during the COVID-19 government-mandated economic shutdowns.

>> **You're interested in diversifying your long-term investments.** You may invest some of your money in bonds as part of a long-term investment strategy, such as for retirement. You should have an overall plan for how you want to invest your money (see Chapter 2). Aggressive younger investors should keep much less of their retirement money in bonds than older folks who are nearing retirement. There's no need during your younger adult years to invest any of your long-term money in bonds so long as you are knowledgeable about and comfortable with the higher short-term risks you are accepting with stocks.

>> **You need income-producing investments.** When you're retired (probably much later in life) or not working, bonds can be useful because they're better at producing current income than many other investments.

WARNING

I don't generally recommend putting your emergency cash reserve in bonds. That's what a money market fund or bank savings/credit union account is for (see Chapters 6 and 7).

Don't put much of your long-term investment money in bonds, either. Bonds are generally inferior investments for making your money grow. Growth-oriented investments — such as stocks, real estate, and your own business — hold the greatest potential to build real wealth.

Comparing other lending investments with bonds

As I explain in Chapter 1, lending investments are those in which you lend your money to an organization, such as a bank, company, or government, that typically pays you a set or fixed rate of interest. Ownership investments, by contrast, provide partial ownership of a company or some other asset, such as real estate, that has the ability to generate revenue and potential profits.

Lending investments aren't the best choice if you really want to make your money grow, but even the most aggressive investors should consider placing some of their money in lending investments. This buffer of money can serve meeting emergency needs and a reservoir to tap when attractive investing opportunities appear.

In this chapter, I focus on bonds, but I'd be remiss if I failed to point out that lending investments are everywhere: banks, credit unions, brokerage firms, insurance companies, and mutual fund companies. Lending investments that you may have heard of include bank accounts (savings and CDs), Treasury bills and other bonds, bond mutual funds and exchange-traded bond funds, mortgages, and *guaranteed-investment contracts* (GICs).

Bonds, money market funds, and bank savings vehicles are hardly the only lending investments. A variety of other companies are more than willing to have you lend them your money and pay you a relatively fixed rate of interest. In most cases, though, you're better off staying away from the investments described in the following sections.

Too many investors get sucked into lending investments that offer higher yields and are pitched as supposedly better alternatives to bonds.

REMEMBER

Risk and return go hand in hand, so higher yields mean greater risk, and vice versa.

One of the allures of nonbond lending investments, such as private mortgages, GICs, and CDs, is that they don't fluctuate in value — at least not that you can see. Such investments appear to be safer and less volatile. You can't watch your principal fluctuate in value because you can't look up the value daily the way you can with bonds and stocks.

But the principal values of your mortgage, GIC, and CD investments really do fluctuate; you just don't see the fluctuations! Just as the market value of a bond drops when interest rates rise, so does the market value of these investments — and for the same reasons. At higher interest rates, investors expect a discounted price on a fixed-interest-rate investment because they always have the alternative of purchasing a new mortgage, GIC, or CD at the higher prevailing rates. Some of these investments are actually bought and sold, and behave just like bonds, among investors in what's known as a secondary market.

TIP

If the normal volatility of a bond's principal value makes you uneasy, try not to follow your investments so closely!

In the sections that follow, I explain common lending investments that are often pitched as bond alternatives with supposedly more stable prices. You can find information on CDs in Chapter 6.

Guaranteed-investment contracts (GICs)

Through your retirement plan at work, you may be pitched to invest in *guaranteed-investment contracts* (GICs). The allure of GICs, which are sold and backed by insurance companies, is that your account value doesn't appear to fluctuate. (Other insurer-backed investments sold to the public through brokers are similar.) Like one-year bank CDs, GICs generally quote you an interest rate for the next year. Some GICs lock in the rate for longer periods, whereas others may change the interest rate several times per year.

Keep in mind that the insurance company that issues the GIC does invest your money, mostly in bonds and maybe a bit in stocks. Like other bonds and stocks, these investments fluctuate in value; you just don't see the fluctuation.

Typically once a year, you receive a new statement showing that your GIC is worth more, thanks to the newly added interest. This statement makes otherwise-nervous investors who can't stand volatile investments feel safe and sound.

The yield on a GIC is usually comparable to those available on short-term, high-quality bonds, yet the insurer invests in long-term bonds and some stocks. The insurer pockets the difference between what these investments generate for the insurer and what the GIC pays you in interest.

The insurer's take can be significant and is generally hidden. Mutual funds and exchange-traded funds are required to report the management fees that they collect and subtract before paying your return, but GIC insurers have no such obligations. By having a return guaranteed in advance (with no chance for loss), you pay heavily with many GICs — an effective fee upward of 2 percent per year — for peace of mind in the form of lower long-term returns.

The high effective fees that you pay to have an insurer manage your money in a GIC aren't the only drawbacks. When you invest in a GIC, your assets are part of the insurer's general assets. Insurance companies sometimes fail, and although they typically merge with healthy insurers if that happens, you can still lose money. The rate of return on GICs from a failed insurance company is often slashed to help restore financial soundness to the company. So the only "guarantee" that comes with a GIC is that the insurer agrees to pay you the promised rate of interest as long as it is able.

Private mortgages

To invest in mortgages directly, you can loan your money to people who need money to buy or refinance real estate. Such loans are known as *private mortgages,* or *second mortgages* if your loan is second in line behind someone's primary mortgage.

You may be pitched to invest in a private mortgage by folks you know in real estate-related businesses. Mortgage and real estate brokers often arrange mortgage investments, and you must tread carefully, because these people have a vested interest in seeing the deal done. Otherwise, the mortgage broker doesn't get paid for closing the loan, and the real estate broker doesn't get a commission for selling a property.

Private mortgage investments appeal to investors who don't like the volatility of the stock and bond markets and who aren't satisfied with the seemingly low returns on bonds or other common lending investments. Private mortgages appear to offer the best of both worlds — stock-market-like returns without the volatility that comes with stocks.

One broker who also happens to write about real estate wrote an article describing mortgages as the "perfect real estate investment" and added that mortgages are a "high-yield, low-risk investment." The writer/broker further gushed that mortgages are great investments because you have "little or no management, no physical labor."

You may know by now that a low-risk, high-yield investment doesn't exist. Earning a relatively high interest rate goes hand in hand with accepting relatively high risk. The risk is that the borrower can default — which leaves you holding the bag. (In the mid to late 2000s, mortgage defaults skyrocketed.) More specifically, you can get stuck with a property that you may need to foreclose on, and if you don't hold the first mortgage, you're not first in line with a claim on the property.

The fact that private mortgages are high-risk should be obvious when you consider why the borrower elects to obtain needed funds privately rather than through a traditional mortgage lender like a bank. Put yourself in the borrower's shoes. As a property buyer or owner, if you can obtain a mortgage through a conventional lender, such as a bank, wouldn't you do so? After all, banks generally give better interest rates. If a mortgage broker offers you a deal where you can, for example, borrow money at 8 percent when the going bank rate is, say, 4 percent, the deal must carry a fair amount of risk.

INVESTIGATE

I recommend that you generally avoid investing in private mortgages. If you really want to invest in such mortgages, you must do some time-consuming homework on the borrower's financial situation. A banker doesn't lend someone money without examining a borrower's assets, liabilities, and monthly expenses, and you shouldn't either. Be careful to check the borrower's credit, and get a large down payment (at least 20 percent). The best circumstance in which to be a lender is if you sell some of your own real estate, and you're willing to act as the bank and provide the financing to the buyer in the form of a first mortgage.

Also recognize that your mortgage investment carries interest-rate risk: If you need to "sell" it early, you'll have to discount it, perhaps substantially if interest rates have increased since you purchased it. Try not to lend so much money on one mortgage that it represents more than 5 percent of your total investments.

If you're willing to lend your money to borrowers who carry a relatively high risk of defaulting, consider investing in high-yield (junk) bond mutual funds or exchange-traded funds instead (see Chapter 10). With these funds, you can at least diversify your money across many borrowers, and you benefit from the professional review and due diligence of the fund management team. You can also consider lending money to family members.

How and Where to Invest in Bonds

You can invest in bonds in one of two major ways: You can invest in a professionally selected and managed portfolio of bonds via a bond mutual fund or exchange-traded fund (ETF), or you can purchase individual bonds.

In this section, I help you decide how to invest in bonds. If you want to take the individual-bond route, I cover that path here, including the purchasing process for various types of bonds such as Treasuries, which are different in that you can buy them directly from the government. If you fall on the side of mutual funds and ETFs, see Chapter 10 for all the details.

Choosing between bond funds and individual bonds

Unless the bonds you're considering purchasing are easy to analyze and homogeneous (such as Treasury bonds), you're generally much better off investing in bonds through a mutual fund or ETF. Here's why:

>> **Diversification is easy with funds and much more difficult with individual bonds.** You shouldn't put your money in a small number of bonds of companies in the same industry or that mature at the same time. It's difficult to cost-effectively build a diversified bond portfolio with individual issues unless you have more than $1 million that you want to invest in bonds.

>> **The best funds are cost-effective; individual bonds cost you more money.** Great bond funds are yours for less than 0.3 percent per year in operating expenses (see Chapter 10). If you purchase individual bonds through a broker, you're going to pay a commission. In most cases, the commission cost is hidden; the broker quotes you a price for the bond that includes the commission. Even if you use a discount broker, these fees take a healthy bite out of your investment. The smaller the amount you invest, the bigger the percentage bite. On a $1,000 bond, the commission fee can equal several percent.

>> **You have better things to do with your time than research bonds and go bond shopping.** Bonds are boring (to most), and bonds and the companies that stand behind them aren't simple to understand. Did you know, for example, that some bonds can be called before their maturity dates? Companies may *call* bonds, which means they repay the principal before maturity to save money if interest rates drop from the level at which the bond was originally issued. After you purchase a bond, you need to do the same things that a good bond fund portfolio manager needs to do, such as track the issuer's creditworthiness and monitor other important financial developments. In addition to the direction of overall interest rates, changes in the financial health of the issuing entity company that stands behind the bond strongly affect the price of an individual bond.

Investing in Treasury bonds

If you want to purchase Treasury bonds, buying them through the Federal Reserve's Treasury Direct program online is generally the lowest-cost method. The Federal Reserve doesn't charge for buying Treasuries through these online accounts (www.treasurydirect.gov).

You may also purchase and hold Treasury bonds through brokerage firms and mutual funds. Brokers typically charge a flat fee for buying a Treasury bond. Buying Treasuries through a brokerage account makes sense if you hold other securities through the brokerage account and you like the ability to quickly sell a Treasury bond that you hold. Selling Treasury bonds held through the Federal Reserve is a hassle, as you must transfer the bonds out to a broker to do the selling for you.

The advantage of a fund that invests in Treasuries is that it typically holds Treasuries of differing maturities, thus offering diversification. You can generally buy and sell no-load (commission-free) Treasury bond funds easily and without fees. Funds, however, do charge an ongoing management fee. (See Chapter 10 for my recommendations of Treasury mutual funds with good track records and low management fees.)

Investing in non-Treasury individual bonds

Purchasing other types of individual bonds, such as corporate and mortgage bonds, is a much more treacherous and time-consuming undertaking than buying Treasuries. Here's my advice for doing it right and minimizing the chance of mistakes:

>> **Buy quality, not yield.** Yes, junk bonds pay higher yields, but they also have a much higher chance of default. Also, did you know what a subprime mortgage was before it was all over the news that defaults were on the rise just as the 2008 financial crisis and severe recession were unfolding? (*Subprime* mortgages are mortgage loans made to borrowers with lower credit ratings who pay higher interest rates because of their higher risk of default.) You're not a professional money manager who's trained to spot problems and red flags; stick with highly rated bonds so you don't have to worry about and suffer through these unfortunate consequences.

>> **Diversify.** Invest in and hold bonds from a variety of companies in different industries to buffer changes in the economy that adversely affect one industry or a few industries more than others. Of the money that you want to invest in bonds, don't put more than 5 percent in any one bond. Diversification requires a large amount to invest, given the size of most bonds, and trading fees erode your investment balance if you invest too little. If you can't achieve this level of diversification, use a bond fund.

>> **Understand that bonds may be called early.** Many bonds, especially corporate bonds, can legally be called before maturity. In this case, the bond issuer pays you back early because it doesn't need to borrow as much money or because interest rates have fallen and the borrower wants to issue new bonds at a lower interest rate. Be especially careful about purchasing bonds that were issued at higher interest rates than those that currently prevail. Borrowers pay off such bonds first.

>> **Shop around.** Just like when you buy a car, shop around for good prices on the bonds you have in mind. The hard part is doing an apples-to-apples comparison, because brokers may not offer exactly the same bonds. Remember that the two biggest determinants of what a bond should yield are its maturity date and its credit rating. Beware of using commission-based brokers. Many of the worst bond-investing disasters have befallen customers of such brokerage firms. Your best bet is to purchase individual bonds through discount brokers.

Evaluating individual bonds you currently hold

Perhaps you've already bought some bonds or inherited them. If you already own individual bonds, and they fit your financial objectives and tax situation, you can hold them until maturity, because you already paid a commission when you purchased them. Selling the bonds before their maturity would just create an additional fee. (When the bonds mature, the broker who sold them to you will probably be more than happy to sell you some more. That's the time to check out good bond funds — see Chapter 10.)

REMEMBER

Don't mistakenly think that your current individual bonds pay the yield that they had when they were originally issued. That yield is the number listed in the name of the bond on your brokerage account statement. As the market level of interest rates changes, the *effective yield* (the interest payment divided by the bond's price) on your bonds fluctuates to rise and fall with the market level of rates for similar bonds. So if rates have fallen since you bought your bonds, the value of those bonds has increased — which in turn reduces the effective yield that you're earning on your invested dollars.

Chapter **10**

Fund Investing: Mutual Funds and Exchange-Traded Funds

This chapter is all about investing through funds — mutual funds and exchange-traded funds (ETFs). Mutual funds are simply pools of money from investors that a mutual fund manager uses to buy a bunch of stocks, bonds, and other assets that meet the fund's investment criteria.

The best ETFs are quite similar to mutual funds — specifically, index mutual funds. Such ETFs generally track a major market index. Some ETFs, however, track narrowly focused indexes, such as an industry group or small country. Others are actively managed and have a changing portfolio over time, just as you would with an actively managed mutual fund.

The most significant difference between a mutual fund and an ETF is that to invest in an EFT, you must buy it through a stock exchange where the ETF trades, just as individual stocks trade. Mutual funds are typically bought through the fund company and don't trade during the trading day but instead close out orders received by 4 p.m. EST.

Different types of funds can help you meet various financial goals. You can use money market funds for something most everybody needs: an emergency savings stash of three to six months' living expenses. Or perhaps you're thinking about saving for a home purchase, retirement, or future educational costs. If so, you can consider some stock and bond funds.

Because efficient funds take most of the hassle and cost out of deciding which companies to invest in, they're among the finest investment vehicles available today. Also, funds enable you to have some of the world's best money managers direct the investment of your money.

In this chapter, I discuss how to match funds to your investing objectives and assemble a portfolio of superior funds. I also cover alternatives to funds.

Understanding the Advantages of Funds

The best funds are superior investment vehicles for people of all economic means, and they can help you accomplish many financial objectives. The following list highlights the main reasons for investing in funds rather than in individual securities. (If you want to invest in individual stocks, see Chapter 8.)

>> **Low cost:** Funds spread the cost of research over many, many investors. The most efficiently managed mutual funds cost less than 1 percent per year in fees and many far lower. (Bonds and money market funds usually cost much less — in the neighborhood of 0.3 percent per year or less.) Some of the larger and more established funds can charge annual fees less than 0.2 percent per year; that's less than a $2 annual charge per $1,000 you invest. The best and lowest cost index funds and ETFs generally charge 0.1 percent per year or less!

>> **Diversification:** Funds generally invest in dozens of securities. Diversification is a big attraction for many investors who choose funds because proper diversification increases the chance that the fund will earn higher returns with less risk. Most funds own stocks or bonds in dozens of companies, thus diversifying against the risk of problems from any single company or sector. Achieving such diversification on your own is difficult and expensive unless you have a few hundred thousand dollars and a great deal of time to invest.

>> **Professional management:** Fund investment companies hire a portfolio manager and researchers whose full-time jobs are to analyze and purchase suitable investments for the fund. These people screen the universe of investments for those that meet the fund's stated objectives. Fund managers are typically graduates of the top business and finance schools, where they learned portfolio management, securities valuation, and securities selection.

Many have additional investing credentials, such as Chartered Financial Analyst (CFA) certification. The best fund managers also typically possess more than ten years' experience analyzing and selecting investments.

For fund managers and researchers, finding the best investments is a full-time job. They do major analysis that you lack the time or expertise to perform. Their activities include assessing companies' financial statements; interviewing company managers to hear the companies' business strategies and vision; examining competitors' strategies; speaking with companies' customers, suppliers, and industry consultants; attending trade shows; and reading industry periodicals.

>> **Achievable investment minimums:** Many mutual funds have minimums of $1,000 or less. Retirement-account investors can often invest with even less. Some funds even offer monthly investment plans so you can start with as little as $50 per month. Heck, some fund companies now have zero minimums on select funds like the Fidelity Zero index funds! ETFs are generally even better in this department because there are no minimums overall, although you need to weigh potential brokerage costs of buying and selling ETF shares. (Some fund companies and brokers do offer their own and certain other companies' ETFs free of brokerage fees.)

>> **Funds to fit varying needs:** You can select funds that match the ratio of risk to reward you need to meet your financial goals. If you want your money to grow over a long period, and if you can handle down as well as up years, choose stock-focused funds. If you seek current income and don't want investments that fluctuate as widely in value as stocks do, consider some bond funds. If you want to be sure that your invested principal doesn't decline in value because you may need to use your money in the short term, select a money market fund. Most investors choose a combination of these types of funds to diversify and to accomplish different financial goals.

>> **High financial safety:** Fund companies can't fail because the value of fund shares fluctuates as the securities in the fund rise and fall in value. For every dollar of securities that they hold for their customers, mutual funds and ETFs have a dollar's worth of securities. The worst that can happen with a fund is that if you want your money, you may get less money than you originally put into the fund due to a market value decline of the fund's holdings — but you won't lose all your original investment. For added security, the specific stocks, bonds, and other securities that a mutual fund buys are held by a *custodian,* a separate organization independent of the mutual fund company. A custodian ensures that the fund management company can't abscond with your funds.

>> **Accessibility:** Funds are set up for people who value their time and don't like going to a local branch office and standing in lines. You can fill out a simple form (often online, if you want) and authorize electronic transfers from your bank or other accounts or write a check to make your initial investment. Then

you typically can make subsequent investments by sending money electronically or other convenient methods. Many fund companies and investment brokerage firms also allow you to transfer money electronically back and forth from your bank account. Selling shares of your mutual fund usually is simple, too. Generally, all you need to do is visit its website, use its app, or call the fund company's toll-free number to make the arrangements.

Maximizing Your Chances for Fund Investing Success

I recommend using some straightforward, commonsense, easy-to-use criteria when selecting funds to greatly increase your chances of fund investing success. The criteria presented in this section have proven to dramatically increase your fund investing returns. (My website, www.erictyson.com, has details on research and studies that validate these criteria.)

Understanding the importance of performance and risk

A common and often costly mistake that many investors make when they select a fund is overemphasizing the importance of past performance. The shorter the time period you analyze, the greater the danger that you'll misuse high past performance as an indicator for a fund's likely future performance.

High past returns for a fund, relative to its peers, are largely possible only if a fund takes more risk or if a fund manager's particular investment style happens by luck to come into favor for a few years. The danger of a fund's taking greater risk in the pursuit of market-beating and peer-beating returns is that it doesn't always work the way you hope. The odds are great that you won't be able to pick the next star before it vaults to prominence in the fund universe. You're more likely to jump into a recently high-performing fund and then be along for the ride when it plummets back to reality.

WARNING

Some funds make themselves look better by comparing themselves with funds that aren't really comparable. The most common ploy starts with a manager investing in riskier types of securities; then the fund company, in its marketing, compares its fund's performance with that of fund companies that invest in less-risky securities. Always examine the types of securities that a fund invests in and then make sure the comparison funds or indexes invest in similar securities.

A fund's historic rate of return or performance is one of several important factors to examine when you select funds. Keep in mind that — as all fund materials must tell you — past performance is no guarantee of future results. In fact, many former high-return funds achieved their results only by taking on high risk and/or benefitting from short-term luck or good fortune. Funds that assume higher risk may sometimes produce higher rates of return, but high-risk funds can easily decline in price faster during market declines.

Examining fund management experience

Although the individual fund manager is important, a manager isn't an island unto himself. The resources and capabilities of the parent company are equally, if not more, important. Managers come and go, but fund companies usually don't.

Different companies maintain different capabilities and levels of expertise with different types of funds. A fund company gains more or less experience than others not only from the direct management of certain fund types, but also through hiring out. Some fund families contract with private money management firms that possess significant experience. In other cases, private money management firms with long histories in private money management — such as Dodge & Cox and Primecap Management — offer funds to the general public, either directly or indirectly through another fund management provider (for example, Primecap manages money in several Vanguard stock funds).

Keeping costs down

The charges that you pay to buy or sell a fund, as well as the ongoing fund operating expenses, have a major effect on the return that you ultimately earn on your fund investments. Given the enormous number of choices available for a particular type of fund, there's no reason to pay high costs.

Fund costs are an important factor in determining the return that you ultimately earn from a fund because fees are deducted from your investment returns. High fees and other charges depress your returns. Here's what I recommend you do regarding fees:

>> **Minimize operating expenses.** All funds charge fees as long as you keep your money in the fund. The fees pay for the costs of running a fund, such as employees' salaries, marketing, website operations, toll-free phone lines, and writing and publishing prospectuses (the legal disclosure of the fund's operations and fees). A fund's operating expenses are invisible to you because they're deducted from the fund's share price on a daily basis. Funds with higher operating expenses tend to produce lower rates of return on average.

Conversely, funds with lower operating costs can more easily produce higher returns for you than comparable types of funds with high costs. This effect makes sense because companies deduct operating expenses from the returns that your fund generates.

INVESTIGATE

Fund companies quote a fund's operating expenses as a percentage of your investment. The percentage represents an annual fee or charge. You can find this number in the fund expense section of a fund's prospectus, usually on a line that says "Total Fund Operating Expense." You also can call the fund's toll-free phone number and ask a representative, or you can find the information at the fund company's website. Make sure a fund doesn't have lower expenses simply because it's waiving them temporarily. (You can ask the fund representative or look at the fees in the fund's prospectus to find this information.)

>> **Use no-load funds.** A *sales load* is a commission paid to brokers and financial planners who work on commission and sell loaded mutual funds. Commissions, or *loads,* generally are about 5 percent of the amount you invest. Sales loads (or 12b-1 fees) are additional and unnecessary costs that are deducted from your investment money. You can find plenty of outstanding *no-load* (commission-free) funds. I recommend a few later in this chapter.

REMEMBER

Invest in funds that have low total operating expenses and that don't charge sales loads. Both types of fees come out of your pocket and reduce your rate of return. Plenty of excellent funds are available at reasonable annual operating-expense ratios (less than 1 percent for stock funds and less than 0.3 percent for bond funds). See my recommendations of specific funds later in this chapter.

Note: Many of the Vanguard funds recommended in this chapter offer Admiral versions that have even lower operating fees for customers who invest at least $50,000, or $10,000 for their tax managed funds that offer Admiral shares, and just $3,000 for their index funds.

Understanding and using index funds

In some funds, the portfolio manager and a team of analysts scour the market for the best securities. These funds are generally known as *actively managed funds.* An index fund, however, simply invests to match the makeup — and, thus, the performance — of an index such as the Standard & Poor's 500 index of 500 large U.S.-company stocks. Index funds, also known as *passively managed funds*, operate with far lower operating expenses because ongoing research isn't needed to identify companies in which to invest.

Index funds deliver relatively solid returns by keeping expenses low, staying invested, and not changing investments (unless changes occur to the securities in the underlying index). With actively managed stock funds, a fund manager can make costly mistakes, such as not being invested when the market goes up, being too aggressive when the market plummets, or just being in the wrong stocks. An actively managed fund can easily underperform the overall market index that it's competing against. Over ten years or more, index funds typically outperform about three-quarters of their peers. Most so-called actively managed funds can't overcome the handicap of high operating expenses that pull down their rates of return.

In addition to lower operating expenses, which help boost your returns, index funds are usually tax-friendlier to invest in when you invest outside retirement accounts. Fund managers of actively managed portfolios, in their attempts to increase returns, buy and sell securities more frequently. This trading, however, increases a fund's taxable capital gains distributions and reduces a fund's after-tax return.

Vanguard is the largest and most successful provider of index funds because it generally maintains the lowest annual operating fees in the business. Vanguard has all types of bond and stock (both U.S. and international) index funds. See my recommended-fund sections later in this chapter.

Understanding exchange-traded funds: Index funds that trade

Index mutual funds, which track particular market indexes and the best of which feature low costs, have been around for decades. Exchange-traded funds (ETFs) represent a twist on index funds. ETFs trade as stocks do and offer some potential advantages over traditional mutual funds, but they also have some potential drawbacks.

As with index funds, the promise of ETFs is low management fees. I say *promise* because the vast majority of ETFs actually have expense ratios higher than those of the best index funds.

In addition to slightly lower expenses, the best ETFs have one possible advantage over traditional index funds: Because ETFs may not be forced to redeem shares to cash and recognize taxable gains (which can happen with an index fund), they may be tax-friendlier for nonretirement-account investors.

If you can't meet the minimum investment amounts for most index funds (typically, several thousand dollars), you face no minimums when buying an ETF, but you must factor in the brokerage costs, if any, of buying and selling ETF shares through your preferred brokerage firm. Suppose you pay a $10 transaction fee through an online broker to buy $1,000 worth of an ETF. That $10 may not sound like much, but it represents 1 percent of your investment and wipes out the supposed cost advantage of investing in an ETF. Because of the brokerage costs, ETFs aren't good vehicles for investors who seek to make regular monthly investments. (*Note:* Some brokers waive brokerage fees for trading their own ETFs and selected other ETFs.)

Here are some drawbacks of ETFs:

>> **The perils of market timing:** Being able to trade in and out of an ETF during the trading day presents challenges. In my experience working with individual investors, most people find it both nerve-racking and futile to try to time their moves in and out of stocks with the inevitable fluctuations that take place during the trading day. In theory, traders want to believe that they can buy at relatively low prices and sell at relatively high prices, but that's far easier said than done.

>> **Brokerage commission every time you trade:** With no-load index funds, you generally don't pay fees to buy and sell. With ETFs, however, because you're actually placing a trade on a stock exchange, you may pay a brokerage commission every time you trade. (***Note:*** Some brokers offer certain ETFs without brokerage charges in the hope of getting your account and making money on other investments or account activity.)

>> **Fluctuating prices:** Because ETFs fluctuate in price based on supply and demand, when you place a trade during the trading day, you face the complication of trying to determine whether the current price on an ETF is above or below the actual value. With an index fund, you know that the price at which your trade was executed equals the exact market value of the securities it holds.

>> **Poorly diversified investments:** Numerous ETFs (that don't invest in an index) invest in narrow segments, such as one specific industry or one foreign country. Such funds undermine the diversification value of fund investing and tend to have relatively high fees.

>> **Excessive risks and costs with leverage:** ETF issuers have come out with increasingly risky and costly ETFs. One particular class of ETFs I especially dislike consists of so-called leveraged ETFs. These ETFs claim to magnify the move of a particular index, such as the Standard & Poor's 500 stock index, by double or triple. So, a double-leveraged S&P 500 ETF is supposed to increase by 2 percent for every 1 percent increase in the S&P 500 index. My

investigations of whether the leveraged ETFs actually deliver on their objectives show that most don't — in fact, they don't even come close. Leveraged ETFs aren't investments; they're gambling instruments for day traders.

Creating and Managing a Fund Portfolio

When you invest money for the longer term, such as for financial independence/retirement, you can choose among the various types of funds that I discuss in this chapter. Most people get a big headache when they try to decide how to spread their money among the choices. This section helps you begin cutting through the clutter for longer-term investing. (I discuss recommended funds for shorter-term goals later in this chapter as well.)

Asset allocation simply means that you decide what percentage of your investments you place, or *allocate,* in bonds versus stocks and international stocks versus U.S. stocks. Asset allocation can include other assets, such as real estate and small business, which are discussed throughout this book.

In your 20s and 30s, time is on your side, and you should use that time to your advantage. You may have many decades before you need to draw on some portion of your retirement-account assets, for example. If some of your investments drop in value over a year or even over several years, the investments have plenty of time to recover before you spend the money during retirement.

TIP

Your current age and the number of years until you retire are generally the biggest factors in your allocation decision. The younger you are and the more years you have before retirement, the more comfortable you should be with volatile, growth-oriented investments, such as stock funds.

Table 10-1 provides my guidelines for allocating fund money that you've earmarked for long-term purposes, such as retirement. It's a simple but powerful formula that uses your current age and the level of risk you're willing to take with your investments.

TABLE 10-1   **Longer-Term Fund Asset Allocation**

Your Investment Attitude	Bond Fund Allocation (%)	Stock Fund Allocation (%)
Play it safe	= Age	= 100 – Age
Middle of the road	= Age – 10	= 110 – Age
Aggressive	= Age – 20	= 120 – Age

Suppose you're an aggressive type who prefers taking a fair amount of risk to make your money grow faster. Using Table 10-1, if you're 30 years old, consider putting 10 percent (30 – 20) into bond funds and 90 percent (120 – 30) into stock funds.

Now divvy up your stock investment money between U.S. and international funds. Here are the portions of your stock allocation that I recommend investing in overseas stocks:

>> 20 percent for a play-it-safe attitude

>> 35 percent for a middle-of-the-road attitude

>> 50 percent for an aggressive attitude

If, in Table 10-1, the 30-year-old aggressive type invests 90 percent in stocks, then she can invest about 50 percent of the stock fund investments (which works out to be around 45 percent of the total) in international stock funds.

So, here's what the 30-year-old aggressive investor's portfolio asset allocation looks like:

Bonds	10 percent
U.S. stocks	45 percent
International stocks	45 percent

Suppose your investment allocation decisions suggest that you invest 50 percent in U.S. stock funds. Which ones do you choose? As I explain in "Picking the best stock funds" later in this chapter, stock funds differ on several levels. You can choose among growth-oriented stocks and funds and those that focus on value stocks, as well as funds that focus on small-, medium-, or large-company stocks. I explain these types of stocks and funds later in this chapter. You also need to decide what portion you want to invest in index funds versus actively managed funds that try to beat the market.

TIP

Deciding how much you should use index versus actively managed funds is really a matter of personal taste. If you're satisfied knowing that you'll get the market rate of return and that you can't underperform the market (after accounting for your costs), index your entire portfolio. On the other hand, if you enjoy the challenge of trying to pick the better managers and want the potential to earn more than the market level of returns, don't use index funds at all. Investing in a happy medium of both, as I do, is always a safe bet.

Identifying the Best Mutual Funds and ETFs

In this section, I explain the different types of funds — stock, bond, and money market — and where to find the best ones. Remember that with stock funds and bond funds, you have the option of investing in ETFs as well as traditional mutual funds.

Investing in the best ETFs

Like the vast majority of investors, you don't need to complicate your life by investing in ETFs. Use them only if you're an advanced investor who understands index funds and you've found a superior ETF for a given index fund that you're interested in.

TIP

I strongly encourage you to employ the buy-and-hold mentality that I advocate throughout this book. Don't hop in and out of ETFs. Also, you should buy only the ETFs that track the broader market indexes and that have the lowest expense ratios. Avoid those that track narrow industry groups or single small countries.

INVESTIGATE

Check whether the ETF you're considering is selling at a premium or discount to its net asset value. You can find this information on the ETF provider's website after the market's close each business day. Morningstar has the information as well, and it's updated throughout the trading day.

The best ETFs, like the best index funds, have low expense ratios. My top picks among the leading providers of ETFs include the following:

>> **Vanguard:** Historically, Vanguard has been the low-cost leader with index funds, and now it has low-cost ETFs as well. If you're interested in finding out more about ETFs, be sure to examine Vanguard's ETFs. Vanguard also offers the Admiral Share class at a minimum of just $3,000 for its index funds that match the low expense ratio on its ETFs (personal.vanguard.com/us/home; 800-662-7447).

>> **iShares:** BlackRock has competitive expense ratios on some domestic ETFs based on quality indexes, such as Russell, Morningstar, S&P, Lehman, Dow Jones, and so on (www.ishares.com; 800-474-2737).

>> **Schwab:** The investment brokerage firm Charles Schwab, which revolutionized the discount brokerage business, offers many very low cost ETFs (www.schwab.com; 800-435-4000).

Picking the best stock funds

Stock funds differ from one another in several dimensions. The following characteristics are what you should pay the most attention to:

>> **Company location:** Stocks and the companies that issue that stock are classified based on the location of their main operations and headquarters. Funds that specialize in U.S. stocks are, not surprisingly, called *U.S. stock funds;* those that focus overseas typically are called *international* or *overseas funds.*

>> **Growth stocks versus value stocks:** Stock fund managers and their funds are categorized by whether they invest in growth or value stocks.

- *Growth stocks* have higher prices in relation to the company's assets, profits, and potential profits. Growth companies typically experience rapidly expanding revenue and profits. These companies tend to reinvest most of their earnings in the company to fuel future expansion; thus, these stocks pay no or low dividends.

- *Value stocks* are priced cheaply in relation to the company's assets, profits, and potential profits. Value stocks tend to pay higher dividends than growth stocks and historically have produced slightly higher average total returns.

>> **Company size:** Another dimension on which a stock fund's stock selection differs is based on the size of the company in which the fund invests: small, medium, or large. The total market value — *capitalization,* or *cap* for short — of a company's outstanding stock defines the categories of the stocks that the fund invests in. Small-capitalization stocks are usually defined as stocks of companies that possess total market capitalization of less than $2 billion. Medium-capitalization stocks have market values of $2 billion to $10 billion. Large-capitalization stocks are those of companies with market values greater than $10 billion. (***Note:*** These definitions can change over time.)

Putting together two or three of these major classifications, you can start to comprehend those lengthy names that are given to various stock funds. You can have funds that focus on large-company value stocks or small-company growth stocks. You can add U.S., international, and global/worldwide funds to further subdivide these categories into more fund types. So, you can have international stock funds that focus on small-company stocks or growth stocks.

TIP

You can purchase several stock funds, each focusing on a different type of stock, to diversify into various types of stocks. Two potential advantages result from doing so:

>> Not all your money rides in one stock fund and with one fund manager.

>> Each of the different fund managers can look at and track particular stock investment possibilities.

The following sections describe the best stock funds that are worthy of your consideration.

U.S. stock funds

Of all the types of funds offered, U.S. stock funds are the largest category. The only way to know for sure where a fund currently invests (or where the fund may invest in the future) is to ask. You can call the fund company that you're interested in to start your information search, or you can visit the company's website. You can also read the fund's annual report. (The prospectus generally doesn't tell you what the fund currently invests in or has invested in.)

Here's my short list of U.S. stock focused funds:

>> Dodge & Cox Stock (800-621-3979; www.dodgeandcox.com)

>> Fidelity Low-Priced Stock (800-544-8544; www.fidelity.com)

>> Harbor Capital Appreciation (800-422-1050; www.harborfunds.com)

>> T. Rowe Price Capital Appreciation and Mid-Cap Value (800-638-5660; www.troweprice.com)

>> Vanguard Total Stock Market Index (and ETF), Primecap, Selected Value, Strategic Equity, Tax-Managed Capital Appreciation, and Tax-Managed Small Capitalization (800-662-7447; www.vanguard.com)

International stock funds

Be sure to invest in stock funds that invest overseas for diversification and growth potential. You usually can tell that you're looking at a fund that focuses its investments overseas if its name contains the word *International*, which typically means the fund's stock holdings are foreign only. If the fund name includes the word *Global* or *Worldwide*, such funds generally hold both foreign and U.S. stocks.

WARNING

Shun foreign funds that invest in just one smaller country. As with investing in a sector fund that specializes in a particular industry, this lack of diversification defeats a major benefit of investing in funds. Funds that focus on specific regions, such as Southeast Asia, are better but generally still problematic because of poor diversification and higher expenses than those of other, more-diversified international funds.

If you want to invest in more geographically limiting international funds, take a look at T. Rowe Price's and Vanguard's offerings, which invest in broader regions, such as investing just in Europe, Asia, and the volatile but higher-growth-potential emerging markets in Southeast Asia and Latin America.

In addition to the risks normally inherent with stock fund investing, changes in the value of foreign currencies relative to the U.S. dollar cause price changes in international stocks. A decline in the value of the U.S. dollar helps the value of foreign stock funds. Conversely, a rising dollar versus other currencies can reduce the value of foreign stocks. Some foreign stock funds hedge against currency changes. Although this hedging helps reduce volatility, it does cost money.

Here are my picks for diversified international funds:

>> Dodge & Cox International (800-621-3979; www.dodgeandcox.com)

>> Fidelity Overseas (800-544-8544; www.fidelity.com)

>> Oakmark International and Global — holds some U.S. stocks (800-625-6275; www.oakmark.com)

>> T. Rowe Price Spectrum Growth — actually a global fund that invests in some foreign stocks (800-638-5660; www.troweprice.com)

>> Tweedy, Browne Global Value — invests in the United States as well (800-432-4789; www.tweedybrowne.com)

>> Vanguard Global Equity (invests in the United States too), International Growth, FTSE All-World ex-US (ETF) and Total International Stock Index (800-662-7447; www.vanguard.com)

Balancing your act: Funds that combine stocks and bonds

Some funds — generally known as *balanced funds* — invest in both bonds and stocks. These funds are usually less risky and less volatile than funds that invest exclusively in stocks. In an economic downturn, bonds usually hold value better than stocks do.

Balanced funds make it easier for investors who are skittish about investing in stocks to hold stocks because they reduce the volatility that normally comes with pure stock funds. Because of their extensive diversification, balanced funds are also excellent choices for an investor who doesn't have much money to start with.

Balanced funds are less appropriate for some investors who purchase funds outside tax-sheltered retirement accounts because these funds pay decent dividends from the bonds that they hold. With the exception of the Vanguard

Tax-Managed Balanced Fund, which holds federal-tax-free bonds, you should avoid balanced funds if you're in a higher tax bracket. Consider buying separate tax-friendly stock funds and tax-free bond funds to create your own balanced portfolio.

Here's my short list of great balanced funds:

>> Dodge & Cox Balanced (800-621-3979; www.dodgeandcox.com)

>> Fidelity Freedom Funds and Fidelity Puritan (800-343-3548; www.fidelity.com)

>> T. Rowe Price Balanced and Retirement Funds (800-638-5660; www.troweprice.com)

>> Vanguard LifeStrategy Funds, Target Retirement Funds, Wellesley Income, and Wellington (800-662-7447; www.vanguard.com)

Finding the best bond funds

Although there are thousands of bond fund choices, not many remain after you eliminate high-cost funds, low-performance funds, and funds managed by fund companies and fund managers with minimal experience investing in bonds (all key points that I address in "Maximizing Your Chances for Fund Investing Success" earlier in this chapter).

Among the key considerations when choosing bond funds are

>> **Years to maturity:** Bond-fund objectives and names usually fit one of three maturity categories: short-, intermediate-, and long-term. You can generally earn a higher yield from investing in a bond fund that holds longer-term bonds, but such bond prices are more sensitive to changes in interest rates. (*Duration,* which quantifies a bond fund's sensitivity to changes in interest rates, is another term you may come across. A fund with a duration of eight years means that if interest rates rise by 1 percent, the fund should decline by 8 percent.)

>> **Bond credit quality:** The lower the issuer's credit rating, the riskier the bond. As with the risk associated with longer maturities, a fund that holds lower-quality bonds should provide higher returns for the increased risk you take. A higher yield is the bond market's way of compensating you for taking greater risk. Funds holding higher-quality bonds provide lower returns but more security.

>> **Fees and costs:** After you settle on the type of bonds you want, you must consider a bond fund's costs, including its sales commissions and annual operating fees. Stick with no-load funds that maintain lower annual operating expenses.

>> **Taxability:** Pay attention to the taxability of the dividends that bonds pay. If you're investing in bonds inside retirement accounts, you want taxable bonds. If you invest in bonds outside retirement accounts, the choice between taxable and tax-free depends on your tax bracket.

>> **Type of bond issuer:** Bonds can be issued by corporations, state and local governments, the federal government, and foreign entities (corporate and governments). Although some bond funds hold an eclectic mix, many focus on specific types of bonds (such as corporate bonds).

TIP

Because bond funds fluctuate in value, invest in them only if you have sufficient money in an emergency reserve. If you invest money for longer-term purposes, particularly retirement, you need to come up with an overall plan for allocating your money among a variety of funds, including bond funds.

The dangers of yield-chasing

When selecting bond funds to invest in, investors are often led astray as to how much they can expect to make. The first mistake is looking at recent performance and assuming that you'll get that return in the future.

Investing in bond funds based on recent performance is particularly tempting immediately after a period where interest rates have declined because declines in interest rates pump up bond prices and, therefore, bond funds' total returns. Remember that an equal but opposite force waits to counteract high bond returns when interest rates rise, which depresses bond prices and returns.

To make performance numbers meaningful and useful, you must compare bond funds that are comparable, such as intermediate-term funds that invest exclusively in high-grade corporate bonds.

INVESTIGATE

Bond funds calculate their yield after subtracting their operating expenses. When you contact a fund company seeking a fund's current yield, make sure you understand what time period the yield covers. Fund companies are supposed to give you the Securities and Exchange Commission (SEC) yield, which is a standard yield calculation that allows for fairer comparisons among bond funds. The SEC yield, which reflects the bond fund's yield to maturity, is the best yield to use when you compare funds because it captures the effective rate of interest that an investor can receive in the future.

If you select bond funds based on advertised yield, you're quite likely to purchase the wrong bond funds. Bond funds and the fund companies that sell them can play more than a few games to fatten a fund's yield. Higher yields make it easier for salespeople and funds to hawk their bond funds. Remember that yield-enhancing shenanigans can leave you poorer. Here's what you need to watch out for:

>> **Lower-credit-quality bonds:** When comparing one bond fund with another, you may discover that one pays a higher yield and decide that it looks better. You may find out later, however, that the higher-yielding fund invests a sizeable chunk of its money in junk (non-investment-grade) bonds, whereas the other fund fully invests only in high-quality bonds.

>> **Longer-maturity bonds:** Bond funds usually can increase their yield just by increasing their maturity a bit. So if one short-term bond fund invests in bonds that mature in an average of two years, and another fund has an average maturity of seven years, comparing the two is comparing apples and oranges.

>> **Return of principal as dividends:** Some funds return a portion of your principal in the form of dividends. This move artificially pumps up a fund's yield but actually depresses its total return. When you compare bond funds, make sure you compare their total return over time in addition to making sure they have comparable portfolios of bonds.

>> **Temporary waivers of expenses:** Some bond funds, particularly newer ones, waive a portion or even all of their operating expenses to inflate the fund's yield temporarily. Bond funds that engage in this practice often quietly end their expense waiver when the bond market is performing well.

Recommended short-term bond funds

Short-term bonds work well for money that you earmark for use in a few years, such as to purchase a home or a car, and for money that you plan to withdraw from your retirement account in the near future.

Short-term bond funds are the least sensitive to interest rate fluctuations in the bond-fund universe. The stability of short-term bond funds makes them appropriate investments for money on which you seek a better rate of return than a money market fund can produce for you. With short-term bond funds, however, you also have to tolerate the risk of losing a percentage or two in principal value if interest rates rise.

TIP

Consider bond funds that pay taxable dividends when you're not in a high tax bracket and when you want to invest inside retirement accounts. My favorite is the Vanguard Short-Term Corporate Bond Index fund (and Vanguard Short-Term Corporate Bond ETF).

U.S. Treasury bond funds may be appropriate if you prefer a bond fund that invests in U.S. Treasuries, which possess the safety of government backing. They're also a fine choice if you're not in a high federal tax bracket but are in a high state tax bracket (5 percent or higher). Vanguard Short-Term Treasury is a good choice. I don't recommend Treasuries for retirement accounts because they pay less interest than fully taxable bond funds.

State- and federal-tax-free short-term bond funds are scarce. If you want short-term bonds, and if you're in a high federal tax bracket but in a low state tax bracket (less than 5 percent), consider investing in these federal-tax-free bond funds (whose dividends are state-taxable):

>> Vanguard Short-Term Tax-Exempt (800-662-7447; www.vanguard.com)

>> Vanguard Limited-Term Tax-Exempt (800-662-7447; www.vanguard.com)

If you live in a state with high taxes, consider checking out the state- and federal-tax-free intermediate-term bond funds (which I discuss in the next section) if you can withstand their volatility.

Recommended intermediate-term bond funds

Intermediate-term bond funds hold bonds that typically mature in a decade or so. They're more volatile than shorter-term bonds but can also be more rewarding. The longer you own an intermediate-term bond fund, the more likely you are to earn a higher return on it than on a short-term fund unless interest rates continue to rise over many years.

WARNING

As an absolute minimum, don't purchase an intermediate-term fund unless you expect to hold it for three to five years — or even longer, if you can. Therefore, you need to make sure the money you put in an immediate-term fund is money that you don't expect to use in the near future.

Taxable intermediate-term bond funds to consider include the following:

>> Dodge & Cox Income (800-621-3979; www.dodgeandcox.com)

>> Doubleline Total Return (877-354-6311; www.doubleline.com)

>> Vanguard Total Bond Market Index and ETF (800-662-7447; www.vanguard.com)

Consider U.S. Treasury bond funds if you prefer a bond fund that invests in U.S. Treasuries, which provide the safety of government backing. You can also invest in them if you're not in a high federal tax bracket but are in a high state tax bracket (5 percent or higher). A couple of my favorites are Vanguard Inflation-Protected Securities and Vanguard Intermediate-Term Treasury. I don't recommend Treasuries for retirement accounts because they pay less interest than fully taxable bond funds.

Consider federal-tax-free bond funds if you're in a high federal tax bracket but a relatively low state tax bracket (less than 5 percent). Good ones include

>> Fidelity Intermediate Municipal Income (800-343-3548; www.fidelity.com)

>> Vanguard Intermediate-Term Tax-Exempt (800-662-7447; www.vanguard.com)

If you're in high federal and state tax brackets, refer to the state- and federal-tax-free bond fund company providers that I mention in the next section.

Recommended long-term bond funds

Long-term bond funds are the most aggressive and volatile bond funds around. If interest rates on long-term bonds increase substantially, you can easily see the principal value of your investment decline 10 percent or more.

Long-term bond funds are generally used for retirement investing in one of two situations by investors who

>> Don't expect to tap their investment money for a decade or more

>> Want to maximize current dividend income and are willing to tolerate volatility

REMEMBER

Don't use long-term bond funds to invest money that you plan to use within the next five years, because a bond-market drop can leave your portfolio short of your monetary goal.

My favorite taxable bond fund that holds longer-term bonds is the Vanguard Long-Term Corporate Bond Index fund (800-662-7447; www.vanguard.com). Also consider the Vanguard Long-Term Corporate Bond ETF.

U.S. Treasury bond funds may be advantageous if you want a bond fund that invests in U.S. Treasuries. They're also great if you're not in a high federal tax bracket but are in a high state tax bracket (5 percent or higher). I recommend Treasuries for nonretirement accounts only because Treasuries pay less interest than fully taxable bond funds. I recommend the Vanguard Long-Term Treasury fund (800-662-7447; www.vanguard.com).

State and federally tax-free bond funds may be appropriate when you're in high federal and state (5 percent or higher) tax brackets. A municipal (federal-tax-free) long-term bond fund that I recommend is Vanguard Long-Term Tax-Exempt. Fidelity, T. Rowe Price, and Vanguard offer good funds for several states. If you can't find a good state-specific fund where you live, or if you're in a high federal tax bracket, you can use the nationwide Vanguard Municipal bond funds.

Considering Alternatives to Investing in Funds

If you're getting into the investment game, you'll likely hear about, and be pitched, some alternatives to investing in funds. In this section, I reveal the truth about those options.

Creating your own fund

On some websites, various services claim that you can invest in a chosen basket of stocks for a low fee and without the high taxes and high fees that come with mutual fund investing.

These "create your own funds" services pitch their investment products as superior alternatives to mutual funds. One such service calls its investment vehicles *folios,* charging you $29 per month ($290 per year paid in advance) to invest in folios, each of which can hold a few dozen stocks that are selected from the universe of stocks that this service makes available. The fee covers trading in your folios that may occur only during two time windows each day that the stock market is open. Thus, in addition to the burden of managing your own portfolio of stocks, you have virtually no control of the timing of your trades during the trading day.

According to my analysis, you'd need to invest more than $150,000 through this folio service to come out ahead in terms of the explicit fees. You also need to be aware of additional fees, which you usually have to search the fine print to find. You may get whacked $30 to wire money out of your account or even $100 to close an account and have it transferred elsewhere!

Evaluating the performance of self-created funds is difficult. Also, unlike mutual funds, these funds have no standards or easily accessible services that report and track the performance of your customized folio.

Robo advisors

Numerous websites offer automated investing services known as *robo advisors.* These sites purport to help you choose an overall investment mix (asset allocation) and then divvy that money up, typically among exchange-traded funds. Over time, the allocations can be tweaked or adjusted based on some predetermined formulas.

For this largely automated service, firms like Acorns, Betterment, SoFi, and WealthFront generally charge around 0.25 percent to 0.5 percent per year of the assets they are managing. Some services offer phone access to financial advisors as something for which you can pay extra.

I believe that you can educate yourself enough about investing in funds and that paying an ongoing fee for such services isn't worth it. Vanguard offers a low cost robo advisor service called "Digital Advisor," which charges 0.15 percent and invests in a handful of Vanguard total market index stock and bond ETFs.

Unit investment trusts

Unit investment trusts (UITs) have much in common with both mutual funds and exchange-traded funds. UITs take a fixed initial amount of money and buy securities that meet the objectives of the UIT. Unlike a mutual fund, however, a UIT doesn't make any changes in its holdings over time. This holding of a diversified portfolio can be advantageous because it reduces trading costs and possible tax bills.

With that said, UITs do suffer from the following major flaws:

» **High commissions:** Brokers like to sell UITs for the same reason they like to pitch load mutual funds: the commissions paid out of your investment. Commissions usually are around 5 percent, so for every $10,000 that you invest in a UIT, $500 comes out of your investment and goes into the broker's pocket. (Although UITs do have ongoing fees, their fees tend to be lower than those of most actively managed mutual funds — typically, in the neighborhood of 0.2 percent per year. The best no-load funds also have reasonable management fees, and some charge even less than UITs charge.)

» **Lack of liquidity:** Especially in the first few years after a particular UIT is issued, you won't readily find an active market in which you can easily sell your UIT. In the event that you can find someone who's interested in buying a UIT that you want to sell, you'll likely have to sell the UIT at a discount from its actual market value at the time.

» **Lack of ongoing management oversight:** Because UITs buy and hold a fixed set of securities until the UITs are liquidated (years down the road), they're more likely to get stuck holding some securities that end up worthless. Compared with the best bond funds, bond UITs are more likely to end up holding bonds in companies that go bankrupt.

Brokerage managed accounts

Brokerage firms offer investment management services for an ongoing fee rather than commissions. (Merrill Lynch is one common example of a brokerage firm.) *Wrap accounts*, or managed accounts, go by a variety of names, but they're the same in one crucial way: For the privilege of investing your money through their chosen money managers, they charge you a percentage of the assets that they're managing for you. These accounts are quite similar to mutual funds except that the accounts don't have the same regulatory and reporting requirements.

These managed accounts tend to have relatively high fees — upward of 2 percent per year of assets under management. No-load mutual funds and ETFs offer investors access to the nation's best investment managers for a fraction of the cost of brokerage managed accounts. Many excellent funds are available for 0.5 percent or less annually.

Hedge funds for the wealthier

Hedge funds, historically investments reserved for big-ticket investors, seem to be like mutual funds in that they typically invest in stocks and bonds. They have the added glamour and allure, however, of taking significant risks and gambles with their investments. Here's how they stack up compared with mutual funds and ETFs:

>> **Hedge funds are often much higher-risk.** When a hedge fund manager bets right, they can produce high returns. When they don't, however, their fund can get clobbered. With short selling, because the value of the security that was sold short can rise an unlimited amount, the potential loss from buying it back at a much higher price can be horrendous. Hedge fund managers have also been clobbered when a previously fast-rising commodity, such as natural gas or copper futures, plunges in value or an investment they make with leverage goes the wrong direction. Several hedge funds went belly-up when their managers guessed wrong. In other words, their investments did so poorly that investors in the fund lost everything. This won't occur with a mutual fund or an ETF.

>> **Hedge funds have much higher fees.** Hedge funds charge an annual management fee of about 1 percent to 2 percent and a performance fee, which typically amounts to a whopping 20 percent of a fund's profits.

>> **Hedge funds have had problems with fraud and lousy returns.** During the severe stock market decline in the late 2000s, numerous hedge funds did poorly. Some funds went under or were exposed to be Ponzi schemes, the most notorious being the fund run by the now deceased Bernie Madoff. According to *Forbes* magazine, "Hedge funds exist in a lawless and risky realm. . . . Hedge funds aren't even required to keep audited books — and many don't." They're often "guilty of inadequate disclosure of costs, overvaluation of holdings to goose reported performance and manager pay, and cozy ties between funds and brokers that often shortchange investors." Objective studies of all hedge fund returns show that they underperform funds, which makes sense, because hedge funds have the burden of much higher fees.

Chapter **11**

Understanding Investment Brokers

As I discuss in Chapter 1, many investment firms vie for your business. In addition to the major fund companies (for example, Fidelity, T. Rowe Price, Vanguard, and so on), investment brokerage firms are worth considering. There's overlap among these firms because the leading fund companies also generally have brokerage offerings and divisions. (And, surely you've seen online ads for a new class of online-only brokers that pitch free trading among other potential perks.)

In this chapter, I focus on brokerage firms and which ones may be worthy of your dollars and investments. I also cut through the hype and tell you the truth about what you're really getting or not getting with various brokers.

Getting Your Money's Worth: Discount Brokers

When you hear the word *discount,* you probably think of adjectives like *cheap, inferior-quality,* and such. However, in the securities brokerage field, the discount brokers who place your trades at substantial discounts can offer you even better value and service than high-cost brokers. The following list offers some of the reasons discount brokers give you more bang for your buck:

>> They can place your trades at a substantially lower price because they have much lower overhead.

>> They tend not to rent the posh downtown office space, complete with mahogany-paneled conference rooms, in order to impress customers.

>> They don't waste tons of money employing economists and research analysts to produce forecasts and predictive reports.

In addition to lower commissions, another major benefit of using discount brokers is that they generally work on salary. Working on salary removes a significant conflict of interest that continues to get commission-paid brokers and their firms into trouble. People who sell on commission to make a living aren't bad people, but given the financial incentives they have, don't expect to receive holistic, in-your-best-interest investing counsel from them.

Assessing the high-commission salespeople's arguments

WARNING

One of the many sales tactics of high-commission brokerage firms is to try to disparage discounters by telling you, "You'll receive poor service from discounters." My own experience, as well as that of others, suggests that in many cases, discounters actually offer *better* service.

Many of the larger discounters with convenient branch offices offer assistance with filling out paperwork and access to independent research reports. From discounters, you also can buy *no-load* (commission-free) mutual funds that are run by management teams that make investment decisions for you. Such funds can be bought from mutual fund companies as well. (See Chapter 10 for more on these mutual funds.)

High-commission firms used to argue that discount brokerage customers received worse trade prices when they bought and sold. This assertion is a bogus argument because all brokerage firms use a computer-based trading system for smaller retail trades. Trades are processed in seconds. High-commission brokers also say that discounters are only "for people who know exactly what they're doing and don't need any help." This statement is also hard to justify, especially given the abundance of financial information and advice available today.

Selecting a discount broker

Which discount broker is best for you depends on what your needs and wants are. In addition to fees, consider how important having a local branch office is to you.

If you seek to invest in mutual funds, the discount brokerage firms that I list in this section offer access to good funds (you can access all exchange-traded funds through a broker because ETFs trade like stocks on exchanges). In addition, these firms offer money market funds into which you can deposit money awaiting investment or proceeds from a sale.

Here are my top picks for discount brokers:

» **Fidelity (800-343-3548); www.fidelity.com):** Fidelity is one of America's largest families of mutual funds, a robust brokerage service, including cash management accounts with banking services and 24/7 customer service. They also have an extensive network of branch offices around the country.

» **Schwab/TD Ameritrade (800-435-4000; www.schwab.com):** Schwab is the nation's largest discount brokerage service, offers 24/7 customer service, and also pioneered offering an extensive mutual fund marketplace of many companies' funds. They have an extraordinary network of local branch offices if that is important to you.

» **T. Rowe Price (800-225-5132; www.troweprice.com):** T. Rowe Price offers a solid family of no-load mutual funds. The company's brokerage fees are competitive and among those on the lower end for discounters. Its six branch offices are primarily in the Baltimore-Washington metro areas, Florida, and Colorado.

» **Vanguard (800-992-8327; www.vanguard.com):** Vanguard is best known for its excellent family of no-load mutual funds, but its discount brokerage services have improved over the years. Vanguard has also reduced its brokerage fees in recent years, and its prices are now near the low end of discount brokers.

REMEMBER

All the preceding firms offer mutual funds from many fund companies in addition to their family of funds (if they have a family of funds). In other words, you may purchase mutual funds that aren't in the T. Rowe Price family of funds through the T. Rowe Price brokerage department. Other discounters certainly have good service and competitive rates, so shop around if you desire. Note, however, that you generally pay a transaction fee to buy funds from firms that don't offer their own family of funds.

If you're going to invest in individual stocks, Schwab and Fidelity deserve more consideration because they offer a comprehensive array of useful and independent research resources, and their brokerage fees in that arena are more competitive. You should also consider some of the online-focused brokers I discuss later in the chapter (see the section "Listing the best online brokers").

CAN FINANCIAL ADVISORS ACCESS BETTER FUNDS THAT AREN'T AVAILABLE TO YOU?

Some financial advisors promote their services in part by saying that they can get you into funds that are sold only through advisors. Please allow me to separate the hype from reality in assessing advisor/institutional funds.

Some investment management companies offer different share classes of some of their funds. Some of these are much-higher-minimum funds (for example, $100,000 or $1,000,000 minimum) that are targeted to wealthy individuals or institutions. Such funds tend to have slightly lower expense ratios, which of course should translate into slightly higher returns for the fund's investors.

Some institutional funds can be accessed only by financial advisors. That said, that doesn't mean that the funds an advisor can get you into are worthy of your investing dollars. Just because a fund restricts access, that doesn't make the fund among the best to invest in (consider the many mediocre and lousy hedge funds).

The bottom line is that access to advisor/institutional funds is a consideration, a minor one, if and only if the advisor is actually doing a good job seeking out funds that are in your best interests and that have the best characteristics. You should evaluate a financial advisor on many factors, especially and including how the advisor is compensated and what conflicts of interest they may have.

Some of the larger fund companies, such as Vanguard and T. Rowe Price, offer lower-expense, higher-minimum-investment fund share classes that are available to anyone who can pay the minimum. For example, Vanguard has "Admiral" funds, which have just $3,000 minimums (for index funds) or $50,000 minimums (for actively managed funds). Through discount and online brokers with good mutual funds networks, you can also access numerous "advisor" and "institutional" share classes of funds which have lower fees for those able to meet those funds' generally higher minimums of investment (for example, $50,000, $100,000, and so on).

Finally, there are also exchange-traded funds (ETFs), such as Vanguard's, that generally have expense ratios that are even lower than or as low as their high-balance Admiral funds without having any minimum investment requirement. That said, be aware that some brokerage firms charge small fees to buy and sell ETFs through a broker.

Checking Out Online Brokers

To get the lowest trading commissions, you generally must place your trades online. Even if you've never visited an online brokerage site, ads for them online, in print publications, and even on national television have surely bombarded you. Visit any website that's remotely related to investing in stocks, and you're sure to find ads for various internet brokers. Anyone familiar with the economics of running a brokerage firm can tell you that technology, when properly applied, reduces a broker's labor costs. Some brokerages, thanks to technology, can now perform *market orders* (which means they'll execute your trade at the best current available price) for a few bucks. And, as I explain in the next section, numerous leading brokerage firms today offer free online trading for most stocks, including ETFs.

Before you jump at the chance to save money by trading online, read the following sections for other considerations that should factor into your choice of an online broker or your decision to trade online at all.

Considering "free" online trades

In recent years, a number of major brokerage firms — Charles Schwab, E*Trade, Fidelity, Interactive Brokers, and Vanguard — have eliminated trading fees on stocks, including exchange-traded funds. These changes have further reduced the attractiveness of upstart app-based trading platforms like Robinhood (discussed further in this section) that previously lured many newer investors with the promise of free trades, which was unique at the time.

Thanks to deregulation decades ago and the relentless advancement of technology, brokerage trading fees have dropped dramatically. Many leading investment companies that I highlight in this chapter and throughout this book offer broad menus of the best investments (mutual funds, exchange-traded funds, stocks, bonds, and so forth). I have explained in this and my other books over the years how to buy the best funds without any trading fees at all, and when fees are levied, they are typically quite low.

But that hasn't stopped some folks from trying to offer even better deals. Hence, the rise of some brokerage firms luring investors by claiming "free" trading. Of course, there is a catch — a brokerage firm can't possibly exist, survive, and continue to stay in business if they don't charge any fees at all for any of their services! And, you should be aware, as I explain later in this section, that some brokers who offer "free" trading get paid by firms that they process their trades through, which can undermine your getting the best price for the security you may be trading. Investors should always consider and evaluate the entire package of services when deciding an investment firm through which to do business.

I have reviewed trading apps like Robinhood that offer "free stock trades" and others including M1Finance, MooMoo, TradeStation, and Webull. Here are several concerns and downsides I've found with what most of these companies offer:

>> It only exists as an app, so there's no way for you to access the company through a traditional desktop (or laptop) computer or through a web-based version.

>> If you need customer service or help resolving a problem on your account, you often have to submit support tickets or deal with a chatbot. If it's available at all, you have greatly limited access to phone assistance and only during normal business hours — after hours, including on weekends, you're stuck using the other options.

>> You can only use the app for taxable accounts — some don't offer retirement accounts like an IRA.

>> They don't offer mutual funds.

>> There are no tools or research to tap into.

>> If you want a paper statement of your account, that may cost you, for example $5 each time you request it.

>> Should you decide to close your account and have it transferred to another broker, they whack you $75 for the privilege of leaving.

And, if that's not enough, consider this. The U.S. Securities and Exchange Commission slapped Robinhood with a $65 million fine in 2020 for failing to disclose payments they received from outside firms for "order flow" that left Robinhood customers worse off (getting lower prices) on trades executed through those firms and with Robinhood benefitting effectively from excessive kickbacks. Robinhood's promise of "free trades" was indeed too good to be true.

REMEMBER

There are no free lunches in the investment world. And, I would not recommend any of the "free" brokerage trading apps I have reviewed to date. They simply have too many deficiencies and drawbacks and won't actually save you money in the long run compared with the best investment and brokerage firms I recommend.

Examining your online trading motives

If trading online attracts you, first examine why. If you're motivated by how easily you can check account balances, beware. Tracking prices daily (or, worse, minute by minute) and frequently checking your account balances leads to addictive trading. Free or low-fee trading doesn't really save you any money if you trade a lot and rack up significant total commissions, and you pay more in capital gains taxes when you sell at a profit. (That's the big problem with some brokerage trading apps supposedly offering free trading; see Chapter 17.) Don't forget that as with trading through a regular brokerage firm, you also lose the *spread* (difference between the bid and ask prices when you trade stocks and bonds) and incur the explicit commission rates that online brokers charge.

Frankly, trading online is also an unfortunately easy way for people to act impulsively and emotionally when making important investment decisions. If you're prone to such actions or if you find yourself tracking and trading investments too closely, stay away from this form of trading and use the internet only to check account information and gather factual information.

Investment websites also push the surging interest in online trading with the pitch that you can beat the market averages and professionals at their own game if you do your own research and trade online. Beating the market and professionals is highly unlikely. You can save some money trading online but perhaps not as much as the hype has you believe. Online trading is good for the convenience and low costs if you're not obsessive about it.

Taking other costs into account

INVESTIGATE

Online brokerage customers often shop for low costs. However, by simply talking with many folks who have traded online and by reviewing online forums where customers speak their minds, I've discovered that shopping merely for low-cost trading prices often causes investors to overlook other important issues. The biggest problem is firms that nickel-and-dime you with fees. For instance, some brokers whack you $20 here and $50 there for services such as wiring money or simply closing your account. Also beware of "inactivity fees" that some brokers levy on accounts that have infrequent trading. So before you sign up with any broker, make sure you examine its entire fee schedule.

Also beware below-market rates on money market accounts at many cut-rate brokers. When you buy or sell an investment, you may have cash sitting around in your brokerage account. Not surprisingly, the online brokers pitching their cheap online trading rates in 3-inch-high numbers don't reveal their money market rates in such large type (if at all). Some don't pay interest on the first $1,000 or so of your cash balance, and even then, some companies pay half a percent to a full percent less than their best competitors. In the worst cases, some online brokers have paid up to 3 percent less during periods of normal interest rates. Under those terms, you'd earn up to $150 less in interest per year if you averaged a $5,000 cash balance during the year.

Looking at service quality

Common complaints among customers of online brokers include slow responses to email queries, long wait times to speak with a live person to answer questions or resolve problems, delays in opening accounts and receiving literature, unclear statements, incorrect processing of trading requests, and slow web response and website outages during periods of heavy traffic. With a number of firms that I called, I experienced phone waits of up to ten minutes and was transferred several times to retrieve answers to simple questions, such as whether the firm carried a specific family of mutual funds.

INVESTIGATE

When you shop for an online broker, check your prospects thoroughly. Here are some things to do:

>> **Call for literature and to see how long it takes you to reach a live human being.** Ask some questions and see how knowledgeable and helpful the representatives are. For nonretirement accounts, if you want to gauge the quality of the firm's year-end account statements, ask prospective brokerages to send you a sample. If you're a mutual fund investor, check out the quality of the funds that the company offers. In other words, don't let the sheer number of funds that the company offers impress you. Also, inquire about the interest rates that the company pays on cash balances. Try sending some questions to the broker's website and see how accurate and timely the response is.

>> **Consider checking online forums to see what current and past customers say about the firms you're considering.** Most online brokers that have been around for more than six months lay claim to a number-one rating with some survey or ranking of online brokers. Place little value on such claims.

>> **Examine what the firm did before it got into the online brokerage business.** Would you rather put your money and trust in the hands of an established and respected financial service company that has been around for a number of years or an upstart firm run by a couple of people hoping to strike it rich on the internet? Transact business only with firms that offer sufficient account insurance (enough to protect your assets) through the Securities Investor Protection Corporation (SIPC).

Listing the best online brokers

Among the e-brokers I've reviewed, my top picks are the following:

Broker	Phone Number	Website
E*Trade	800-387-2331	etrade.com
Fidelity	800-343-3548	fidelity.com
Interactive Brokers	800-442-2757	interactivebrokers.com
T. Rowe Price	800-638-5660	troweprice.com
Vanguard	800-992-8327	vanguard.com
Schwab/TD Ameritrade	800-454-9272	schwab.com

4

Investing in Real Estate, Small Business, and Other Investments

IN THIS PART . . .

Master real estate basics, starting with a home in which you live and then moving along to real estate you own and rent out.

Understand real estate financing and deal-making strategies.

Invest in small business, including starting your own small business and buying or investing in someone else's.

Delve into some less-conventional investments, including annuities, life insurance, gold and other commodities, and collectibles.

Chapter **12**

Seeking Shelter and Appreciation in Real Estate

Thinking of a home in which you live as an investment may seem like a poor idea to some folks. In many parts of the country, home prices suffered in the late 2000s and early 2010s, and, of course, that wasn't the first time that home prices suffered a notable decline.

Although homes may require plenty of financial feeding, over the course of your adult years, owning rather than renting a home can potentially make and save you money. The pile of mortgage debt seems daunting in the years just after your purchase, but someday your home may be among your biggest assets.

Like stocks, real estate does well over the long term but doesn't go continuously higher. Astute investors take advantage of down periods; they consider these periods to be times to buy at lower prices, just as many do when their favorite retailers are having a sale.

Comparing Owning a Home to Renting

As financial decisions go, deciding whether and when to buy a home is pretty challenging. You have plenty of financial considerations to contend with, as well as personal issues. Psychologically, many folks equate buying a home with settling down — and dare I say possibly becoming more like your parents — eek! After all, you'll be coming home to your home day after day, year after year. You can always move, of course, but doing so can be costly and time-consuming, and as a homeowner, you'll have a financial obligation to deal with.

In this section, I cover the important issues to consider when comparing buying to renting.

Weighing financial considerations

You've probably already heard some arguments regarding the supposed financial benefits of owning a home. These benefits include the notion of buying and owning a home for the tax breaks, as well as the thought that paying rent is analogous to throwing your money away.

REMEMBER

The biggest homeownership costs are mortgage interest and property taxes, and in the United States, these costs are generally tax-deductible subject to some limitations. The tax breaks, however, are already largely factored into the higher cost of owning a home, so you should never buy a home just because of the tax breaks.

Renting isn't necessarily like throwing your money away. In fact, renting can have several benefits, including the following:

>> **Renting sometimes costs less (sometimes much less) than owning.** In the mid-2000s, in some parts of the country with really inflated home prices, renting a given property cost about half as much as owning that same property (a monthly comparison even after factoring in the tax benefits of owning).

>> **You may be able to save more toward your personal and financial goals if you can rent at a relatively low cost.** You can invest, for example, in other financial assets such as stocks, bonds, and funds (and may be able to do so through tax-favored accounts).

>> **Renting has potential emotional and psychological rewards.** You usually have more flexibility to pack up and move on as a renter. You may have a lease to fulfill, but you may be able to renegotiate it if circumstances require you to move. As a homeowner, you have some major monthly payments to take care of. To some people, this responsibility feels like a financial ball and chain. After all, you have no guarantee that you will be able to sell your home in a timely fashion or at the price you desire if you want or need to move.

WARNING

Renting does have at least one big drawback: exposure to inflation (cost-of-living increases). As the cost-of-living increases, unless you live in a rent-controlled unit, your landlord can keep increasing your rent. By contrast, if you're a home-owner, your largest monthly expense — the mortgage payment — doesn't increase, assuming that you buy your home with a fixed-rate mortgage. Your property taxes, homeowner's insurance, and maintenance expenses are exposed to inflation, but these expenses are usually much smaller in comparison with your monthly mortgage payment.

Considering costs and your time frame

You face significant costs when buying and selling a home. My analysis suggests that you probably need at least three to five years of low to moderate appreciation to recoup your transaction costs. Some of the expenses you face when buying and selling a home include the following:

>> **Agent's commission:** Real estate agents generally charge a commission of 5 percent to 7 percent of the purchase price. Even if the seller is technically paying the commission out of the proceeds that they receive from selling a home, both the buyer and seller of a home are effectively paying commissions because those costs are built into the home's sale price. (You may be able to reduce these costs somewhat by doing the selling yourself, but a buyer may offer less, knowing that you're not having to pay commission.)

>> **Inspection fees:** When you buy a property, you should hire a professional to thoroughly check it out. Good inspectors can help you identify problems with the plumbing, heating, electrical systems, foundation, roof, pests like termites, and so on. Property inspections typically cost at least a few hundred dollars up to $1,000 for larger homes.

>> **Moving expenses:** Moving costs vary wildly, but you can count on spending hundreds to thousands of dollars. Costs increase with the distance you have to go and the amount of stuff you have, of course.

>> **Mortgage costs:** The costs of getting a mortgage include such items as the *points* (upfront interest — about 1 percent to 2 percent of the loan amount), application and credit report fees, and appraisal fees.

>> **Title insurance:** When you buy a home, you and your lender will want to protect yourselves against the small probability that the property seller doesn't actually legally own the home that you're buying. Title insurance protects you financially from unscrupulous sellers. Although title insurance costs vary by area, 0.5 percent of the purchase price of the property is about average.

On top of all these transaction costs of buying and then selling a home, you face maintenance expenses — repairs, cosmetic work, and so on — during your years of home ownership. To cover the typical transaction and maintenance costs of homeownership, the value of your home needs to appreciate about 15 percent over the years that you own it for you to be as well off financially as if you'd continued renting. Counting on that kind of appreciation in case you need or want to move elsewhere in a few years is risky.

Some people invest in real estate even when they don't expect to live in the home long, and they may consider turning their home into a rental if they move within a few years. Doing so can work well financially in the long haul, but don't underestimate the responsibilities and potential downsides that come with rental property. See the section "Investing in Investment Real Estate" later in this chapter.

Deciding when to buy

If you're considering buying a home, you may be concerned about whether home prices are poised to rise or fall. No one wants to purchase a home that then plummets in value. And who wouldn't like to buy just before prices surge higher?

It's not easy to predict what's going to happen with real estate prices in a particular town or neighborhood over the next few years. Ultimately, the economic health and vitality of an area drive the demand and prices for homes in that area. An increase in jobs, particularly ones that pay well, increases the demand for housing, and when demand goes up, so do prices.

If you buy your first home when you're in your 20s or 30s, you will likely be a homeowner for many decades. Over such a long time, you will surely experience numerous ups and downs. But you'll probably see more ups than downs, so don't be too concerned about trying to predict what's going to happen to the real estate market in the near term and whether prices may fall a little. You should do a basic rent-versus-buy comparison, of course, to see whether the properties you're considering offer decent value or not. For example, to note a recent shift in home prices, a silver lining of the late-2000s decline in home prices is that homes were more affordable than they had been in a long time and offered better value versus renting in many areas. Since then in most parts of the country, housing prices have increased to reach new all-time highs.

That said, at particular times in your life, you may be ambivalent about buying a home. Perhaps you're not sure whether you'll stay put for five years. Therefore, part of your home-buying decision may hinge on whether current home prices versus the costs of renting in your local area offer you a good value. The state of the job market, the number of home listings for sale, and the level of real estate prices compared with rent are useful indicators of the housing market's health.

TIP

Trying to time your purchase has more importance if you think you may move within a few years. In that case, be especially careful to avoid buying in a market where home prices are relatively high compared with rental costs. If you expect to move so soon, renting generally makes sense because of the high transaction costs of buying and selling real estate.

THE IMPACT OF COVID-19 ON REAL ESTATE

Early in the pandemic, in most areas, home transactions greatly slowed as prospective home buyers were stuck in their apartments or homes and sellers (and their agents) weren't interested in having potential buyers trapsing through their homes for sale. In subsequent months, however, a surge of activity became apparent, especially outside of densely populated cities that were suffering long government-mandated shutdowns.

What was the point, after all, of staying in such cities if you couldn't partake of the usual or even any amenities (eating out, going to entertainment venues, and so on) that drew you to live in the city originally? A significant rise in crime in many of these cities also contributed to a desire to flee.

I've observed one of the unfortunate consequences of long draconian lockdowns is the harmful impact it has had on many young adults. (Locking down healthy, working-age adults has been misguided and hasn't protected the elderly, especially in nursing homes.)

Those who can afford to do so and are able to work remotely have chosen in many cases to relocate from locked-down cities to surrounding suburban areas. This has driven up rents and home prices in those surrounding areas as some who could afford to buy were motivated to do so, while having a depressing effect on city rents and real estate values.

Will these trends continue? Some employers may be willing to allow some or even many of their employees to work remotely, but I don't see this changing economy wide. The reality is that many employers see benefits to getting employees together in a professional work environment, and many workers see value in that as well. It can be lonely and isolating to work at home, and in many companies, it's harder to collaborate with and relate to co-workers through just a small video displaying on your computer screen. The pandemic will subside, and life will return to a greater sense of normal, so I wouldn't simply extrapolate that the unusual conditions that happened during the height of the pandemic will persist for years to come.

That said, it will take some cities years to recover economically from the lockdowns that they employed and suffered. However, renters in those cities may enjoy somewhat reduced rent compared to pre-pandemic levels.

Figuring Your Home-Buying Budget

Buying a home is a long-term financial commitment. You'll probably take out a 15- or 30-year mortgage to finance your purchase, and the home you buy will need maintenance over time. So before you decide to buy, take stock of your overall financial health, determine how large a down payment you'll need, and understand how much lenders will be willing to lend you.

Getting your financial house in order

To qualify for a mortgage, you need good credit and a stable, reliable source of employment income. Mortgage lenders will tell you the maximum amount that you're qualified to borrow. Just because they offer you that maximum amount, however, doesn't mean you should borrow that much.

Buying a home without considering your other monthly expenditures and long-term goals may cause you to end up with a home that dictates much of your future spending. Have you considered, for example, how much you need to save monthly to reach your goals? How about the amount you want to spend on your current lifestyle?

If you want to continue your current lifestyle, you have to be honest with yourself about how much you can really afford to spend as a homeowner. First-time home buyers in particular run into financial trouble when they don't understand their current spending.

WARNING

Buying a home can be a wise decision, but it can also be a huge burden. Also, you can buy all sorts of nifty things for a home. Some people prop up their spending habits with credit cards — a dangerous practice. So before you buy a property or agree to a particular mortgage, be sure you can afford to do so and that it fits with your overall plans and desires.

Determining your down payment

When deciding how much to borrow for a home purchase, keep in mind that most lenders require you to purchase private mortgage insurance (PMI) if your down payment is less than 20 percent of your home's purchase price. PMI protects the lender from getting stuck with a property that may be worth less than the mortgage you owe, in the event that you default on your loan. On a moderate-size loan, PMI can add hundreds of dollars per year to your payments.

If you have to purchase PMI to buy a home with less than 20 percent down, keep an eye on your home's value and your loan balance. Over time, your property should appreciate, and your loan balance should decrease as you make monthly payments. After your mortgage represents 80 percent or less of the market value of the home, you can get rid of the PMI. Doing so usually entails contacting your lender and paying for an appraisal.

WARNING

I've never liked interest-only loans, which entice cash-strapped buyers with lower monthly payments because all the initial payments go toward interest. These loans typically have higher interest rates and fees than conventional mortgages do, and they cause some buyers to take on more debt than they can handle. (After a certain number of years, the payment amount jumps higher when the principal and interest begin to be repaid together.)

What if you can afford to make more than a 20 percent down payment? How much should you put down then? (This problem is rare; most buyers, especially first-time buyers, struggle to get a 20 percent down payment together.) The answer depends on what else you can or want to do with the money. If you're considering other investment opportunities, determine whether you can expect to earn a higher rate of return on those other investments versus the interest rate that you'd pay on the mortgage. (Forget about the tax deduction for your mortgage interest for now. The interest is generally/mostly deductible but remember that the earnings from your investments are ultimately taxable.)

REMEMBER

All investments come with risk. If you prefer to put down just 20 percent and invest more money elsewhere, that's fine. Just don't keep the extra money (beyond an emergency reserve) under the mattress, in a savings account, or in bonds with a lower yield than your mortgage's interest rate. Invest in stocks, real estate, or other growth investments. Otherwise, you don't have a chance of earning a higher return than the cost of your mortgage; therefore, you'd be better off paying down your mortgage.

Doing lenders' calculations

Mortgage lenders calculate the maximum amount that you can borrow to buy a home. All lenders want to gauge your ability to repay the money that you borrow, so you have to pass a few tests.

For a home in which you will live, lenders total your monthly housing expenses. They define your housing costs as

Mortgage payment + Property taxes + Insurance

Note: Lenders don't consider maintenance and upkeep expenses (including utilities) in owning a home, but of course, you will incur these expenses as a homeowner.

Assessing consumer debt

Although lenders may not care where you spend money outside your home, they do care about your other debt. A lot of other debt, such as consumer debt on credit cards or auto loans and student loans, diminishes the funds that are available to pay your housing expenses. Lenders know that having other debt increases the possibility that you may fall behind or actually default on your mortgage payments.

If you have consumer debt and student loans that require monthly payments, lenders calculate another ratio to determine the maximum that you can borrow for a home. Lenders add the amount you need to pay monthly on your other debt to your monthly housing expense.

WARNING

Consumer debt is bad news, even without considering the fact that it hurts your qualification for a mortgage. Consumer debt is costly and encourages you to live beyond your means. Unlike the interest on mortgage debt, consumer debt interest isn't tax-deductible. Student loans are also generally better to carry than consumer debt because up to $2,500 in student loan interest is tax deductible.

Get rid of your consumer debt as soon as possible. Curtail your spending and adjust to living within your means. If you can't live within your means as a renter, you likely won't be able to do it as a homeowner either.

Determining homeownership tax savings

Your mortgage interest and property taxes are deductible, subject to limitations, on IRS Form 1040, Schedule A of your personal federal income tax return. When you calculate the costs of owning a home, subtract the tax savings to get a more complete and accurate sense of what homeownership will cost you.

Effective 2018, due to the Tax Cuts and Jobs Act, the tax benefits of home ownership were somewhat reduced, especially for those buying more expensive properties subject to higher property tax bills. The biggest change is that property taxes combined with your state income tax is now limited to a $10,000 annual deduction. And, the mortgage interest deduction now may be claimed on up to $750,000 of mortgage debt, which obviously doesn't affect most home buyers.

Down the road, also know that eligible homeowners can exclude a large portion of their gain on the sale of a principal residence from taxable income: up to $250,000 for single taxpayers and up to $500,000 for married couples filing jointly. Because of the new tax bill, determining the tax savings you may realize from home ownership has become much more complicated. Here's a shortcut that works reasonably well in determining your tax savings in home ownership: Multiply your federal tax rate by the portion of your property taxes up to $10,000 when combined with your annual state income tax payments, and the portion of your mortgage payment on up to $750,000 of mortgage debt.

Note: Even if you're under the $750,000 threshold, not all of your mortgage payment is tax-deductible — only the portion of the mortgage payment that goes toward interest. However, in the early years of your mortgage, nearly all of your payment goes toward interest. On the other hand, you may earn state tax benefits from your deductible mortgage interest and property taxes, which I am ignoring here in this simplified analysis.

If you want to more accurately determine how home ownership may affect your tax situation, get out your tax return and try plugging in some reasonable numbers to estimate how your taxes will change. You can also speak with a tax advisor.

TIP

When you finally buy a home, refigure how much you need to pay in income tax, because your mortgage interest and property tax deductions can help lower your income tax bill. If you work for an employer, ask your payroll/benefits department for Form W-4. If you're self-employed, you can complete a worksheet that comes with Form 1040-ES. (Call 800-829-3676 for a copy.) Many new home buyers don't bother with this step, and they receive a big tax refund on their next filed income tax return. Although getting money back from the Internal Revenue Service may feel good, it means that at minimum, you gave the IRS an interest-free loan. In the worst-case scenario, the reduced cash flow during the year may cause you to accumulate other debt or miss out on contributing to tax-deductible retirement accounts.

Shopping for Your Home

Be realistic about how long it may take you to get up to speed about different areas and to find a home that meets your various desires. If you're like most people, with a full-time job that allows only occasional evenings and weekends free to look for a house, three to six months is a short period to research and see possible areas in which to live, settle on an area, and actually find and successfully negotiate for a property. Six months to a year isn't unusual or slow.

Remember that you're talking about an enormous purchase that you'll come home to daily. Buying a home can also involve a lot of compromise when you buy with other family members, particularly spouses.

Real estate agents can be a big barrier to taking your time with this monumental decision. Some agents are pushy; they just want to make a sale and get their commission. Don't work with such agents as a buyer because they can make you stressed and broke. If necessary, begin your search without an agent to avoid this outside pressure.

In this section, I discuss your housing choices, how to research communities, and finally how to check out homes and value them.

Understanding your housing options

If you're ready to begin shopping for a home, to help focus your search, you should make some decisions about what and where to buy. Here are the most common types of housing you will encounter:

>> **Single-family homes:** If you grew up in the suburbs, you probably saw plenty of single-family homes, even if you didn't live in one. This type of home is a detached house on a piece of land. Lots may be small or large, but the land is 100 percent yours, and the house is separate from other neighboring properties.

>> **Condominiums:** These properties typically are apartment-style units that are on top of and adjacent to one another. Many condo buildings were originally apartments that were converted to condos through the sale of ownership of separate units. When you purchase a condominium, you purchase a specific unit as well as a share of the common areas (the pool, landscaping, entry and hallways, laundry room, and so on).

>> **Townhomes:** Townhomes are attached or row homes. A townhome is essentially a cross between a condominium (because it's attached, sharing a roof and some walls) and a single-family house (because it has its own yard).

>> **Cooperatives:** Cooperatives (or co-ops) resemble apartment and condominium buildings. When you buy a share in a cooperative, you own a share of the entire building, including some living space. Unlike in a condo, you generally need to get approval from the cooperative association if you want to remodel or rent your unit to a tenant. In some co-ops, you must even gain approval from the association to sell your unit to a proposed buyer.

Co-ops generally are much harder to obtain loans for and to sell, so I don't recommend that you buy one unless you get a good deal and are certain you can obtain a loan.

With the exception of single-family homes in the preceding list, the other types of housing are shared housing. This type of housing generally gives you more living space for your dollars. This value makes sense, because a good chunk of the cost of a single-family home is the land on which the home sits. Land is good for decks, recreation, and children's playgrounds, but you don't live "in" land the way you do in your home. Shared housing maximizes living space for the housing dollars that you spend.

Another possible benefit of shared housing is that in many situations, you're not personally responsible for general maintenance. Instead, the homeowners' association (which you pay into) takes care of it. If you don't have the time, energy, or desire to keep up a property, shared housing can make sense. Shared housing units may also give you access to recreation facilities, such as a pool, tennis courts, and exercise equipment.

From an investment perspective, shared housing isn't best. Single-family homes generally appreciate more than shared housing does. Part of the reason for that is that shared housing is easier to build and to overbuild, and the greater supply tends to keep prices from rising as much. On the demand side, single-family homes tend to attract more potential buyers. Most folks, when they can afford it, prefer a stand-alone home, especially for the increased privacy.

TIP

If you can afford a smaller single-family home instead of a larger shared-housing unit and don't balk at maintaining a home, buy a single-family home. Shared housing makes more sense for people who don't want to deal with maintenance and who value the security of living in a larger building with other folks. (Recognize that you may not like or even feel comfortable with everyone living in a given shared housing complex.) Shared-housing prices tend to hold up better in developed urban environments. If possible, avoid shared housing units in suburban areas, where the availability of developable land makes building many more units possible, thus increasing the supply of housing, and slowing growth in value.

Researching communities

You may have an idea about the type of property and location that interests you or that you think you can afford. Even if you've lived in an area for a while and think that you know it well, be sure to explore different types of properties in a variety of locations before you start to narrow your search.

INVESTIGATE

Thinking that you can know what an area is like from anecdotes or from a small number of personal experiences can be a mistake. Anecdotes and people's perceptions often aren't accurate reflections of the facts. Check out the following key items in an area you're considering:

>> **Amenities:** Ideally, you don't spend all your time at work, slaving away to make your monthly mortgage payment. I hope you have time to use parks, recreation facilities, and so on. Walk and drive around the neighborhoods

you're interested in to get a sense of these attractions. Most real estate agents enjoy showing their favorite neighborhoods. Talk to folks you know in the areas you're considering. Visit those cities' and towns' websites.

>> **Catastrophic risks:** Are the neighborhoods in which you're considering buying a home prone to floods, tornadoes, mudslides, fires, or earthquakes? Although homeowner's insurance, with proper supplements, can protect you financially, consider how you may deal with such catastrophes emotionally. Insurance addresses only the financial pain of a home loss. You can't eliminate all risks, but you can get educated about catastrophic risks. The U.S. Geological Survey (www.usgs.gov) has maps that show earthquake risks, and the Federal Emergency Management Agency (www.fema.gov) has flood-risk maps. Insurance companies and agencies can also tell you what they know about risks in particular areas.

>> **Crime:** Cities and towns keep all sorts of crime statistics for neighborhoods, so use them! Call the local police department or get local crime data online at sites like www.neighborhoodscout.com.

>> **Development:** Check with the planning office in towns that you're considering living in to find out what types of new developments and major renovations are in the works. Planning people may also be aware of problems in particular areas.

>> **Property taxes:** What will your property taxes be? Property tax rates vary from community to community. Check with the town's assessment office or with a good real estate agent.

>> **Schools:** If you have kids, you care about this issue a lot. Unfortunately, many people make snap judgments about school quality without getting the facts. Visit schools where possible, talk to parents and teachers, and discover what goes on at the schools.

REMEMBER

Consider school quality even if schools aren't important to you because they can affect the resale value of your property.

Checking out and valuing a home

Over many months, you may see dozens of homes for sale. Use these viewings as an opportunity to find out what specific homes are worth. Odds are that the listing price isn't what a house is actually worth. Property that's priced to sell usually does sell. Properties left on the market are often overpriced. The listing prices of such properties may reflect what an otherwise greedy or uninformed seller and their agent hope that some fool will pay.

Of the properties that you see, keep track of the prices they end up selling for. (Good agents can provide this information.) Properties usually sell for less than the listed price. Keeping track of selling prices gives you a good handle on what properties are really worth and a better sense of what you can afford.

INVESTIGATE

After you set your sights on a home you like, thoroughly check out the surroundings. Go back to the neighborhood in which the property is located at different times of the day and on different days of the week. Take a walk around and see if you can strike up a conversation or two with folks who live there and perhaps meet some of your potential neighbors. Ask questions. Talk to property owners as well as renters. Because they don't have a financial stake in the area, renters are often more forthcoming with negative information about an area.

After you decide where and what to buy, you're ready to try to put a deal together. To do so, you need to understand mortgages, negotiations, and inspections. I cover these issues and many more in the latest edition of *Home Buying Kit For Dummies* (Wiley), which I cowrote with Ray Brown.

Investing in Investment Real Estate

If you've already bought your own home (and even if you haven't), using real estate as an investment may interest you. Real estate investing, like the stock market and small-business investments, has long generated tremendous wealth for many investors.

Real estate is like other types of ownership investments, such as stocks, in that you have an ownership stake in an asset. Although you have the potential for significant profits, don't forget that you also accept greater risk. Like stocks, real estate goes through good and bad performance periods. Most people who make money investing in real estate do so because they invest in and hold property over many years.

WARNING

Real estate investing isn't for everyone. You should avoid real estate investments that involve managing property if you're pressed for time. Buying and owning investment property and being a landlord can take a lot of time. If you fail to do your homework before purchasing real estate, you can end up overpaying — or buying a heap of trouble. You can hire a property manager to help with screening and finding good tenants, as well as troubleshooting problems with the building you purchase, but this step costs money and still requires some time involvement. Also, remember that most tenants don't care for a property the same way that property owners do. If every little scratch or carpet stain sends your blood pressure soaring, being a landlord may not be for you.

In this section, I discuss how to make wise real estate investments.

Understanding real estate investment's appeal

Many people build their wealth by investing in real estate. Some people focus exclusively on property investments, but many others build their wealth through the companies they started or through other avenues and then diversify into real estate investments.

Real estate, like all investments, has its pros and cons. Investing in real estate is time-intensive and carries risks. Do it because you enjoy the challenge and because you want to diversify your portfolio. Don't take this route because you seek a get-rich-quick outlet. Here are some of the reasons why people pursue real estate investments:

>> **Ability to add value:** Perhaps you can fix up a property or develop it further and raise the rental income and resale value. Through legwork, persistence, and good negotiating skills, you may also be able to make money by purchasing a property below its fair market value.

>> **Appreciation and income:** You can make money from investment real estate through appreciation and from rental income in excess of your expenses. The appreciation of your properties compounds without taxation during your ownership. You don't pay tax on this profit until you sell your property, and even then, you can roll over your gain into another investment property to avoid paying tax. The federal tax rate on gains from property held more than one year (known as *long-term capital gains*) are taxed at a reduced rate — currently, a maximum of 20 percent (and possibly an additional 3.8 percent if you're a high-income earner subject to the Obamacare investment income surtax). You also seek to rent out your investment property at a profit based on the property's rental income in excess of its expenses (mortgage, property taxes, insurance, maintenance, and so on). Over time, your operating profit, which is subject to ordinary income tax, should rise as you increase your rental prices faster than your expenses.

>> **Leverage:** Real estate is different from most other investments because you can generally borrow up to 75 percent of the value of the property to buy it. Thus, you can use your down payment of 25 percent of the purchase price to buy, own, and control a much larger investment; this concept is called *leverage*. You hope, of course, that the value of your real estate goes up; if it does, you make money on your original dollars invested as well as on the money that you borrowed. Leverage can also work against you when prices decline.

>> **Limited land:** There's a limited supply of buildable, desirable land, and as the population grows, demand for land and housing continues to grow. Land and what you can do with it are what make real estate valuable.

>> **Longer-term focus:** One problem with investing in the stock market is that prices are constantly changing. Because all you need to do is tap your phone app, click your computer mouse, or call a toll-free phone number to place your sell or buy order, some stock market investors fall prey to irrational snap judgments. While the real estate market is constantly changing, short-term, day-to-day, and week-to-week changes are invisible (although some real estate–pricing websites are calculating updated prices, of questionable accuracy, more often). If prices do decline over months and years, you're much less likely to sell real estate in a panic. Preparing a property for sale and eventually getting it sold take a good deal of time, and this barrier to selling quickly helps you keep your perspective.

Sizing up real estate investment options

If you think you're cut out to be a landlord and are ready for the responsibility of buying, owning, and managing rental real estate, you have numerous real estate investment options to choose among.

Some investors prefer to buy properties, improve them, and then move on. Ideally, however, you should plan to make real estate investments that you hold for many years, perhaps into your retirement years. But what should you buy? Following is my take on various real estate investments.

Real estate investment trusts

Real estate investment trusts (REITs) are entities that generally invest in different types of property, such as shopping centers, apartments, and other rental buildings. For a fee, REIT managers identify and negotiate the purchase of properties that they believe are good investments; then they manage these properties, including handling all tenant relations.

REITs are a good way to invest in real estate if you don't want the hassles and headaches that come with directly owning and managing rental property. You can research and purchase shares in individual REITs, which trade as securities on the major stock exchanges. An even better approach is to buy a mutual fund or exchange–traded fund that invests in a diversified mixture of REITs.

Residential housing

If you're willing to be a landlord, your best bet for real estate investing is to purchase residential property. People always need places to live. Residential housing is easier to understand, purchase, and manage than most other types of property, such as office and retail property. If you're a homeowner, you already have experience locating, purchasing, and maintaining residential property.

The most common residential housing options are single-family homes, condominiums, and townhouses. You can also purchase multiunit buildings. Consider the following issues when you decide what type of property to buy:

>> **Appreciation potential:** Look for property where simple cosmetic and other fixes may allow you to increase rents and increase the market value of the property. Although condos may be easier to maintain, they tend to appreciate less than homes or apartment buildings do, unless the condos are located in a desirable urban area.

>> **Cash flow:** The difference between the rental income that you collect and the expenses that you pay out is known as your *cash flow*. As time goes on, generating a positive cash flow usually gets easier as you pay down your mortgage debt and increase rents.

>> **Maintenance:** Condominiums are generally the lowest-maintenance properties because most condominium associations deal with issues such as roofing, landscaping, and so on for the entire building. Note that as the owner, you're still responsible for maintenance that's needed inside your unit, such as servicing appliances, interior painting, and so on. Be aware, though, that some condo complexes don't allow rentals. With a single-family home or apartment building, you're responsible for all the maintenance. You can hire someone to do the work, but you still have to find the contractors and coordinate, oversee, and pay for the work they do.

>> **Tenants:** Single-family homes with just one tenant (which could be a family, a couple, or a single person) are simpler to deal with than a multiunit apartment building that requires the management and maintenance of multiple renters and units.

TIP

Unless you really want to minimize maintenance responsibilities, avoid condominium investments. Similarly, apartment-building investments are best left to sophisticated investors who like a challenge and can manage more complex properties. Single-family home investments are generally more straightforward for most people. Be sure you run the numbers on your rental income and expenses to see whether you can afford the negative cash flow that may occur in the early years of ownership.

Land

If having tenants and maintaining a building is a lot of work, you can consider investing in land. Over time, in areas experiencing economic and building growth and using up available land, land values may appreciate well. That said, unrented land tends to underperform leased real estate because there is no income. (An exception — farmland — is used to grow crops.)

Although land doesn't require upkeep and tenants, it does require financial feeding. Investing in land can be problematic for the following reasons:

>> **Identifying many years in advance which communities will experience rapid population and job growth isn't easy.** Land in those areas that people believe will be the next hot spot often already sells at a premium. If property growth doesn't happen, appreciation will dry up.

>> **Investing in land is a cash drain.** Because it costs money to purchase land, you also have a mortgage payment to make. Mortgage lenders charge higher interest rates on loans to purchase land because they see it as a more speculative investment.

>> **You don't get depreciation tax write-offs because land isn't depreciable.** You also have property tax payments to meet. With land investments, you don't receive income from the property to offset these expenses.

>> **If you someday decide that you want to develop the property, it can cost a great deal of money.** Obtaining a loan for development is challenging and more expensive (because it's riskier for the lender) than obtaining a loan for a developed property.

If you decide to invest in land, be sure you meet the following criteria:

>> **You can afford it.** Tally up the annual carrying costs so you can see what your cash drain may be. What are the financial consequences of this cash outflow? Will you be able to fund your tax-advantaged retirement accounts, for example? If you can't, count the lost tax benefits as another cost of owning land.

>> **You understand what further improvements the land needs.** Running utility lines, building roads, landscaping, and so on all cost money. If you plan to develop and build on the land you purchase, research what these things may cost. Remember that improvements almost always cost more than you expect.

>> **You know its zoning status.** The value of land depends greatly on what you can develop on it, so thoroughly understand the land's zoning status and what you can — and can't — build on it before you buy. Also research the disposition of the planning department and nearby communities. Areas that are antigrowth and antidevelopment are less likely to be good places for you to invest in land, especially if you need permission to do the type of project you have in mind.

Be aware that zoning can change for the worse. Sometimes a zoning alteration can reduce what you can develop on a property and, consequently, the property's value.

>> **You've researched the local economic and housing situations.** Buy land in an area that's home to rapidly expanding companies and that has a shortage of housing and developable land.

Commercial real estate

If you're really motivated and willing to roll up your sleeves, you may want to consider commercial real estate investments (such as small office buildings or strip malls). Generally, however, you're better off *not* investing in such real estate, because it's much more complicated than investing in residential real estate. It's also riskier from an investment and tenant-turnover perspective. When tenants move out, new tenants sometimes require extensive and costly improvements to the space they want to rent.

In addition to considering investing in commercial real estate when your analysis of the local market suggests that it's a good time to buy, consider it when you can use some of the space to run your own small business. Just as owning your home can be more cost-effective than renting over the years, so is owning commercial real estate if you buy at a reasonably good time and hold the property for many years.

So how do you evaluate the state of your local commercial real estate market? Examine the supply-and-demand statistics over recent years. Determine how much space is available for rent and how that number has changed over time. Also discover the vacancy rate and find out how it has changed in recent years. Finally, investigate the rental rates, usually quoted as a price per square foot. Ask your local commercial property real estate agent for this data or for the local sources where you can find it.

Here's one way to tell that purchasing a commercial property in a certain area is a bad idea: The supply of available space has increased faster than demand, leading to falling rental rates and higher vacancies. A slowing local economy and an increasing unemployment rate also spell trouble for commercial real estate prices. Each market is different, so make sure you check out the details of your area.

Conducting real estate investing research

In the following sections, I explain what to look for in a community and area where you seek to invest in real estate. Investing in real estate closer to home is best because you're probably more familiar with the local area, allowing you to have an easier time researching and managing the properties.

Assessing employment vitality

Invest in real estate in communities that maintain diverse job bases. If the local economy relies heavily on jobs in a small number of industries, that dependence increases the risk of your real estate investments. The Bureau of Labor Statistics (www.bls.gov) compiles this type of data for metropolitan areas and counties.

Also determine which industries are most heavily represented in the local economy. Areas that have a greater concentration of high-growth and higher-paying industries stand a greater chance of faster price appreciation.

Finally, check out the unemployment situation, and examine how the jobless rate has changed in recent years. Good signs to look for are declining unemployment and increasing job growth. The Bureau of Labor Statistics also tracks this data.

Evaluating the realty market's health

The price of real estate, like the price of anything else, is driven by supply and demand. The smaller the supply and the greater the demand, the higher prices climb. An abundance of land and available credit, however, inevitably leads to overbuilding. When the supply of anything expands at a much faster rate than demand, prices usually fall.

Upward pressure on real estate prices tends to be greatest in areas with little buildable land. In addition to buildable land, consider these important real estate market indicators to gauge the health of a particular market:

>> **Building permits:** The trend in the number of building permits tells you how the supply of real estate properties may soon change. A long and sustained rise in permits over several years can indicate that the supply of new property may dampen future price appreciation.

>> **Vacancy rates:** If few rentals are vacant, you can assume that the area has more competition and demand for existing units, which bodes well for future real estate price appreciation. Conversely, high vacancy rates indicate an excess supply of real estate, which may put downward pressure on rental rates as many landlords compete to attract tenants.

>> **Listings of property for sale and number of sales:** Just as the construction of many new buildings is bad for future real estate price appreciation, increasing numbers of property listings are an indication of potential trouble. A sign of a healthy real estate market is a decreasing and relatively low level of property listings, indicating that the demand from buyers meets or exceeds the supply of property for sale from sellers. When the cost of buying is relatively low compared with the cost of renting, more renters can afford and choose to purchase, thus increasing the number of sales.

>> **Rental rates:** The trend in rental rates that renters are willing and able to pay over the years is a good indication of the demand for housing. When the demand for housing keeps up with the supply of housing and the local economy continues to grow, rents generally increase. This increase is a positive sign for continued real estate price appreciation. Beware of buying rental property that's subject to rent control; the property's expenses may rise faster than you can raise the rents.

Valuing property and financial projections

INVESTIGATE

Crunching some numbers to figure what revenue and expenses a rental property may have is one of the most important exercises that you can go through when determining a property's worth and making an offer. Here are some key things to do:

>> **Estimate cash flow.** Cash flow is the difference between the money that a property brings in and what goes out for its expenses.

>> **Value property.** Estimating a property's cash flow is an important first step in figuring a property's value, but a building's cash flow doesn't provide enough information for you to decide intelligently whether to buy a particular real estate investment. Property valuations are most often done by appraisers, who value property for a living, or real estate agents, who can do an analysis of comparable property sales.

For more details on investing in real estate, see the latest edition of *Real Estate Investing For Dummies* (Wiley), which I cowrote with Robert S. Griswold.

IN THIS CHAPTER

» Choosing your best real estate investment financing

» Finding an excellent real estate agent

» Negotiating and inspecting your deals

» Making smart property selling decisions

Chapter **13**

Financing and Putting Together Real Estate Investment Deals

I n this chapter, I discuss issues such as understanding and selecting mortgages, working with real estate agents, negotiating, and other important details that help you put a real estate deal together. I also provide some words of wisdom about taxes and selling your property that may come in handy down the road.

Financing Your Real Estate Deals

Unless you're affluent or buying a low-cost property, you likely need to borrow some money via a mortgage to make the purchase happen. Without financing, your dream to invest in real estate remains just that: a dream. So first you have to maximize your chances of getting approved for a loan. Shopping wisely for a good mortgage can save you thousands, perhaps even tens of thousands, of dollars in interest and fees. Don't get saddled with a loan that you may not be able to afford someday and that could push you into foreclosure or bankruptcy.

Achieving loan approval

Even if you have perfect or near-perfect credit, you may encounter financing problems with some properties. And, of course, not all real estate buyers have a perfect credit history, tons of available cash, and no debt. Because of the soft real estate market in the late 2000s and the jump in foreclosures around that time, lenders tightened credit standards to avoid making loans to people likely to default. If you're one of those borrowers who end up jumping through more hoops than others to get a loan, don't give up hope. Few borrowers are perfect from a lender's perspective, and many problems are fixable.

TIP

To head off some potential rejections before you apply for a loan, disclose to your lender anything that may cause a problem. For example, if you already know that your credit report indicates some late payments from when you were out of the country for several weeks five years ago, write a note/email to your preferred lender or mortgage broker that explains this situation.

Fixing down payment blues

Many people, especially when they make their first real estate purchase, are strapped for cash. In order to qualify for the most attractive financing, lenders typically require that your down payment be at least 20 percent of the property's purchase price. Investment property loans may require 25 to 30 percent down for the best terms. In addition, you need reserve money to pay for other closing costs, such as title insurance and loan fees.

TIP

If you don't have 20-plus percent of a property's purchase price available, don't despair. You can still own real estate with the following strategies:

» **Take out private mortgage insurance.** Some lenders may offer you a mortgage even though you can put down only, say, 10 percent of the purchase price. These lenders will likely require you to purchase *private mortgage insurance* (PMI) for your loan, however. This insurance generally costs a few hundred dollars per year and protects the lender if you default on your loan. When you have at least 20 percent equity in the property, you can generally eliminate the PMI.

» **Dip into your retirement savings.** You may be able to borrow against your retirement account balance through your employer's retirement savings plan under the condition that you repay the loan within a set number of years. Subject to eligibility requirements, first-time homebuyers can make penalty-free withdrawals of up to $10,000 from IRA accounts. (**Note:** You still must pay regular income tax on the withdrawal.)

>> **Postpone your purchase.** If you don't want the cost and strain of extra fees and bad mortgage terms, you can postpone your purchase. Go on a financial austerity program and boost your savings further.

>> **Consider lower-priced properties.** Lower-priced properties can help keep down the purchase price and the required down payment.

>> **Find a partner.** Sharing the financial obligations with a partner often makes buying real estate easier. Just make sure you write up a legal contract to specify what happens if a partner wants out. Family members sometimes make good partners. Your parents, grandparents, and even your siblings may have some extra cash they'd like to loan, invest, or give to you as a gift!

>> **Look into seller financing.** Some property owners or developers may finance your purchase with as little as 5 to 10 percent down. However, you can't be as picky about such seller-financed properties because a limited supply is available. Many that are available need work or haven't yet sold for other reasons.

Boosting your credit score

Late payments, missed payments, or debts that you never bothered to pay can tarnish your credit report and squelch a lender's desire to offer you a mortgage. If you're turned down for a loan because of your less-than-stellar credit history, find out the details of why by requesting (at no charge to you) a copy of your credit report from the lender that turned down your loan.

TIP

If you think your credit history may be a problem as you're looking for a loan, the first thing to do is get the facts. By law, you're entitled to one free credit report per year from each of the three consumer credit reporting companies — Equifax, Experian, and TransUnion. You can get all three reports at once or space them out throughout the year (checking in on one each at four-month intervals for example). The companies have set up one central website where you can access these reports (www.annualcreditreport.com), or you can call toll-free at 877-322-8228. Just be careful not to buy the ongoing credit monitoring services these companies will pitch you.

If you do find credit report problems, explain them to your lender. If the lender is unsympathetic, try calling other lenders. Tell them your credit problems upfront and see whether you can find one willing to offer you a competitive rate loan. Mortgage brokers may also be able to help you shop for lenders in these cases. (I discuss working with mortgage brokers later in this chapter.)

Sometimes you may feel that you're not in control when you apply for a loan. In reality, however, you can fix a number of credit problems yourself, and you reap great rewards (access to better loan terms, including lower interest rates) for doing so. And you can often explain away those that you can't fix. Remember that some lenders are more lenient and flexible than others. Just because one mortgage lender rejects your loan application doesn't mean all the others will as well.

TIP

If you discover erroneous information on your credit report, you can request that it be fixed by disputing the incorrect information on the credit bureaus' websites. If specific creditors are the culprits, contact them, too. Keep notes from your conversations, and make sure you follow up and put your case in writing (emails leave an excellent documentation trail) and add your comments as necessary to your credit report if a lender isn't cooperative in fixing what you believe is a problem/mistake. If the customer service representatives you talk with are no help, send a letter to the president of each company. Let the head honcho know that their organization caused you problems in obtaining credit. For more information on examining and disputing items on your credit report and managing credit in general, check out the Federal Trade Commission's website at www.ftc.gov/credit.

Besides late or missed payments, another common credit problem is having too much consumer debt at the time you apply for a mortgage. The more consumer debt you rack up (including credit card and auto loan debt), the less mortgage credit you qualify for. If you're turned down for a mortgage, consider it a wake-up call to get rid of your high-cost debt. Hang on to the dream of buying real estate and plug away at paying off your debts before you attempt another foray into real estate.

To find out more about how credit scores work and techniques to improve yours, see the latest edition of my book *Personal Finance For Dummies* (Wiley).

Addressing a low appraisal

Even if you have sufficient income, a clean credit report, and an adequate down payment, a lender may deny your loan if the appraisal of the property that you want to buy comes in lower than what you agreed to pay for the property.

TIP

If you still like the property, renegotiate a lower price with the seller by using the low appraisal to strengthen your case. You need to follow a different path should you encounter a low appraisal on a property that you already own and are refinancing. If you have the cash available, you can simply put more money down to get the loan balance to a level for which you qualify. If you don't have the cash, you may need to try another lender or forgo the refinance until you save more money or until the property value rises. (I discuss refinancing in more detail later in this chapter.)

Handling insufficient income

If you're self-employed or have changed jobs, your current income may not resemble your past income or, more importantly, your income may be below what a mortgage lender likes to see given the amount that you want to borrow. A way around this problem, although challenging, is to make a larger down payment.

TIP

If you can't make a large down payment, another option is to get a co-signer for the loan. For example, your relatives may be willing to sign with you. As long as they aren't overextended themselves, they may be able to help you qualify for a larger loan than you can get on your own. As with partnerships, put your agreement in writing so no misunderstandings occur.

Debating fixed-rate versus adjustable-rate mortgages

Two major types of mortgages exist: those with a fixed interest rate and those with an adjustable rate. Your choice depends on your financial situation, how much risk you're willing to accept, and the type of property you want to purchase. For example, obtaining a fixed-rate loan on a property that lenders perceive as a riskier investment is more difficult than getting an adjustable-rate mortgage for the same property.

Understanding fixed-rate mortgages

Fixed-rate mortgages, which are typically for a 15- or 30-year term, have interest rates that stay fixed or level — you lock in an interest rate that doesn't change over the life of your loan. Because the interest rate stays the same, your monthly mortgage payment stays the same. You have nothing complicated to track and no uncertainty. Fixed-rate loans give people peace of mind and payment stability.

WARNING

Fixed-rate mortgages do, however, carry risks. If interest rates fall significantly after you obtain your mortgage and you're unable to refinance, you face being stuck with a higher-cost mortgage, which could be problematic if you lose your job or the value of your property decreases. (This scenario — declining interest rates and falling real estate values — happened to plenty of people in the late 2000s.) Even if you're able to refinance, you'll probably have to spend significant time and money to complete the applications and forms.

Analyzing adjustable-rate mortgages (ARMs)

In contrast to a fixed-rate mortgage, an *adjustable-rate mortgage* (ARM) carries an interest rate that varies over time, based on a formula the lender establishes, and is set and clearly disclosed at the time you take out the mortgage. Such a mortgage begins with one interest rate, and you may pay different rates for every year, possibly even every six months or month, that you hold the loan. Thus, the size of your monthly payment fluctuates. Because a mortgage payment makes a large dent in most property owners' bank accounts, signing up for an ARM without fully understanding how the rate can change is risky and can be fiscally foolish.

The advantage of an ARM is that if you purchase your property during a period of higher interest rates, you can start paying your mortgage with a relatively low initial interest rate, compared with fixed-rate loans. (With a fixed-rate mortgage, a mortgage lender takes extra risk in committing to a fixed interest rate for 15 to 30 years. To be compensated for accepting this additional risk, lenders charge a premium with fixed-rate mortgages in case interest rates, which they have to pay on their source of funds in the form of deposits, move much higher in future years.) If interest rates decline, an ARM allows you to capture many of the benefits of lower rates without the cost and hassle of refinancing.

BEWARE OF BALLOON LOANS

Balloon loans generally start the way traditional fixed-rate mortgages start. You make level payments based on a long-term payment schedule — over 15 or 30 years, for example. But at a predetermined time, usually within ten years of the loan's inception, the remaining loan balance becomes fully due.

Balloon loans may save you money because they have a lower interest rate than a longer-term fixed-rate mortgage and you pay that interest over a shorter period of time. However, balloon loans are dangerous; your financial situation can change, and you may not be able to refinance when your balloon loan is due. What if you lose your job or your income drops? What if the value of your property drops and the appraisal comes in too low to qualify you for a new loan? What if interest rates rise and you can't qualify at the higher rate on a new loan? You're still going to have to pay off your balloon loan when it comes due.

Sometimes, balloon loans may be the only option for the buyer (or so the buyer thinks). Buyers are more commonly backed into these loans during periods of high interest rates. When a buyer can't afford the payments on a conventional mortgage and really wants a particular property, a seller may offer a balloon loan.

Warning: Shun balloon loans. Consider a balloon loan if, and only if, you've really done your homework to exhaust other financing alternatives, and you're certain you can refinance when the balloon comes due. If you take a balloon loan, get one with as much time as possible, preferably ten years, before it becomes due.

Deciding between fixed and adjustable mortgages

You can't predict the future course of interest rates. Even the professional financial market soothsayers and investors can't predict where rates are heading. If you could foretell interest rate movements, you could make a fortune investing in bonds and interest-rate futures and options. So cast aside your pundit cap and ask yourself the following two vital questions to decide whether a fixed or adjustable mortgage will work best for you.

What financial risks can you handle?

How much of a gamble can you take with the size of your monthly mortgage payment? For example, if your job and income are unstable and you need to borrow an amount that stretches your monthly budget, you can't afford much risk. If you're in this situation, stick with fixed-rate mortgages because you likely won't be able to handle a large increase in interest rates and the payment on an ARM.

If, on the other hand, you're in a position to take the financial risks that come with an adjustable-rate mortgage, you have a better chance of saving money with an adjustable loan rather than a fixed-rate loan. Your interest rate starts lower and stays lower if the market level of interest rates remains unchanged. Even if rates go up, they'll likely come back down over the life of your loan. If you can stick with your adjustable-rate loan for better and for worse, you may come out ahead in the long run.

Adjustables also make more sense if you borrow less than you're qualified for. Or perhaps you regularly save a sizable chunk — more than 10 percent — of your monthly income. If your income significantly exceeds your spending, you may feel less anxiety about fluctuating interest rates. If you do choose an adjustable loan, you may be more financially secure if you have a hefty financial cushion (at least six months' to as much as a year's worth of expenses reserved) that you can access if rates go up.

TIP

Almost all adjustables limit, or *cap,* the rise in the interest rate that your loan allows. Typical caps are 2 percent per year and 6 percent over the life of the loan. Ask your lender to calculate the highest possible monthly payment that your loan allows. The number that the lender comes up with is the *lifetime cap,* the payment you face if the interest rate on your loan goes to the highest level allowed. If you can't afford the highest-allowed payment on an adjustable-rate mortgage, don't take one. You shouldn't take the chance that the rate won't rise that high — it can, and you could lose the property.

Don't take an adjustable mortgage just because the lower initial interest rates allow you to afford the property that you want to buy (unless you're absolutely certain your income will rise to meet future payment increases). Instead, set your sights on a property that you can afford to buy with a fixed-rate mortgage.

How long do you anticipate keeping the mortgage?

Saving interest on most adjustables is usually a certainty in the first two or three years. By nature, an adjustable-rate mortgage starts at a lower interest rate than a fixed-rate mortgage. However, if rates rise while you hold an ARM, you can end up giving back the savings that you achieve in the early years of the mortgage.

If you aren't going to keep your mortgage for more than five to seven years, you'll probably end up paying more interest to carry a fixed-rate mortgage. Also consider a hybrid loan, which combines features of fixed- and adjustable-rate mortgages. For example, the initial rate may hold constant for several years and then adjust once a year or every six months thereafter. Such loans may make sense for you if you foresee a high probability of keeping your loan seven years or less but want some stability in your monthly payments. The longer the initial rate stays locked in, the higher the interest rate.

Finding your best fixed-rate mortgage

You may think that comparing one fixed-rate loan to another is simple because the interest rate on a fixed-rate loan is the rate you pay every month over the entire life of the loan. And as with your number of car accidents and the number of times that your boss catches you showing up late for work, a lower number (or interest rate) is better, right?

Unfortunately, banks generally charge an upfront interest fee, known as *points,* in addition to the ongoing interest over the life of the loan. Points are actually percentages: One point is equal to 1 percent of the loan amount. So when a lender tells you a quoted loan has 1.5 points, you pay 1.5 percent of the amount you borrow as points. On a $100,000 loan, for example, 1.5 points cost you $1,500. The interest rate on a fixed-rate loan must always be quoted with the points on the loan, if the loan has points.

You may want to take a higher interest rate on your mortgage if you don't have enough cash to pay for a lot of points, which you pay upfront when you close the loan. On the other hand, if you're willing and able to pay more points, you can lower your interest rate. You may want to pay more points because the interest rate on your loan determines your payments over a long period of time — 15 to 30 years.

Suppose one lender quotes you a rate of 5.75 percent on a 30-year fixed-rate loan and charges one point (1 percent). Another lender, which quotes 6 percent for 30 years, doesn't charge any points. Which is better? The answer depends on how long you plan to keep the loan.

The 5.75 percent loan is 0.25 percent less than the 6 percent loan. However, it takes you about four years to earn back the savings to cover the cost of that point because you have to pay 1 percent (one point) upfront on the 5.75 percent loan. So if you expect to keep the loan more than four years, go with the 5.75 percent option. If you plan to keep the loan less than four years, go with the 6 percent option.

TIP

To make it easier to perform an apples-to-apples comparison of mortgages from different lenders, get interest rate quotes at the same point level. For example, ask each lender for the interest rate on a loan for which you pay one point. And remember that if a loan has no points, it's sure to have a higher interest rate. I'm not saying that no-point loans are better or worse than comparable loans from other lenders. Just don't get sucked into a loan because of a no-points sales pitch. Lenders who spend big bucks on advertising these types of loans rarely have the best mortgage terms.

All things being equal, no-point loans make more sense for refinances because points aren't immediately tax-deductible as they are on purchases. (You can deduct the points that you pay on a refinance *only* over the life of the mortgage.) On a mortgage for a property that you're purchasing, a no-point loan may help if you're cash poor at closing.

Consider a no-point loan if you can't afford more out-of-pocket expenditures now or if you think you'll keep the loan only a few years. Shop around and compare different lenders' no-point loans.

Landing an appropriate adjustable-rate mortgage

Selecting an ARM has a lot in common with selecting a home to buy. You need to make trade-offs and compromises. In the following sections, I explain the numerous features and options — caps, indexes, margins, and adjustment periods — that you find with ARMs. (These aren't issues with fixed-rate loans.)

Understanding the start rate

Just as the name implies, your *start rate* is the rate that your adjustable mortgage begins with. Think of the start rate as a teaser rate — the initial rate on ARMs is often set artificially low to entice you. Don't judge an ARM by this rate alone! You won't pay this attractively low rate for long. With ARMs, interest rates generally rise as soon as the terms of the mortgage allow. Even if the market level of interest rates doesn't change, your adjustable rate is destined to increase. An increase of 1 or 2 percentage points above the start rate is common.

The formula for determining the rate caps and the future interest rates on an adjustable-rate mortgage (see the next section) are far more important in determining what a mortgage will cost you in the long run. For more on rate caps, see the section "Analyzing adjustments" later in this chapter.

Assessing your future interest rate

The first thing you need to ask a mortgage lender or broker about an adjustable-rate mortgage is the exact formula it uses for determining the future interest rate on your particular loan. You need to know how a lender figures your interest rate changes over the life of your loan.

All adjustables are based on the following general formula, which specifies how the interest rate is set on your loan in the future:

Index + Margin = Interest rate

The *index* determines the base level of interest rates that the mortgage contract specifies in order to calculate the specific interest rate for your loan. Indexes are generally (but not always) widely quoted in the financial press.

For example, suppose that the current index value for a given loan is equal to the 6-month Treasury bill index, which is, say, 2 percent. The *margin* is the amount added to the index to determine the interest rate that you pay on your mortgage. Most loans have margins of around 2.5 percent. Thus, the rate of a mortgage driven by the following formula — 6-month Treasury bill rate + 2.5 percent — is set at 2 + 2.5 = 4.5 percent. This figure is known as the *fully indexed rate.* If the advertised start rate for this loan is just 3 percent, you know that if the index (6-month Treasuries) stays at the same level, your loan will increase to 4.5 percent.

Compare the fully indexed rate to the current rate for fixed-rate loans. During particular time periods, you may be surprised to discover that the fixed-rate loan is at about the same interest rate or even a tad lower. This insight may cause you to reconsider your choice of an adjustable-rate loan, which can, of course, rise to an even higher rate in the future.

Making sense of common ARM indexes

The different indexes vary mainly in how rapidly they respond to changes in interest rates. Some common indexes include the following:

>> **Treasury bills:** *Treasury bills,* which are often referred to as T-bills, are IOUs (bonds) that the U.S. government issues. Most adjustables are tied to the interest rate on 6-month or 12-month T-bills. T-bill interest rates move relatively quickly.

>> **Certificates of deposit:** *Certificates of deposit,* or CDs, are interest-bearing bank investments that lock you in for a specific period of time. ARMs are usually tied to the average interest rate that banks are currently paying on 6-month CDs. Compared with Treasury bills, CDs tend to respond moderately quickly to changes in the market's level of interest rates.

>> **London Interbank Offered Rate Index (LIBOR):** This index is an average of the interest rates that major international banks charge one another to borrow U.S. dollars in the London money market. LIBOR tends to move and adjust similarly to CDs with changes in interest rates.

If you select an adjustable-rate mortgage that's tied to one of the faster-moving indexes, you take on more of a risk that the next adjustment will reflect interest rate increases. Because you take on this risk, lenders cut you breaks in other ways, such as through lower caps or points. If you want the security of an ARM tied to a slower-moving index, you pay for that security in one form or another, such as through a higher start rate, caps, margin, or points.

REMEMBER

Trying to predict interest rates is risky business. When selecting a mortgage, keeping sight of your financial situation is far more important than trying to guess future interest rates.

Analyzing adjustments

After the initial interest rate expires, the interest rate on an ARM fluctuates based on the loan formula that I discuss earlier in the chapter. Most ARMs adjust every 6 or 12 months, but some adjust as frequently as monthly. In advance of each adjustment, the lender sends you a notice telling you your new rate.

All things being equal, the less frequently your loan adjusts, the less financial uncertainty you have in your life. However, mortgages with less-frequent adjustments usually have a higher starting interest rate.

Almost all adjustables come with an *adjustment cap,* which limits the maximum rate change (up or down) at each adjustment. On most loans that adjust every 6 months, the adjustment cap is 1 percent. In other words, the interest rate that the loan charges can move up or down no more than one percentage point in a given adjustment period.

Loans that adjust more than once per year usually limit the maximum rate change that's allowed over the entire year as well. On the vast majority of such loans, 2 percent is the annual rate cap. Likewise, almost all adjustables come with *lifetime caps*. These caps limit the highest rate allowed over the entire life of the loan. Adjustable loans commonly have lifetime caps 5 to 6 percent higher than the initial start rate.

WARNING

Never take an ARM without rate caps! Doing so is worse than giving a credit card with an unlimited line of credit to one of your kids. When you want to take an ARM, you must identify the maximum payment that you can handle. If you can't handle the highest allowed payment, don't look at ARMs.

Avoiding negative amortization ARMs

WARNING

As you make mortgage payments over time, the loan balance you still owe is gradually reduced, or *amortized. Negative amortization* — increasing your loan balance — is the reverse of this process. Some ARMs allow negative amortization. How can your outstanding loan balance grow when you continue to make mortgage payments? This phenomenon occurs when your mortgage payment is less than it really should be.

Some loans cap the increase of your monthly payment but don't cap the interest rate. Thus, the size of your mortgage payment may not reflect all the interest you owe on your loan. So rather than paying the interest you owe and paying off some of your loan balance (or principal) every month, you end up paying off some, but not all, of the interest you owe. Thus, lenders add the extra, unpaid interest you still owe to your outstanding debt.

Negative amortization resembles paying only the minimum payment that your credit card bill requires. You continue to rack up finance charges (in this case, greater interest) on the balance as long as you make only the artificially low payment. Taking a loan with negative amortization defeats the whole purpose of borrowing an amount that fits your overall financial goals.

REMEMBER

Avoid adjustables with negative amortization. Most lenders and mortgage brokers aren't forthcoming about telling you when they're pitching a particular loan, so be sure to explicitly ask whether a loan includes negative amortization. You find negative amortization more frequently on loans that lenders consider risky. If you have trouble finding lenders that will deal with your financial situation, make sure you're especially careful.

Understanding other mortgage fees

INVESTIGATE

In addition to points and the ongoing interest rate, lenders tack on all sorts of other upfront charges when processing your loan. Get an itemization of these other fees and charges in writing from all lenders that you're seriously considering. (I explain how to find the best lenders for your needs in the next section.) You need to know the total of all lender fees so you can accurately compare different lenders' loans and determine how much closing on your loan will cost you. These other mortgage fees can pile up in a hurry. Here are the common ones you may see:

>> **Application and processing fees:** Most lenders charge a few hundred dollars to work with you to complete your paperwork and funnel it through their loan evaluation process. If your loan is rejected, or if it's approved and you decide not to take it, the lender needs to cover its costs. Some lenders return this fee to you upon closing with their loan.

>> **Credit report charge:** Most lenders charge you for the cost of obtaining your credit report, which tells the lender whether you've repaid other loans on time. Credit report fees typically run about $75.

>> **Appraisal fee:** The property for which you borrow money needs to be valued. If you default on your mortgage, a lender doesn't want to get stuck with a property that's worth less than you owe. The cost for an appraisal typically ranges from several hundred dollars for most residential properties to as much as $1,000 or more for larger investment properties.

Some lenders offer loans without points or other lender charges. However, remember that if they don't charge points or other fees, they charge a higher interest rate on your loan to make up the difference. Such loans may make sense for you when you lack the cash to close a loan or when you plan to keep the loan for just a few years.

TIP

To minimize your chances of throwing money away applying for a loan that you may not qualify for, ask the lender whether he sees any reason your loan request may be denied. (Also consider getting pre-approved which any lender you're considering using should be able to do for you.) Be sure to disclose any problems on your credit report or any problems with the property that you're aware of. Lenders may not take the time to ask about these sorts of things in their haste to get you to complete their loan applications.

Finding the best lenders

You can easily save thousands of dollars in interest charges and other fees if you shop around for a mortgage deal. Whether you do research on your own or hire someone good to help you, you should definitely shop around because a lot of money is at stake! I discuss both options in the next two sections.

Shopping through a mortgage broker

A competent mortgage broker can be a big help in getting you a good loan and closing the deal, especially if you're too busy or uninterested to dig for a good deal on a mortgage. A good mortgage broker also stays abreast of the many different mortgages in the marketplace. They can shop among lots of lenders to get you the best deal available. The following list presents some additional advantages to working with a mortgage broker:

>> An organized and detail-oriented mortgage broker can help you through the process of completing all those tedious forms that lenders require.

>> Mortgage brokers can help polish your loan package so the information you present is most favorable yet truthful.

>> The best brokers can help educate you about various loan options and the pros and cons of available features.

INVESTIGATE

A mortgage broker typically gets paid a percentage, usually 0.5 to 1 percent, of the loan amount. This commission is generally negotiable, especially on larger loans that are more lucrative. So be sure to ask what the commission is on loans that a broker pitches. Some brokers may be indignant that you ask, but that's their problem. You have every right to ask. After all, it's your money.

WARNING

Be careful when you choose a mortgage broker because some brokers are lazy and don't shop the market for the best current rates. Even worse, some brokers direct their business to specific lenders so they can take a bigger cut or commission.

Even if you plan to shop on your own, talking to a mortgage broker may be worthwhile. At the very least, you can compare what you find with what brokers say they can get for you. But again, be careful. Some brokers tell you what you want to hear — that they can beat your best find — and then can't deliver when the time comes.

If your loan broker quotes you a really good deal, ask who the lender is. (However, do be aware that most brokers refuse to reveal this information until you pay the necessary fee to cover the appraisal and credit report.) You can then check with the actual lender to verify the interest rate and points that the broker quotes you and make sure you're eligible for the loan.

Shopping by yourself

Many mortgage lenders compete for your business. Although having a large number of lenders to choose from is good for keeping interest rates lower, it also makes shopping a chore, especially if you're going it alone (instead of using a broker). But there's no substitute for taking the time to speak with numerous lenders and exploring the range of options.

Real estate agents may refer you to lenders with whom they've done business. Just keep in mind that those lenders don't necessarily offer the most competitive rates; the agent simply may have done business with them in the past or received client referrals from them.

INVESTIGATE

You can get a sense of current rates and start searching for a good deal by visiting internet sites, such as HSH Associates (www.hsh.com), Bankrate (www.bankrate.com), and Realtor.com (www.realtor.com) that provide current rates and lender ads. Use them as a starting point and then call the lenders that list the best rates.

Refinancing for a better deal

When you buy a property, you take out a mortgage based on your circumstances and available loan options at that time. But things change. Maybe interest rates have dropped, or you have access to better loan options now than when you first purchased. Or perhaps you want to tap into some of your real estate equity for other investments.

If interest rates drop and you're able to refinance, you can lock in interest rate savings. But getting a lower interest rate than the one you got when you took out your original mortgage isn't reason enough to refinance your mortgage. When you refinance a mortgage, you have to spend money and time to save money. So you need to crunch a few numbers to determine whether refinancing makes financial sense for you.

TIP

Calculate how many months it will take you to recoup the costs of refinancing, such as appraisal costs, loan fees and points, title insurance, and so on. You also have to consider tax issues. For example, if the refinance costs you $2,000 to complete and reduces your monthly payment by $100, it may appear that you can recoup the cost of the refinance in 20 months. However, because you lose some tax write-offs if you reduce your mortgage interest rate and payment, you can't simply look at the reduced amount of your monthly payment.

For a better estimate without spending hours crunching numbers, take your tax rate as specified in Chapter 4 (for example, 28 percent) and reduce your monthly payment savings on the refinance by this amount. That means, continuing with the preceding example, that if your monthly payment drops by $100, you're actually saving only around $72 a month after you factor in the lost tax benefits. So it takes about 28 months ($2,000 divided by $72), not 20 months, to recoup the refinance costs.

REMEMBER

Consider refinancing when you can recover the costs of the refinance within a few years or less and you don't plan to move (or sell your investment property) in that time frame. If it takes longer to recoup the refinance costs, refinancing may still make sense if you anticipate keeping the property and mortgage that long. If you estimate that breaking even will take more than five to seven years, refinancing is probably too risky to justify the costs and hassles.

Refinancing a piece of real estate that you own to pull out cash for some other purpose can make good financial sense because under most circumstances, mortgage interest is tax-deductible. Perhaps you want to purchase another piece of real estate, start or purchase a business, or get rid of an auto loan or some high-cost credit card debt. The interest on consumer debt isn't tax-deductible and is usually at a much higher interest rate than what mortgage loans charge you.

WARNING

Be careful that you don't borrow more than you need to accomplish your financial goals. For example, just because you can borrow more against the equity in your real estate doesn't mean you should do so to buy an expensive new car or take your dream vacation.

USING A HOME EQUITY LOAN

Home equity loans, also known as *second mortgages,* allow you to borrow against the equity in your home in addition to the mortgage you already have (a first mortgage).

A home equity loan may benefit you if you need more money for just a few years or if your first mortgage is at such a low interest rate that refinancing it to get more cash would be too costly. Otherwise, I advise you to avoid home equity loans.

If you need a larger mortgage, why not refinance the first one and wrap it all together? Home equity loans have higher interest rates than comparable first mortgages because they're riskier from a lender's perspective. They're riskier because the first mortgage lender gets first claim against your property if you file bankruptcy or you default on the mortgage.

Interest on home mortgage loans, including home equity loans, of up to $750,000 (first or second residences) is tax-deductible. The interest deduction on home equity loans is limited to loans taken out to buy, build, or substantially improve the taxpayer's home.

Working with Real Estate Agents

If you're like most people, when you purchase real estate, you enlist the services of a real estate agent. A good agent can help screen property so you don't spend all your free time looking at potential properties, negotiating a deal, helping coordinate inspections, and managing other pre-closing items.

Recognizing agent conflicts of interest

All real estate agents (good, mediocre, and awful) are subject to a conflict of interest because of the way they're compensated: on commission. I respect real estate agents for calling themselves what they are. They don't hide behind an obscure job title, such as "shelter consultant." (Many financial "planners," "advisors," or "consultants," for example, actually work on commission and sell investments and life insurance and therefore are really stockbrokers and insurance brokers, not planners or advisors.)

REMEMBER

Real estate agents aren't in the business of providing objective financial counsel. Just as car dealers make their living selling cars, real estate agents make their living selling real estate. Always remember this fact as a prospective home buyer.

The pursuit of a larger commission may encourage an agent to get you to do things that aren't in your best interest, such as the following:

>> **Buy, and buy sooner rather than later:** If you don't buy, your agent doesn't get paid for all the hours she spends working with you. The worst agents fib and use tricks to motivate you to buy. They may say, for example, that other offers are coming in on a property that interests you, or they may show you a bunch of dumps and then one good listing that has much of what you're looking for to motivate you to buy the nicer property.

>> **Spend more than you should:** Because real estate agents get a percentage of the sales price of a property, they have a built-in incentive to encourage you to spend more on a property than what fits comfortably with your other financial objectives and goals. An agent doesn't have to consider or care about your other financial needs.

>> **Purchase their company's listings:** Agents also have a built-in incentive (higher commission) to sell their own listings. So don't be surprised when an agent pushes you in the direction of one of her own company's properties.

>> **Buy outside their territory of experience and expertise:** Real estate agents typically work a specific territory. As a result, they usually can't objectively tell you the pros and cons of the surrounding region which may be what you're interested in and the best fit for your desires.

>> **Use people who scratch their backs:** Some agents refer you to mortgage brokers, lenders, inspectors, and title insurance companies that have referred customers to them. Some agents also solicit and receive referral fees (or bribes) from mortgage lenders, inspectors, and contractors to whom they refer business.

Selecting a good agent

A mediocre, incompetent, or greedy agent can be a real danger to your finances. Whether you're hiring an agent to work with you as a buyer or as a seller, you want someone who's competent and with whom you can get along. Working with an agent costs a good deal of money, so make sure you get your money's worth out of them.

TIP

Interview several agents and check references. Ask agents for the names and contact information of at least three clients with whom they've worked in the past six months in the geographical area in which you're looking. By narrowing the period during which they worked with these references, you maximize the chances of speaking with clients other than the agent's all-time-favorite clients.

As you speak with an agent's references, ask about these traits in any agent that you're considering working with, whether as a buyer or as a seller:

>> **Full-time employment:** Some agents work in real estate as a second or even third job. Information in this field changes constantly, so keeping track of it is challenging on a full-time basis. It's hard to imagine a good agent being able to stay on top of the market on a part-time basis while working full-time elsewhere.

>> **Experience:** Hiring someone with experience doesn't necessarily mean looking for an agent who's sold real estate for decades. Many of the best agents come into the field from other occupations, such as business and teaching. Agents can acquire some sales, marketing, negotiation, and communication skills in other fields. However, keep in mind that some experience in real estate or a related field does count.

>> **Honesty and integrity:** You need to trust your agent with a lot of information. If the agent doesn't level with you about what a neighborhood or particular property is really like, you suffer the consequences.

>> **Interpersonal skills:** An agent must get along not only with you but also with a whole host of other people who are involved in a typical real estate deal: other agents, property sellers, inspectors, mortgage lenders, and so on. An agent needs to know how to put your interests first without upsetting others.

>> **Negotiation skills:** Putting a real estate deal together involves negotiation. Is your agent going to exhaust all avenues to get you the best deal possible? Most people don't like the sometimes aggravating process of negotiation, so they hire someone else to do it for them. Be sure to ask the agent's former client references how the agent negotiated for them.

>> **High quality standards:** Sloppy work can lead to big legal or logistical problems down the road. If an agent neglects to recommend an inspection, for example, you may get stuck with undiscovered problems after the deal is done and paid for.

Agents who pitch themselves as buyers' brokers claim they work for your interests. However, agents who represent you as a buyer's broker still get paid only when you buy. And agents still get paid a commission that's a percentage of the purchase price. So they still have an incentive to sell you a piece of real estate that's more expensive because their commission increases.

WARNING

Some agents market themselves as *top producers*, meaning that they sell a relatively larger volume of real estate. This title doesn't matter much to you, the buyer. In fact, you may use this information as a potential red flag for an agent who focuses on completing as many deals as possible. Such an agent may not be able to give you the time and help you need to get the house you want.

BUYING WITHOUT A REAL ESTATE AGENT

You can purchase property without an agent if you're willing to do some additional legwork. You need to do the things that a high-quality real estate agent does, such as searching for properties, scheduling appointments to see those properties, determining fair market value, negotiating the deal, and coordinating inspections.

If you don't work with an agent, have a real estate attorney review the various contracts. Having someone else not vested in the transaction look out for your interests helps your situation. Real estate agents generally aren't legal experts, so getting legal advice from an attorney is generally better. (In fact, in some states, you need to hire an attorney in addition to the real estate agent.)

One possible drawback to working without an agent is performing the negotiations yourself. Negotiating can be problematic if you lack these skills or get too caught up emotionally in the situation.

When you buy a home, you need an agent who is patient and allows you the necessary time to educate yourself and who helps you make the decision that's best for you. The last thing you need is an agent who tries to push you into making a deal.

You also need an agent who's knowledgeable about the local market and community. If you want to buy a home (or investment property) in an area where you don't currently live, an informed agent can have a big impact on your decision.

TIP

Finding an agent with financing knowledge and contacts is a plus for buyers, especially first-time buyers or those with credit problems. Such an agent may be able to refer you to lenders that can handle your type of situation, which can save you a lot of legwork.

Putting Your Deal Together

After you locate a property you want to buy and you understand your financing options, the real fun begins. At this point, you have to put the deal together. The following sections discuss key things to keep in mind.

Negotiating basics

When you work with an agent, she usually carries the burden of the negotiation process. But even if you delegate that responsibility to your agent, you still should have a strategy in mind. Otherwise, you may overpay for real estate. Here's what I recommend that you consider:

>> **Find out about the property and the owner before you make your offer.** How long has the property been on the market? What are its flaws? Why is the owner selling? The more you understand about the property you want to buy and the seller's motivations, the better your ability to draft an offer that meets everyone's needs. Some listing agents love to talk and will tell you the life history of the seller. Either you or your agent may be able to get a listing agent to reveal helpful information about the seller.

>> **Bring facts to the bargaining table; get comparable sales data to support your proposed price.** Too often, homebuyers and their agents pick a number out of the air when they make an offer. If you were the seller, would you be persuaded to lower your asking price in such a case? Pointing to recent and comparable home sales to justify your offer price strengthens your case.

REMEMBER

Price is only one of several negotiable items. Sometimes sellers fixate on selling their homes for a certain amount. Perhaps they want to get at least what they paid for it several years ago. You may get a seller to pay for certain repairs or improvements or to offer you an attractive loan without all the extra fees that a bank charges. Also, be aware that the time for closing on the purchase is a bargaining point. Some sellers may need cash fast and may concede other terms if you can close quickly. Likewise, the real estate agent's commission is negotiable.

>> **Try to leave your emotions out of any property purchase.** Being objective rather than emotional regarding a purchase is easier said than done, and it's hardest to do when buying a home in which you'll live. So do your best not to fall in love with a property. Keep searching for other properties even when you make an offer because you may be negotiating with an unmotivated seller.

Inspecting the property

Unless you've built homes and other properties and performed contracting work yourself, you probably have no idea what you're getting yourself into when it comes to furnaces and termites.

TIP

Spend the money and take the time to hire inspectors and other experts to evaluate the major systems and potential problem areas of the home. Because you can't be certain of the seller's commitment, I recommend you do the inspections *after* you've successfully negotiated and signed a sales contract. Even though you won't have the feedback from the inspections to help with this round of negotiating, you can always go back to the seller with the new information. Make your purchase offer contingent on a satisfactory inspection.

Hire people to help you inspect the following features of the property:

>> Overall condition of the property (for example, look for peeling paint, level floors, appliances that work properly, and so on)

>> Electrical, heating and air conditioning, and plumbing systems

>> Foundation

>> Roof

>> Pest control and dry rot

>> Seismic/slide/flood risk

Inspection fees often pay for themselves. If you uncover problems you weren't aware of when you negotiated the original purchase price, the inspection reports give you the information you need so you can go back and ask the property seller to fix the problems or reduce the property's purchase price.

Never accept a seller's inspection report as your only source of information. When a seller hires an inspector, which some sellers do before listing their house for sale, they may hire someone who isn't as diligent and critical of the property. Review the seller's inspection reports if available, but please, please, please also get your own evaluation! And beware of inspectors who are popular with real estate agents. They may be popular because they don't bother to document all the property's problems.

As with other professionals whose services you retain, interview a few different inspection companies. Ask which systems they inspect and how detailed of a report they can prepare for you. Consider asking the company that you're thinking of hiring for customer references. Ask for names and phone numbers of three people who used the company's services within the past six months. Also request from each inspection company a sample of one of its reports.

TIP

The day before you close on the purchase, take a brief walk-through of the property to make sure everything is still in the condition it was before and that all the fixtures, appliances, curtains, and other items the contract lists are still there. Sometimes, sellers ignore or don't recall these things, and consequently, they don't leave what they agreed to leave in the sales contract.

Shopping for title insurance and escrow services

Mortgage lenders require *title insurance* to protect against someone else claiming legal title to your property. For example, when a husband and wife split up, the one who remains in the home may decide to sell and take off with the money. If the title lists both spouses as owners, the spouse who sells the property (possibly by forging the other's signature) has no legal right to do so. The other spouse can come back and reclaim rights to the home even after it has been sold. In this event, both you and the lender can get stuck holding the bag. (If you're in the enviable position of paying cash for a property, buying title insurance is still wise to protect your investment, even though a mortgage lender won't prod you to do so.)

TIP

Title insurance and escrow charges vary from company to company. (*Escrow charges* pay for neutral third-party services to ensure that the instructions of the purchase contract or refinance are fulfilled and that everyone gets paid.) Don't simply use the company that your real estate agent or mortgage lender suggests — shop around. When you call around for title insurance and escrow fee quotes, make sure you understand all the fees. Many companies tack on all sorts of charges for things such as courier fees and express mail. If you find a company with lower prices and want to use it, consider asking for an itemization in writing so you don't receive any unpleasant surprises.

An insurance company's ability to pay claims is always important. Most state insurance departments monitor and regulate title insurance companies. Title insurers rarely fail, and most state departments of insurance do a good job of shutting down financially unstable ones. Check with your state's department if you're concerned. You can also ask the title insurer for its ratings from insurance-rating agencies.

Selling Real Estate

Buying and holding real estate for the long term really pays off. If you do your homework, buy in a good area, and work hard to find a fairly priced or underpriced property, why sell it quickly and incur all the selling costs, time, and hassle to locate and negotiate another property to purchase?

WARNING

Some real estate investors like to buy properties in need of improvement, fix them up, and then sell them and move on to another. Unless you're a contractor or experienced real estate investor and have a real eye for this type of work, don't expect to make a windfall or even to earn back more than the cost of the improvements. The process of buying, fixing, and flipping can be profitable, but it's not as easy as the home-improvement television shows and some books would have you believe. In fact, you're more likely to erode your profit through the myriad costs of frequent buying and selling. The vast majority of your profits should come from the long-term appreciation of the overall real estate market in the communities in which you own property.

Use the reasons that you bought in an area as a guide for considering selling. Review the criteria that I discuss in Chapter 12 as a guideline. For example, if the schools in the community are deteriorating and the planning department is allowing development that will hurt the value of your property and the rents that you can charge, you may have cause to sell. Unless you see significant problems like these in the future, holding good properties over many years is a great way to build your wealth and minimize transaction costs.

Negotiating real estate agents' contracts

Most people use an agent to sell real estate. As I discuss in "Selecting a good agent" earlier in this chapter, selling and buying a home (or investment property) require agents with different strengths. When you sell a property, you want an agent who can get the job done efficiently and for the highest possible sales price.

TIP

As a seller, seek agents who have marketing and sales expertise and who are willing to put in the time and money necessary to sell your house. Don't be impressed by an agent just because she works for a large company. What matters more is what the agent can do to market your property.

When you list a property for sale, the contract that you sign with the listing agent includes specification of the commission that you pay the agent if she succeeds in selling your property. In most areas of the country, agents usually ask for a 6 percent commission for single-family homes. In an area with relatively low-priced housing, agents may ask for 7 percent. For small multifamily properties and commercial properties, commissions often hover around the 3 to 5 percent range.

REMEMBER

Regardless of the commission an agent says is "typical," "standard," or "what my manager requires," always remember you can negotiate commissions. Because the commission is a percentage, you have a much greater ability to get a lower commission on a higher-priced property. If an agent makes 6 percent selling both a $200,000 and a $100,000 property, the agent makes twice as much on the $200,000 property. Yet selling the higher-priced property doesn't usually take twice as much work.

If you live in an area with generally higher-priced properties, you may be able to negotiate a 5 percent commission. For really expensive properties, a 4 percent commission is reasonable. You may find, however, that your ability to negotiate a lower commission is greatest when an offer is on the table. Because of the cooperation of agents who work together through the multiple listing service (MLS), if you list your real estate for sale at a lower commission than most other properties, some agents won't show it to prospective buyers. For this reason, you're better off having your listing agent cut their take instead of cutting the commission you pay to a real estate agent who brings a buyer for your property.

TIP

In terms of the length of the listing agreement, 3 months is reasonable. If you give an agent too long to list your property (6 to 12 months), the agent may simply toss your listing into the multiple listing database and not expend much effort to get your property sold. Practically speaking, you can fire your agent whenever you want, regardless of the length of the listing agreement, but a shorter listing may motivate your agent more. A shorter listing period also allows you to more easily part company with your agent if he doesn't do a good job and to move on to someone who will.

Selling without an agent

The temptation to sell real estate without an agent is usually to save the commission that an agent deducts from your property's sale price. If you have the time, energy, and marketing experience, you can sell sans agent and possibly save some money.

WARNING

The major problem with attempting to sell real estate on your own is that you can't list it in the MLS, which, in most areas, only real estate agents can access. If you're not listed in the MLS, many potential buyers never know that your home is for sale. Agents who work with buyers don't generally look for or show properties that are for sale by owner or listed with discount brokers.

Besides saving you time, a good agent can help ensure you're not sued for failing to disclose known defects of your property. If you decide to sell on your own, contact a local real estate legal advisor who can review the contracts. Take the time to educate yourself about the many facets of selling property for top dollar. Read the latest edition of *House Selling For Dummies,* which I co-authored with Ray Brown (published by Wiley).

Chapter **14**

Taking Your Talents to the Small-Business Arena

Many people's American Dream isn't a 9-to-5 job working for someone else, especially a large company, for the duration of their career. A lot of these folks dream of starting and running their own business. Making plenty of money, being their own boss, and having flexibility in setting their hours are often part of the dream.

I've known plenty of dreamers over the years, as well as those who achieved their dream. This chapter is designed to help you to invest in yourself by making the most of your working years and figuring out how to pursue entrepreneurial endeavors, if that's what you desire. That might include a side gig. I also discuss alternative ways to invest in small business that don't involve starting a business from scratch.

Investing in Your Career

Some people aren't going to enjoy — or be successful — as entrepreneurs. The simple truth and reality is that some folks are better off working for someone else. Plenty of people are happy or content as employees. There are many solid companies that need and want good employees, so you should be able to find a desirable job if you have skills, a good work ethic, the structure of a well-run company, and the ability to get along with others.

The global economy is increasingly competitive, and those whose skills don't measure up will have a harder time finding the best jobs at the best wages. Well-paying, interesting jobs are out there, but applicants must have the right kind of background and training.

You can make the most of your income-earning ability and invest in your career in a variety of ways:

>> **Get useful experience.** You probably have in your mind at least a dream job (such as working for a particular company or organization). The reality, however, is you may not have the requisite training and experience to land the dream job right now. So you have to figure out what jobs will allow you to tap your talents and help you gain needed experience to realize your dream.

>> **Read.** One of the reasons you don't need an advanced degree or even a costly four-year liberal-arts undergraduate college degree to succeed in business is that you can find out a lot on your own. You can gain insight by doing, but you can also gain expertise by reading. A good bookstore or well-stocked library has no entrance requirements, such as a high grade-point average or SAT score. A good book costs a heck of a lot less than taking college or graduate courses!

REMEMBER

You can read lots of "content" online. Just be sure you understand the quality and source of what you're consuming. If something is "free," investigate how the purveyor ultimately makes money and what its bias and agenda may be.

>> **Continue your education.** If you haven't completed your college or graduate degree and the industry you're in values those who have, consider investing the time and money to finish your education. Speak with others who have taken that path, and see what they have to say. Also, check out the increasing numbers of online courses being offered on sites like www.academicearth. org, www.coursera.org, www.edx.org, and www.udemy.com.

>> **Work hard.** Be willing to work extra hours and take on more responsibility. Those who take extra initiative and then deliver really stand out in a company where many people working on a salary have a time-clock, 9-to-5 mentality. Be careful, however, that the extra effort doesn't contribute to workaholism,

an addiction that causes folks to neglect important personal relationships and their own health. Don't bite off more than you can chew; otherwise, your supervisors won't have faith that they can count on you to deliver. Find ways to work smarter, not just longer, hours.

Deciding to Start Your Own Business

Should you start your own business? It's often a difficult decision for most people, and it's the first question you should answer before turning your business idea into the reality of your start-up company. In addition to helping you decide whether to start your own business, in this section I discuss a potentially attractive alternative: being an entrepreneur inside an established company.

Weighing your options

Of all your small-business options, starting your own business involves the greatest amount of work. Although you can perform this work on a part-time basis in the beginning, most people end up working in their business full-time.

For most of my working years, I've run my own business, and overall, I really like it. In my experience counseling small-business owners, I've seen many people of varied backgrounds, interests, and skills achieve success and happiness running their own businesses.

Most people perceive starting their own business as the riskiest of all small-business investment options. But if you get into a business that uses your skills and expertise, the risk isn't nearly as great as you may think.

TIP

Instead of leaving your job cold turkey and trying to build your business from scratch, you may be able to make progress by getting a side gig up and running initially. Many an entrepreneur has laid a nice foundation for his business over a couple of years by building up his sideline business in this fashion.

You can start many businesses with little money by leveraging your existing skills and expertise. If you have the time to devote to building sweat equity, you can build a valuable company and job. As long as you check out the competition and offer a valued product or service at a reasonable cost, a principal risk with your business is that you won't do a good job of marketing what you have to offer.

Sometimes entrepreneurial advocates imply that running your own business or starting your own not-for-profit organization is the greatest thing in the world and that all people would be happy owning their own businesses if they just set their minds to it. Starting and running a business aren't for everyone, though. The good news: Other options may offer you the best of both worlds.

Entrepreneuring at a company

Wouldn't it be great if you could have a job that gave you the challenge and upside of running your own business, with the security and support that come with a company environment? This combination does exist — if you can manage an entrepreneurial venture at a company.

If you're able to secure an entrepreneurial position inside a larger company, in addition to gaining significant managerial and operational responsibility, you can negotiate your share of the financial success that you help create. The parent company's senior management wants you to have the incentive that comes from sharing in the financial success of your endeavors. Bonuses, stock options, and the like are often tied to a division's performance.

For more small-business options beyond starting your own business or leading an entrepreneurial effort inside an established company, see "Considering Small-Business Investment Options" later in this chapter.

Turning a Business Idea into Reality

Ideas are a dime a dozen. I'd love to see you turn your best ideas into reality. To make that happen, you should develop a business plan, lay the groundwork financially and emotionally to leave your job, and determine how you're going to finance your new venture. I cover these topics in this section.

Drawing up your business plan

If you're motivated to start your own business, the next step is to prepare a business plan. Your business plan should be a working document or blueprint for the early days, months, and years of your business. It should enable you to plan your goals, apply for and obtain loans, and show potential investors (if you need them) what you plan to do with any money they would invest in or loan to your business.

TIP

The amount of detail that your plan needs depends on your goals and the specifics of your business. A simple, more short-term-focused plan of ten pages or less is fine if your goal is a "smaller" small business. However, if your goal is to grow, hire employees, and open multiple locations, your plan generally needs to be more substantial (30 to 50 pages) to address longer-term issues. If you want to solicit outside investors, a longer business plan is usually a necessity.

As you put together your business plan and evaluate your opportunities and challenges, keep your ears and eyes open. Expect to do research, and speak with other entrepreneurs and people in the industry. Most folks will spend time talking with you as long as they realize that you don't want to directly compete with their businesses.

What follows are the highlights your business plan should cover:

>> **The executive summary:** An executive summary is a two-page or so summary of your entire business plan that you can share with interested investors who don't have the time and desire to wade through a lengthy plan. The executive summary whets the prospective investor's appetite by touching on the highlights of your entire plan.

>> **Business-concept definition:** What do you want your business to do? What product or service do you want to offer? Your concept doesn't need to be unique to survive in the business world. The existence of plenty of other businesses doing what you want to do validates the potential for your small-business ideas. I'm not suggesting that an innovative idea lacks merit. Indeed, a creative idea gives you the chance to hit it big, and being the first person to successfully develop a new idea can help you achieve big success.

>> **Your objectives:** Before starting your firm, think about your objectives, or what you're seeking to achieve. Your objectives will likely evolve over time. Most for-profit businesses, not surprisingly, seek to maximize profits. Other common objectives can include working with people you like and respect, educating others, and improving an industry or setting a higher standard. You can't accomplish these loftier objectives without profits, of course, and doing these things isn't inconsistent with generating greater profits.

>> **Understanding of the marketplace:** The single most important area to understand is the marketplace in which your business competes. To be successful, your business must not only produce a good product or service but also reach customers and persuade them to buy your product at a price at which you can make a profit. So you must understand your desired customers and their needs. Discern what the competition has to offer, as well as its strengths and weaknesses. You also need to understand government regulations that affect the type of business that you're considering.

>> **Plans to deliver your service or product:** How are you going to provide your product or service to your customers? If you want to manufacture a product, you definitely need to scope out the process you're going to use. Otherwise, you have no idea how much time the manufacturing process may take or what the process may cost. As your business grows and you hire employees to provide services or create your products, the more you document what you do, the better your employees can replicate your good work.

>> **Plans to market your service or product:** How much will you charge for your services and products? How will you position your products and services compared with the competition? Where will you sell your product or service? Finding and retaining customers is vital to any business owner who wants her company to grow and be profitable. One simple, inexpensive way to stay in touch with customers you've dealt with or others who have made inquiries and expressed interest in your company's offerings is via a mailing list. Software and websites give you fast, efficient ways to keep customer mailing lists up to date.

>> **Plans to organize and staff your business:** Many small businesses are one-person operations — so much the better for you if that's what you desire, because you'll have none of the headaches of hiring, payroll, and so on. But if you hope to grow your business and would rather manage the work being done instead of doing all of it yourself, you'll eventually want to hire people. Give some thought now to the skills and functional areas of expertise that future hires will need. If you want to raise money, the employment section of your business plan is essential to show your investors that you're planning long-term. Also consider what legal form of organization — sole proprietorship, partnership, limited liability company, and so on — your business will adopt. This decision affects how the business is taxed and what its liabilities are in the event of a lawsuit, among other important issues.

>> **Financial projections:** An idea may become a business failure if you neglect to consider, or are unrealistic about, the financial side of the business you want to start. Financial projections are mandatory, and knowledgeable investors will scrutinize them if you seek outside money. Before the revenue begins to flow in, you incur expenditures as you develop and market your products and services. Therefore, you need to understand what you must spend money on and the approximate timing of the needed purchases. Preparing an estimated income statement that summarizes your expected revenue and expenses is a challenging and important part of your business plan.

A balance sheet details a company's assets and liabilities. A detailed balance sheet isn't as important as tracking your available cash, which will likely be under pressure in the early years of a business because expenses can continue to exceed revenue for quite some time. A complete balance sheet is useful for a business that owns significant equipment, furniture, inventory, and so on.

After you research and evaluate the needs of your prospective business, at some point you need to decide whether to actually start your business. If you really want to, you can conduct and analyze market research and crunch numbers until the cows come home. Even if you're a linear, logical, analytic, quantitative kind of person, you ultimately need to make a gut-level decision: Do you jump in the water and start swimming, or do you stay on the sidelines and remain a spectator? In my opinion, watching isn't nearly as fun as doing. If you feel ready but have some trepidation, that's normal.

Mind you, I'm not trying to present a rosy view of entrepreneurship. Plenty of small businesses fail, and plenty of small-business owners end up losing rather than making money.

Plotting to leave your job

You may never discover that you have the talent to run your own business, and perhaps have a good idea to boot, unless you prepare yourself financially and psychologically to leave your job. Financial and emotional issues cause some aspiring entrepreneurs to remain chained to their employers and cause those who do break free to soon return to their bondage.

On the financial side, plan for a reduction in the income that you bring home from work, at least in the early years of your business. Do all you can to reduce your expenses to a level that fits the entrepreneurial life that you want to lead.

In addition to reducing your spending before and during the period that you start your business, figure out how to manage the income side of your personal finances. One way to pursue your entrepreneurial dreams is to continue working part-time in a regular job while you work part-time at your own business. If you have a job that allows you to work part-time, seize the opportunity. Just be sure that the outside work you're doing doesn't conflict with your regular job.

Another option is to completely leave your job but line up work that provides a decent income for a portion of your weekly work hours. Consulting for your old employer is a time-tested first "entrepreneurial" option with low risk.

For many people, walking away from their employer's benefits (including insurance, retirement funds, and paid time off) is both financially and emotionally challenging. Benefits are valuable, but you may be surprised by how efficiently you can replicate them in your own business:

>> **Health insurance:** The first option to explore is whether your existing coverage through your employer's group plan can be converted to individual coverage (through COBRA). Also, get proposals for individual coverage from

major health plans in your area. Take a high deductible, if available, to keep costs down. Having a high-deductible health plan, which is defined (for 2021) as an individual plan with a deductible of at least $1,400 or a family plan with a minimum $2,800 deductible for the tax year (this amount increases over time with inflation), qualifies you to contribute money to a health savings account (HSA). Contributions to an HSA reduce your current year's taxable income, and the money compounds without taxation over time. Withdrawals aren't taxed so long as you use the money for qualified healthcare expenses, which are broadly defined.

>> **Long-term disability insurance:** Your greatest asset probably is your ability to earn money. Long-term disability (LTD) insurance protects your work income in the event of a disability. Before you leave your job, secure an individual LTD policy. After you leave your job and are no longer earning steady income, you won't qualify for a policy. Check with any professional associations that you belong to or could join to see whether they offer LTD plans. Association plans are sometimes less expensive because of the group's purchasing power.

>> **Life insurance:** If you have dependents who count on your income, you need life insurance. You can generally purchase a life insurance policy on your own for less money than additional coverage through your employer would cost.

>> **Retirement savings plans:** If your employer offers retirement savings programs, such as a 401(k) plan or a pension plan, don't despair about not having these in the future. One of the best benefits of self-employment is the availability of SEP-IRAs, which allow you to sock away up to 20 percent of your net income on a tax-deductible basis. With employees, the decision is a bit more complicated but often still a great idea.

Financing your business

While creating your business plan (discussed earlier in the chapter), you should estimate your business's start-up and development costs. Luckily, you can start many worthwhile small businesses with little capital, but you will need capital — and for some businesses, significant amounts.

Here are proven, time-tested methods of financing your business:

>> **Bootstrapping:** *Bootstrapping* simply means that a business lives within its own means and without external support. This funding strategy generally forces a business to be more resourceful and less wasteful. Bootstrapping is also a great training mechanism for producing cost-effective products and services. It offers you the advantage of getting into business with little capital.

Misconceptions abound about how much money a company needs to achieve its goals and sources of funding. The vast majority of small businesses obtain their initial capital from personal savings, relatives, and friends rather than from outside sources, such as banks and venture capital firms. Crowdfunding made possible on numerous websites like Kickstarter, Indiegogo, and Fundable is another avenue to explore.

Eventually, a successful, growing company may want outside financing to expand faster. Raising money from investors or lenders is much easier after you demonstrate that you know what you're doing, that a market exists for your product or service, and you've been a responsible steward of others' money invested in your business thus far.

>> **Taking out business loans:** If you're starting a new business or have been in business for just a few years, borrowing, particularly from banks, may be difficult. Borrowing money is easier when you don't really need to do so. No one knows this fact better than small-business owners. To borrow money from a bank, you generally need a business plan, three years of financial statements and tax returns for the business and its owner, and projections for the business. Seek out banks that are committed to and understand the small-business marketplace.

TIP

The U.S. Small Business Administration (SBA) offers workshops and counseling services for small-business owners. Its SCORE (Service Corps of Retired Executives) consulting services (www.score.org; 800-634-0245) provide free advice and critiques of business plans, as well as advice on raising money for your business. For more information on the SBA's services and how to contact a local office, call 800-827-5722 or visit its website at www.sba.gov.

If you don't have luck with banks or the SBA, credit unions can be a source of financial help. They're often more willing to make personal loans to individuals.

>> **Borrowing from relatives and friends:** Because they know you and (ideally) like and trust you, your family members and friends may seem like good sources of investment money for your small business. They also likely have the added advantage of offering you better terms than a banker, wealthy investor, or a venture capitalist. Be sure to prepare and sign a letter of agreement that spells out the terms of the investment or loan and that states that you had a candid discussion with all involved as to the risks and downside if things don't work out the way you hope.

>> **Tapping investors for an equity investment:** Beyond family members and friends, wealthy individuals are your next best source of capital if you want an equity investor. An *angel investor* is a wealthy individual who invests in small companies and has a track record of success in funding somewhat-similar businesses. Angels bring things to the table besides money, such as strategic advice and helpful business contacts.

Finding folks who may be interested in investing requires persistence and creativity. Try consulting tax advisors and attorneys you know who may have contacts, and network with successful entrepreneurs in similar fields. Also consider customers or suppliers who like your business and believe in its potential.

Considering Small-Business Investment Options

Only your imagination limits the ways you can make money with small businesses. Choosing the option that best meets your needs isn't unlike choosing other investments, such as in real estate or in the financial markets. In this section, I discuss the major ways you can invest in small business, including what's attractive and not so attractive about each option.

Buying an existing business

If you don't have a specific idea for a business that you want to start, but you have business management skills and an ability to improve existing businesses, another option is to consider buying an established business.

WARNING

Although you don't have to go through the riskier start-up period if you take this route, you'll likely need more capital to buy a going enterprise. You also need to be able to deal with potentially sticky personnel and management issues. The history of the organization and the way things work predate your potential ownership of the business. If you don't like making hard decisions, firing people who don't fit with your plans, and persuading people to change the way they did things before you arrived on the scene, buying an existing business likely isn't for you. Also realize that some of the good employees may be loyal to the old owner and his style of running the business, so they may split when you arrive.

Some people perceive that buying an existing business is safer than starting a new one, but buying someone else's business can actually be riskier. You have to put out far more money upfront, in the form of a down payment, to buy a business. And if you don't have the ability to run the business, and it does poorly, you may lose much more financially. Another risk is that the business may be for sale for a reason. Perhaps it's not very profitable, it's in decline, or it's generally a pain in the posterior to operate.

Good businesses that are for sale don't come cheaply. If the business is a success, the current owner has removed the start-up risk from the business, so the price of the business should include a premium to reflect this reduced risk. If you have the capital to buy an established business and the skills to run it, consider going this route.

Investing in someone else's business

If you like the idea of profiting from successful small businesses but don't want the day-to-day responsibility of managing the enterprise, you may want to invest in someone else's small business. Although this route may seem easier, fewer people are actually cut out to be investors in other people's businesses.

Consider investing in someone else's business if the following points describe you:

>> **You have sufficient assets:** You need enough assets so that what you invest in small, privately held companies is a small portion (20 percent or less) of your total financial assets.

>> **You can afford to lose what you invest:** Unlike with investing in a diversified stock fund, you may lose all of your investment when you invest in a small, privately held company.

>> **You're astute at evaluating financial statements and business strategies:** Investing in a small, privately held company has much in common with investing in a publicly traded firm. A main difference is that private firms aren't required to produce comprehensive, audited financial statements that adhere to certain accounting principles the way public companies are. Thus, you have a greater risk of not receiving sufficient or accurate information when you evaluate a small, private firm. (There are also liquidity differences, in that with a small, private company, you may not be able to sell out when you want and at a fair current price.)

Putting money into your own business (or someone else's) can be a high-risk but potentially high-return investment. The best options are those that you understand well. If you hear about a great business idea or company from someone you know and trust, do your research and use your best judgment. That company or idea may be a terrific investment.

INVESTIGATE

Before investing, read and review the business plan. Thoroughly check out the people who are running the business. Talk to others who don't have a stake in the investment; you can benefit from their comments and concerns. Remember, though, that many a wise person has rained on the parade of what turned out to be a terrific business idea.

Looking at franchises

Purchasing a good franchise can be your ticket into the world of small-business ownership. Franchising makes up a huge part of the business world. Companies that franchise — such as Papa John's, Jiffy Lube, 7-Eleven stores, Gymboree, Century 21 Real Estate, Supercuts, Holiday Inn, Avis, Smoothie King, Chick-fil-A, Subway, Servpro, RE/MAX, and Foot Locker — account for more than $1 trillion in sales annually.

When you purchase a *franchise*, you buy the local rights to a specified geographic territory to sell the company's products or services under the company's name and to use the company's system of operation. In addition to an up-front franchisee fee, franchisers also typically charge an ongoing royalty.

Here are the primary advantages that come with a good franchise:

>> **Proven business:** A company that has been in business for several years and has successful franchisees proves the demand for the company's products and services and shows that the company's system for providing those products and services works. As a franchise owner, you benefit from and share in the experience that the parent company has gained over the years.

>> **Name-brand recognition:** Some consumers recognize the company name of a larger and successful franchise company and may be more inclined to purchase its products and services. The comfort that comes from dealing with such firms may stem from the influence of advertisements, recommendations of friends, or familiarity with a business's services in another part of the country. Most freestanding small businesses for sale in a community lack this name-brand recognition.

>> **Centralized purchasing power:** You would hope and expect that a corporation made up of hundreds of locations buys supplies at a low price. (Volume purchasing generally leads to bigger discounts.) In addition to possibly saving franchisees money on supplies, the parent company can take the hassle out of figuring out where and how to purchase supplies. Again, most unattached small businesses that you could buy won't offer this advantage. However, quality business associations can provide some of these benefits.

REMEMBER

When you purchase a new franchise, as with starting a business, you must find customers. However, the parent company should have a track record and multiple locations with customers. (You can also purchase existing franchises from owners who want to sell, and these businesses come complete with customers.)

Buying a franchise isn't for everyone. Here are some common problems that may cause you to reconsider buying a franchise:

>> **You're not the franchise type.** When you buy a franchise, you buy into an established system. If you're the creative type who likes to experiment and change things, you may be an unhappy franchisee. Unlike starting your own business, where you can get into the game without investing lots of your time and money, buying a franchise that you end up not enjoying can make for an expensive learning experience.

>> **You may be locked in to buying overpriced supplies.** Centralized, bulk purchasing through the corporate headquarters supposedly saves franchisees time and money on supplies and other expenditures. Some franchisers, however, take advantage of franchisees through large markups on proprietary items that franchisees must buy from the franchisers.

>> **The franchise is unproven.** If the company's concept hasn't stood the test of time, don't make yourself a guinea pig. Some franchisers show more interest in simply selling franchises to collect the upfront franchise money. Reputable franchisers want to help their franchisees succeed so they can collect an ongoing royalty from the franchisees' sales. In the worst cases, franchisers engage in fraud and sell next to nothing, except the hopes of getting rich quick.

TIP

Do your due diligence before you agree to buy a franchise. You may be tempted to cut corners when reviewing a franchise from a long-established company. Don't. You may not be right for the specific franchise, or perhaps the "successful" company has mostly been good at keeping problems under wraps.

Beware the pitfalls of multilevel marketing companies

Franchises and *multilevel marketing* companies have some similarities: Both offer a prepackaged and defined system for running a business. Although both types may be worth your exploration, significant obstacles can trip you up, especially with multilevel marketing companies (MLM).

MLM companies, sometimes known as *network companies,* can be thought of as a poor person's franchise. I know dozens of people, from clients I've worked with to students I've taught in my courses, who have been sorely disappointed with the money and time they've spent on MLM companies.

In companies that use multilevel marketing, representatives who work as independent contractors recruit new representatives, known in the industry as your *downline,* as well as solicit customers. For those weary of traditional jobs, the appeal of multilevel marketing is obvious. You can work at home, part-time if you want. You have no employees. You don't need any experience. Yet you're told you can still make big bucks ($10,000, $25,000, $50,000, or more per month).

WARNING

A big problem to watch out for when dealing with MLM companies is the business equivalent of the *pyramid scheme* — businesses that exist to sign up other people. Beware of MLM companies that advocate the following: "Sell directly to those you have direct influence over. The system works great because you don't need to resell month after month. It's an opportunity for anybody; it's up to that person how much work he wants to put into it."

Think twice before you sign up relatives, friends, and co-workers. A danger in doing business with those people you have influence over is that you put your reputation and integrity on the line. You could be putting your friendships and family relations on the line as well.

REMEMBER

The bottom line on any network marketing "opportunity" is to remember that it's a job. No company is going to pay you a lot of money for little work. As with any other small-business venture, if you hope to earn a decent income, multilevel marketing opportunities typically require at least three to five years of low income to build up your business. Most people who pay to buy into networks make little money, and many quit and move on.

INVESTIGATE

Any MLM company examination should start with the company's product or service. How does its product or service stack up to the competition on price and quality? Remember that due diligence requires digging for facts and talking to people who don't have a bias or reason to sell to you. Through the Better Business Bureau website (www.bbb.org), examine the MLM company's complaint record. Be skeptical of multilevel marketing systems unless the company has a long track record and many people who are happy. In other words, assume that an MLM company isn't worth pursuing until your extensive due diligence proves otherwise.

Quality multilevel marketing companies are the exception and make sense for people who really believe in and want to sell a particular product or service and don't want to or can't tie up a lot of money buying a franchise or other business. Just remember to check out the MLM company and realize that you won't get rich in a hurry — or probably ever.

IN THIS CHAPTER

» **Checking out call options**

» **Digging into gold and other commodities**

» **Considering cryptocurrencies**

» **Surveying collectibles**

» **Exploring annuities and cash value life insurance**

Chapter **15**

Exploring Other Investment Vehicles

I n the earlier chapters of this book, I present and discuss a pretty wide range of investments that are time-tested. You've probably already heard of and been pitched other or alternative investments. The vast majority of these alternative investments are flawed due to high fees, lousy performance, or worse.

In this chapter, I discuss the most common of these alternative investments: options, gold and other commodities, currencies and cryptocurrencies, collectibles, and annuities and cash-value life insurance. In each case, I explain each investment's redeeming qualities as well as its flaws.

Calling on Options

In recent years, I'm finding that some young people are using options, like call options, to try and make big money quickly. If you don't understand call options, it would probably be better if I didn't actually explain them to you — I'd rather you stay away from them! But, here's a simple example to show you how they work.

Suppose you're intrigued by the field of online gaming software development and you hear about the company Unity Software and its stock. You look and see that the stock is trading at $150 per share. Instead of buying the stock, though, you could buy some call options for the stock. Their $180 call options, which expire in about ten months, are going for $32 per share. Suppose before those options expire the stock zooms higher and hits $300 per share. Your call options would be worth at least $120 per share now so you'd have nearly quadrupled your money — a far greater percentage move than you would have enjoyed in the stock. If the stock instead treads water or goes down, your options will end up expiring worthless and you will have lost all the money you invested in them.

REMEMBER

With options, you are making a short-term bet or gamble on the price of a particular stock rather than making an investment for the years ahead. So, you not only have to be right about the specific stock you are choosing, but you also have to be correct about the specific (short-term) timing of your investment.

As you can see, call options can be really exciting because you can make really high returns if you pick the right stock at the right time and it goes up by a large amount. But, that's more like gambling than investing, and more often than not, you will lose money on call options or not make very much. And, they will likely make you a nervous wreck as they entice you to constantly watch the stock market and the stocks and call options that you own.

Considering Gold and Other Precious Metals

Of all the commodities, gold and silver have gotten the most attention over time, especially in recent decades. Gold and silver are also known as *precious metals.*

Gold and silver have served as mediums of exchange or currency over thousands of years because they have tangible value and can't be debased the way that paper currencies can (by printing more money). These precious metals are used in jewelry and manufacturing.

As investments, gold and silver tend to perform well during bouts of inflation, especially when the inflation is unexpected. During the 1970s, for example, when inflation zoomed into the double-digit range in the United States and stocks and bonds went into the tank, gold and silver prices skyrocketed more than 500 percent.

Precious-metals prices have zoomed upward again since 2000. From less than $300 per ounce, gold hit more than $1,900 per ounce in the early 2010s, as some feared the return of inflation due to excessive government debt, government stimulus spending, and expansion of the printed money supply. During this period, silver jumped from just over $4 per ounce to a high of $45 per ounce. After those runups, however, gold and silver dropped dramatically in value and now a decade later, gold is just getting back near its prior highs while silver still has quite a way to go.

Although precious metals may shine for a decade, over the long, long term, they're lousy investments. They don't pay any dividends, and their price increases may at best just keep up with, but not ahead of, increases in the cost of living. Consider the fact that even when gold breached $1,900 per ounce in 2011, it was still below the inflation-adjusted levels it had reached more than 30 years ago. To reach those levels, gold would have to rise to more than $2,500 an ounce! According to Professor Jeremy Siegel's research on investment returns, which goes back more than two centuries (to 1802), gold's average annual rate of return has been just 2.1 percent, which translates into a return of just 0.7 percent per year ahead of the rate of inflation. So, those who have invested in gold over the long term have just barely kept up with and slightly ahead of inflation.

Although investing in precious metals is better than keeping cash in a piggy bank or stuffing it in a mattress, the long-term investment returns aren't nearly as good as those of bonds, stocks, and real estate. One way to earn better long-term returns is to invest in a fund containing the stocks of gold and precious-metals companies. Two such funds to consider are Fidelity Select Gold and Vanguard Global Capital Cycles.

Fidelity Select Gold (trading symbol FSAGX) has been in existence since 1985 and has returned 5.1 percent per year on average. The Vanguard Global Capital Cycles fund (trading symbol VGPMX; formerly the Vanguard Precious Metals and Mining fund) invests partially in companies that benefit from increased demand for physical assets such as gold, other precious metals, and minerals. At least 25 percent of the fund is invested in precious metals and mining securities. It also focuses on opportunities to invest in companies with scarce, high-quality infrastructure assets — typically in utilities and telecommunications — that are viewed as irreplaceable and therefore have enduring value. Since its inception in 1984, this fund's annualized rate of return is 4.2 percent, which is less than half the return you'd expect from a stock-focused fund but is nearly double the annualized rate of return of gold over the long term.

There are numerous other commodities that you can "invest" in, but the long-term data shows terrible returns. Sure, there can be short periods where a particular commodity's price zips higher, but you will do poorly generally with these over time.

GOLD AND COLLECTIBLES DON'T GET FAVORABLE CAPITAL GAINS TAX TREATMENT

While gold and other precious metals have increased in value over the years, they've produced returns significantly below stocks and even bonds. And unbeknownst to most investors, the profits on precious metals aren't eligible for the low 20-percent tax rate cap on long-term capital gains (for investments held more than one year). Collectibles, which include precious metals, are taxed at 28 percent, which further reduces the subpar return on gold and other precious metals.

Historically, investors haven't been allowed to own gold and other collectibles in retirement accounts. However, investors in precious metals were happy to hear that in 2007, the IRS ruled that investors could own precious metal ETFs in retirement accounts since ETFs are shares of ownership and not a direct stake in a precious metal.

"This ruling hinges on the ETF being formed as a trust. The shareholders of the ETF do not have claims on the bullion owned by the fund and can't ask for distributions of the metal," says Bob Carlson, who publishes the *Retirement Watch* newsletter.

However, a more recent IRS ruling contained bad tax news for investors holding gold and other precious ETFs in taxable (nonretirement) accounts: ". . . If the investor sells shares in the ETF, the investor is treated as selling his or her share of the metal backing the shares. When the investor owned the shares for more than one year, the gains are taxed at the 28 percent rate" rather than the lower long-term capital gains tax rate, says Carlson.

Of course, if you own the ETF in a retirement account, you lose all possible preferential capital gains tax treatment. Upon withdrawal from a retirement account, all profits are taxed as ordinary income.

Should You Invest in Currencies and Cryptocurrencies?

Those who frequently predict doom and gloom and the demise of particular civilizations and governments like to highlight the fact that government-created currency, like the U.S. dollar, can be increased and expanded simply by creating more of it. Just look at the large government deficits that occurred during periods like the severe 2008 financial crisis and recession and the 2020 COVID-19 government-mandated economic shutdowns.

Again, looking at historic data going back over 200 plus years, we see that the U.S. dollar has depreciated by a whopping 95 percent after adjusting for increases in the cost of living. That works out to losing about 1.4 percent per year on average. Other currencies generally show similar long-term patterns so "investing" in currencies has been a long-term loser.

When you invest in stocks, you're actually getting some exposure to and diversification with currencies around the world which in theory reduces your overall stock market risk a bit. When you invest in U.S. companies, especially larger ones, they often do some business overseas. Foreign stock funds, of course, invest in overseas companies which do most if not all of their business in foreign countries and in foreign currencies.

Now, let's talk a bit about the "newer" currencies that are generating more interest among some younger adults — cryptocurrencies. Bitcoin, the most well-known and highly traded cryptocurrency, has been making headlines as its price climbs to ever dizzying heights. It recently hit more than $61,000 per coin. But there are literally thousands — more than 9,100 at recent count — of other cryptocurrencies.

So, what exactly are these cryptocurrencies? For starters, none of them are actually a coin — that's a marketing gimmick used by many to make it sound like real currency. Bitcoin and other similar cryptocurrencies only exist in the online world. Bitcoin's creators say that they have limited the number of Bitcoins that can be mined and put into online circulation to about 21 million.

As its promoters have talked up its usefulness and dizzying rise, many people who have Bitcoins and various other cryptocurrencies continue to hold onto them like shares of stock in the next Amazon, Apple, or Tesla, hoping for and expecting further steep price increases. People don't hoard real currencies with similar pie-in-the-sky hopes for large investment returns. And for good reason, because as I just discussed, real currencies depreciate over the years, not appreciate!

Outside of Bitcoin and Ethereum, the vast majority of other cryptocurrencies have depreciated in recent years. Many cryptocurrencies have crashed and burned — losing 90 percent or more of their value — as the number of cryptocurrencies has mushroomed over recent years.

WARNING

Online cryptocurrency transactions can be done anonymously, and they can't be contested, disputed, or reversed. So, if you buy something using cryptocurrencies and have a problem with the item you bought, that's too bad — you have no recourse, unlike, for example, a purchase made on your credit card. The clandestine nature of many cryptocurrencies makes them attractive to folks trying to hide money or engaged in illegal activities (criminals, drug dealers, and the like).

And hackers create another real danger — your cryptocurrency could be stolen as has happened to numerous Bitcoin and other crypto holders.

So, what is a given cryptocurrency worth? Cryptocurrencies generally have no inherent value; there are a small number of so-called stable coins linked to or backed by another asset or traditional currency. Tether is an example of a stable/crypto coin, which is linked to the U.S. dollar. Digix Gold Token is an example of a crypto/stable coin linked to gold (actually one gram of gold per token/coin).

Contrast cryptocurrencies with no inherent value of linkage with that with gold. Not only has gold had a long history of being used by some as a medium of exchange, but gold also has commercial and industrial uses. Furthermore, gold costs real money to mine out of the ground, which provides a floor of support under the price of gold in the range of $1,200 to $1,300 per ounce, not far below the price of gold at about $1,750 per ounce at the time of this writing.

While the supply of Bitcoin is currently artificially limited, Bitcoin is hardly unique — it's one of thousands of cryptocurrencies. So, if another cryptocurrency is easier to use online and perceived as attractive (in part because it's far less expensive), Bitcoin will tumble in value.

REMEMBER

Even though Bitcoin has been the most popular cryptocurrency in recent years (it accounts for about 50 to 60 percent of the market value of all cryptocurrencies), few merchants actually accept it. And, to add insult to injury, Bitcoin users get whacked with unfavorable conversion rates, which add greatly to the effective price of items bought with Bitcoin.

I can't tell you what will happen to Bitcoin's or any other cryptocurrencies' price next month, next year, or next decade. But I can tell that it has virtually no inherent value as a digital currency, so those paying big bucks for a particular cryptocurrency will likely eventually be extremely disappointed. There are more than 9,100 of these cryptocurrencies, and the field keeps growing as creators hope to get in on the ground floor of the next cryptocurrency that they hope will soar in value. And, in that respect, they actually share something in common with collectibles.

Contemplating Collectibles

The term *collectibles* is a catch-all category for antiques, art, autographs of famous folks, baseball cards, clocks, coins, comic books, diamonds, dolls, gems, photographs, rare books, rugs, stamps, vintage wine, writing utensils, and a whole host of other items. In this section, I discuss the appeal and reality of investing in collectibles.

Understanding the allure of collectibles

The best returns that collectibles investors reap come from the ability to identify, years in advance, items that will become popular. Do you think you can do that? You may be the smartest person in the world, but you should know that most dealers can't tell what's going to rocket to popularity in the coming decades.

Dealers make their profits the same way other retailers do — from the spread or markup on the merchandise they sell. The public and collectors have fickle, quirky tastes that no one can predict.

You can find out enough about a specific type of collectible to become a better investor than the average person, but you have to be among the best such collectors to have a shot at earning decent returns. To get to this level of expertise, you need to invest hundreds, if not thousands, of hours reading, researching, and educating yourself about your specific type of collectible.

Don't get me wrong: There's nothing wrong with spending money on collectibles. Just don't fool yourself into thinking that they're investments (more on their actual returns in the next section). You can sink lots of your money into these non-income-producing, poor-return "investments." At their best as investments, collectibles give the wealthy a way to buy quality stuff that doesn't depreciate.

Seeing the realities of collectibles and their returns

Although connoisseurs of fine art, antiques, and vintage wine wouldn't like the comparison of their pastime with buying old playing cards, collectibles generally are objects with little intrinsic value. Wine is just a bunch of old, mushed-up grapes. A painting is simply a canvas and some paint that at retail would set you back a few bucks. Stamps are small pieces of paper, usually less than an inch square. What about baseball cards? Heck, my childhood friends and I used to stick them between our bike spokes (the crummiest players' cards, of course)!

REMEMBER

I'm not trying to diminish contributions that artists and others make to the world's culture. And I know that some people place a high value on some of these collectibles. But true investments that can make your money grow — such as stocks, real estate, or a small business — are assets that can produce income and profits.

Because collectibles have little inherent value, they're fully exposed to the whims and speculations of buyers and sellers. As history has shown, of course, and as I discuss elsewhere in the book, the prices of particular stocks, real estate, and businesses can be subject to the whims and speculations of buyers and sellers, too, especially in the short term. Over the long term, however, securities' market prices return to reality and sensible valuations. Also, a real investment can provide a return to you even if no one ever buys it from you.

Here are some other major problems with collectibles:

>> **Large markup costs:** The spread between the price that a dealer pays for an object and the price for which he sells the same object is often around 100 percent. Sometimes, the difference is even greater, particularly if a dealer is the second or third middleman in the chain of purchase. So at minimum, your purchase typically must double in value just to get you back to even, and a value may not double for 10 to 20 years or more!

>> **Substantial other costs:** If the markups aren't bad enough, some collectibles incur all sorts of other costs. If you buy more-expensive pieces, for example, you may need to have them appraised. You may have to pay storage and insurance costs as well. And unlike the case with markup, you pay some of these fees year after year of ownership.

>> **Costly mistakes of nonexpert buyers:** Sometimes, you may overpay even more for a collectible because you didn't realize some imperfection or inferiority of the item. Worse, you may buy a forgery. Even reputable dealers have been duped by forgeries. Also, you may make storage mistakes that cause your collectible to deteriorate over time. Damage from sunlight, humidity, temperatures that are too high or too low, and a whole host of vagaries can ruin the quality of your collectible. Insurance doesn't cover this type of damage or negligence on your part.

>> **Terrible returns:** Even if you ignore the substantial costs of buying, holding, and selling, the average returns that investors earn from collectibles rarely keep ahead of inflation, and they're generally inferior to returns from stocks, real estate, and small-business investing.

Objective return data on collectibles is hard to come by. Never, ever trust so-called "data" that dealers or the many collectibles trade publications provide.

Considering advice on buying collectibles

If you want to buy collectibles and can afford to do so, you have my blessing. Here are some tips to keep in mind to make the most of your efforts:

>> **Do your homework.** Use a comprehensive resource to research, buy, sell, maintain, and improve your collectible, such as the books by Ralph and Terry Kovel or their website at www.kovels.com.

>> **Collect for your love of the collectible, your desire to enjoy it, or your interest in finding out about or mastering a subject.** In other words, don't collect these items because you expect high investment returns, because you probably won't get them.

>> **When you know what you want, buy direct and eliminate the middle-man where possible.** In some cases, you may be able to buy directly from the artist.

>> **Check collectibles that are comparable to the one you have your eye on, shop around, and don't be afraid to negotiate.** An effective way to negotiate after you decide what you like is to make your offer to the dealer or artist by phone. Because the seller isn't standing right next to you, you don't feel pressure to decide immediately.

>> **Get a buy-back guarantee.** Ask the dealer (who thinks that the item is such a great investment) for a written guarantee to buy the item back from you within five years, if you opt to sell it, for at least the same price you paid for it.

>> **Keep quality items that you and your family have purchased, and hope that someday they'll be worth something.** Keeping these quality items is the simplest way to break into the collectibles business. The complete sets of baseball cards I gathered as a youngster are now (30-plus years later) worth hundreds of dollars, and one is worth $1,000!

Understanding Annuities and Cash-Value Life Insurance

Odds are that if you're looking to make investments, you'll be pitched various types of investment vehicles by folks who are licensed to sell insurance products. In this section, I discuss two of the most common vehicles: annuities and cash-value life insurance.

Availing yourself of annuities

Annuities are contracts that insurance companies back. If you, the annuity holder (investor), should die during the so-called accumulation phase (before receiving payments from the annuity), your designated beneficiary is guaranteed reimbursement of the amount of your original investment.

Annuities, like Individual Retirement Accounts (IRAs), allow your capital to grow and compound tax-deferred. You defer taxes until you withdraw the money. Unlike with an IRA, which has an annual contribution limit of $6,000, you can deposit as much as you want into an annuity in any year — even millions of dollars, if you've got them! As with a Roth IRA, however, you get no upfront tax deduction for your contributions.

WARNING

The problem with annuities is that insurance agents try to sell them to many folks who won't benefit from them — and the vast majority of folks won't be in a position to benefit from them.

If you've contributed all you're allowed to contribute to your IRA and your employer's retirement accounts, and you still want to put more money into retirement accounts, you might consider annuities.

TIP

Don't consider contributing to an annuity until you've fully exhausted your other retirement account investing options, including all possible Roth accounts. The reason: Annuity contributions aren't tax-deductible, and annuities carry higher annual operating fees to pay for the small amount of insurance that comes with them. Roth accounts are superior to an annuity because you don't pay income tax on your withdrawn investment earnings from Roth accounts. Because of their higher annual expenses, annuities generally make sense only if you have 15 or more years to wait until you need the money.

Considering cash-value life insurance

If you have dependents, you may need life insurance. The key question to ask yourself and your family is how they would fare if you died and they no longer had your employment income. You need life insurance if your family is dependent on your income from work and would be unable to maintain its current standard of living with your passing.

Term life insurance is pure insurance protection and the best choice for the vast majority of people. The other major type of life insurance is *cash-value coverage*, which includes a life insurance death benefit (as does a term policy), as well as a savings and investment feature.

You generally can't combine insurance with investing when you buy an auto, disability, or homeowner's policy, so why can you with life insurance? You can thanks to an exemption in the tax code.

WARNING

Insurance companies and agents who sell their products and earn commissions favor cash-value life insurance. The reasons are pretty simple: Cash-value life insurance costs much more and provides heftier profits for insurance companies and commissions to the agents who sell it.

You should consider getting cash-value life insurance only if your net worth is high enough that you anticipate having an estate-planning "problem." When you buy a cash-value policy and place it in an irrevocable life insurance trust, the death benefits can pass to your heirs free of federal estate taxes.

Under current tax law, you can leave up to $11.7 million free of federal estate taxes to your heirs. If you're married, you can pass on double these amounts through the use of a bypass trust. So, most people don't have an estate-planning situation that warrants cash-value life insurance.

5

The Part of Tens

Make use of the best investment information sources.

Master investment concepts that contribute greatly to investing success.

Understand the keys to success when using investing apps.

Chapter **16**

Ten Things to Know about Investing Resources

E verywhere you look or listen, you'll find plenty — and I mean plenty — of investing opinions and advice. Some of it may be great information but not a good fit for you. Much of it is mediocre or downright awful, biased, uninformed, and misleading.

In this chapter, I highlight ten important things you should know and do to evaluate investing resources and get the best and right information for you.

Get Educated to Discern the Best from the Rest

With the tremendous increase in the coverage of investing, more and more "journalists" and self-anointed experts are writing about increasingly technical issues — often in areas in which they have little or even no expertise. (This type of reporting is true in traditional print publications but especially so online.) Some writers provide good information and advice. Unfortunately, many others dish out bad, biased, and/or mediocre advice.

How can you know what information is good and who you can trust? Although I suggest my favorite resources later in this chapter, I know you'll encounter many investment resources, and you need to know how to tell the best from the rest. The answer rests in educating yourself. The more knowledgeable you are about sound and flawed investment strategies, the better able you are to tell good from not-so-good investment resources.

Beware "Free"

Too many folks get suckered into supposedly free resources when looking for investing information and advice. The internet is filled with tons of apparently "free" investing websites and blogs, and if you turn on your television or radio, you come across mountains of seemingly "free" stuff. Someone is paying for all this "free" content, of course, and it's all available for some reason.

Most of the free internet sites are run by investment companies or someone else (such as small-time money managers) with something to sell. What these sites give away is nothing but subtle and not-so-subtle advertising for whatever products and services they sell. Also, watch out for free sites that make money through referrals. *Affiliates* are companies that provide referral fees and income for business that websites direct their way, and such payments create major conflicts of interest for the websites. For that reason, a website shouldn't receive affiliate fees when recommending a financial product or service.

Many investing books also contain thinly veiled advertisements. Some so-called authors choose to write books that are the equivalent of infomercials for something else — such as high-priced seminars — that they really want to sell you. Such writers aren't interested in educating and helping you as much as they're seeking to sell you something else. So, for example, an author may write about how complicated the investing markets are, saying that investing is too complicated to do on your own and that you really need a personal investment manager like the author.

Understand the Influence of Advertising

Whether on the internet, on television, in print, or on the radio, advertising often compromises the quality of the investment advice it accompanies. I won't say that you can't find some useful investment resources in media with lots of advertising.

These resources, however, are exceptions to the rule that sources with lots of advertising contain little valuable information and advice.

Many organizations, such as newspaper and magazine publishing companies and radio and television stations that accept ads, say that their ad departments are separate from their editorial departments. The truth, however, is that in most of these organizations, advertisers wield influence over the content. At minimum, the editorial environments at these organizations must be perceived as being conducive to the sale of the advertisers' products.

Another problem, especially prevalent online, is the merging of editorial and advertising content into *advertorials,* whereby a company or person pays a fee to a website to place provided content that's really an ad in disguise. This practice is unethical, especially when it isn't clearly and boldly disclosed.

WARNING

The influence of advertisers prevents readers, viewers, and listeners from getting the truth and best advice. Specifically, some media organizations and publishers simply won't make derogatory comments about advertisers, and sometimes they highlight and praise investment companies that are big advertisers.

Value Quality over Quantity

Talk about information overload! Blogs on the topic of investing continue to multiply. You can't peruse most publications or turn on the television or radio without bumping into articles, stories, segments, and entire programs devoted to investment issues.

The internet introduced a whole new medium. Now, at a relatively low cost, anyone can publish "content" online. The number of television channels has mushroomed as a result of cable television. Flip through your cable channels at any hour of the day, and you see infomercials that promise to make you a real estate tycoon or stock market millionaire in your spare time. These communications options are primarily structured around selling advertising rather than offering quality content. The accessibility of these communications media allows just about anyone with an animated personality or access to a computer to appear to be an expert. Much of the advice out there can easily steer you in the wrong direction.

Because investment information and advice is so widespread and constantly growing, knowing how to sift through it is just as important as hearing what the best resources are today. When chosen wisely, the best investing resources can further your investment knowledge and enable you to make better decisions. Quality is more important than quantity. Later in this chapter, I name the best investment resources that I'm familiar with.

Know How to Check Out a Resource

The best thing to do when you encounter a financial website, blog, radio or television program, or other resource for the first time is scrutinize it.

All things being equal, you have a greater chance of finding quality content when subscriber fees account for the bulk of a company's revenue and advertising accounts for little or none of the revenue. This generalization, of course, is just that: a generalization. Some publications that derive a reasonable portion of their revenue from advertising have some good columns and content. Conversely, some relatively ad-free sources aren't very good.

Deciphering a writer's philosophy and agenda is important in determining whether he provides quality information. Readers of my books, for example, can clearly understand my philosophies about investing. I advocate buying and holding, not trading and gambling. I explain how to build wealth through proven vehicles, including stocks, real estate, and small-business ownership.

Unfortunately, many venues and programs don't make it as easy for you to see or hear their operating beliefs. You have to do some homework. With a radio program, for example, you probably have to listen to at least portions of several shows to get a sense of the host's investment philosophies.

Examine the backgrounds, including professional work experience and education credentials, of a resource's writers, hosts, or anchors. If such information isn't given or easily found, consider this omission to be a red flag. People who have something to hide or who lack solid credentials usually don't promote their backgrounds. Also, don't blindly accept presented qualifications as being honest or truthful.

WARNING

Other red flags include publications and programs that make investing sound overly complicated and that imply — or say outright — that you won't succeed or do as well if you don't hire a financial advisor or follow your investments like a hawk.

Beware Hype and Exaggeration

There's an old news-media expression that says, "If it bleeds, it leads." Translation: Jarring, violent, or blood-and-gore stories attract attention.

Too often, this is the case in financial reporting too. If the stock market drops quickly or there's a disappointing economic report, you're sure to hear about it over and over again. Ditto for political scandals.

I'm not suggesting that only good news be reported. But frequently, negative events are blown out of proportion and hyped to garner more attention. Don't get carried away by the hype or be misled into believing that much of this short-term news should impact your important and longer-term investing decisions.

Don't Assume Quoted Experts Know Their Stuff

Historically, one way that investment journalists have attempted to overcome technical gaps in their knowledge has been to interview and quote experts in the field. Although these quotes may add to the accuracy and quality of a story, journalists who aren't experts themselves often have difficulty discerning qualified experts from posers and charlatans.

One common example of this phenomenon is that many investment writers quote unproven advice from investment-newsletter writers. As I discuss later in this chapter, the predictive advice of many newsletter writers is often poor, causing investors to earn lower returns and miss investment gains due to frequent trading. Journalists who simply parrot this type of information and provide an endorsement that unqualified sources are "experts" do readers an immense disservice.

Investigate Gurus' Claims

The tremendous growth in the number of people talking and writing about investing on websites, on cable television, and on radio means that more pundits are making claims about the value of their predictions. Unfortunately, many publications and media outlets that interview and give airtime to these pundits fail to independently investigate most such claims.

You don't need predictions and soothsayers to make sound investing choices. If you choose to follow this "expert" advice and you're lucky, little harm will be done. But more often than not, you can lose lots of money by following a pundit's predictions.

Never accept a guru's performance claims as valid. These claims should always be verified through an independent source. Visit the "Guru Watch" section of my website, www.erictyson.com, for analysis of many of the popular gurus in the media today.

Don't Believe Investment-Newsletter Claims

Especially in the investment-newsletter business, you'll see and hear lots of extraordinary performance claims. Private money managers, who aren't subject to the same scrutiny and auditing requirements as fund managers, can do the same.

Be especially wary of any newsletters making claims of high returns. According to the *Hulbert Financial Digest,* over the many decades it was published, the worst investment newsletters underperformed the market averages by dozens of percentage points; some would even have caused you to lose money during decades when the financial markets performed extraordinarily well (like the 1980s and 1990s).

Also be aware that plenty of gurus and newsletters will tout many strategies, investments, and funds, and then continue to hype only the one or two that happen to do well. The strategy or back-tested model may in fact have a good track record over a given period, but it may be cherry-picked and unlikely to succeed in the future.

Don't believe a track record unless a reputable accounting firm with experience doing such audits has audited it. Stay far away from publications that purport to be able to tell what's going to happen next. No one has a crystal ball.

Check Out and Keep Up with My Favorite Resources

I've come across a lot of resources over the years. Some have stood the test of time and offer worthwhile perspectives and insights. Here are some of the best for you to consider:

>> **CorporateInformation:** If you want to pick your own stocks, this site, at www.corporateinformation.com, has a treasure-trove of information, but subscription fees aren't cheap.

>> **Morningstar:** The premium content here, which is more moderately priced, covers all types of funds and most stocks. Go to www.morningstar.com.

>> *A Random Walk Down Wall Street: The Time-Tested Strategy for Successful Investing* **by Burton G. Malkiel (W.W. Norton):** I first read this classic in a college economics course, and this book has gotten better over the years with its new editions.

>> **The SEC:** The U.S. Securities and Exchange Commission (www.sec.gov) provides free access to the regulatory-required filings of investment funds and public companies.

>> **St. Louis Federal Reserve Economic Data:** This site, at fred.stlouisfed.org, has lots of interesting economic research and tons of historic economic.

>> *Stocks for the Long Run: The Definitive Guide to Financial Market Returns & Long Term Investment Strategies* **by Jeremy J. Siegel (McGraw Hill):** This terrific book details investing in stocks around the globe over the long run.

>> **Value Line:** Value Line has generations of experience providing concise summaries for the stocks of public companies. Most subscriptions run at least several hundred dollars per year. Check out www.valueline.com.

>> **Vanguard:** The leading no-load mutual fund company, Vanguard has plenty of user-friendly and readable information on its website at www.vanguard.com.

>> **Eric Tyson:** I regularly digest the best financial information and advice and then post the latest on my website at www.erictyson.com. Some content is free, and premium content is available at a relatively low cost.

Chapter **17**

Ten Essential Tips for Investing Success

nvesting appears to be complicated and complex. But if you can take some relatively simple concepts to heart and adhere to them, you can greatly increase your success.

In this chapter, I present my ten favorite, time-tested principles of investing success. Following these principles will pay you big dividends (and capital gains) for many years to come.

Regularly Save and Invest 5 Percent to 10 Percent of Your Income

Unless you enjoy a large inheritance, you should consistently save 5 percent to 10 percent of the money you're earning. When should you start doing this? I say, as soon as you begin earning money on a regular basis.

Preferably, invest through a retirement savings account to reduce your taxes and ensure your future financial independence. You can reduce both your current federal and state income tax (on the contributions) as well as these ongoing taxes (on the investment earnings).

The exact portion of your income you should be saving is driven by your goals and by your current financial assets and liabilities. Take the time to crunch some numbers to determine how much you should be saving monthly.

Understand and Use Your Employee Benefits

The larger the employer, the more likely it is to offer avenues for you to invest conveniently through payroll deduction, and with possible tax benefits and discounts. Some companies enable you to buy company stock at a reduced price.

Often, the most valuable benefit you have is a retirement savings plan, such as a 401(k) plan that enables you to make contributions and save on your current income taxation. Also, after the money is in the account, it can compound and grow over the years and decades without taxation until you withdraw from it.

Be sure to review and consider your employer's insurance benefits. Doing so is of value since insurance coverages, especially health insurance, are costly to buy solely on your own. In addition to helping pay for a portion of the cost, your employer may get better pricing on some types of policies (for example, disability insurance) than what you could get on your own.

TIP

If you're self-employed, be sure to establish and use a retirement plan (see Chapter 2). Also take time to learn about the best investment options available to you — and use them.

Thoroughly Research Before You Invest

The allure of large expected returns too often is the enticement that gets novices hooked on a particular investment. That's a whole lot more appealing than researching an investment. But research you must if you want to make an informed decision.

Be sure you understand what you're investing in. Don't purchase any financial product that you don't understand. Ask questions and compare what you're being offered with the best sources I recommend. Beware of purchasing an investment on the basis of an advertisement or a salesperson's solicitation.

Shun Investments with High Commissions and Expenses

The cost of the investments you buy is an important variable you can control. All fees must be disclosed in a prospectus, which you should always review before making any investment.

WARNING

Companies that sell their investment products through aggressive sales techniques generally have the worst financial products and the highest fees and commissions.

Invest the Majority of Your Long-Term Money in Ownership Investments

When you're young, you have plenty of time to let your investments compound and grow. Likewise, you have time to recover from setbacks.

So with your long-term money, focus on investments that have appreciation potential, such as stocks, real estate, and your own business. When you invest in bonds or bank accounts, you're simply lending your money to others and will earn a return that probably won't keep you ahead of inflation and taxes.

Avoid Making Emotionally Based Financial Decisions

Successful investors keep their composure when the going gets tough. You need the ability and wisdom to look beyond the current environment, understanding that it will change in the months and years ahead.

You don't want to panic and sell your stock holdings after a major market correction, for example. In fact, you should consider such an event to be a buying opportunity for stocks. Be especially careful about making important financial decisions after a major life change, such as marriage, the birth of a child, a divorce, job loss, or a death in your family.

Make Investing Decisions Based on Your Plans and Needs

Your investment decisions should come out of your planning and your overall needs, goals, and desires. This requires looking at your overall financial situation first and then coming up with a comprehensive plan.

Don't be swayed and influenced by the predictive advice offered by various investment pundits or the latest news headlines and concerns. Trust that you know yourself and your financial situation better than anyone else does.

Tap Information Sources with High Quality Standards

You need to pare down the sources you use to keep up with investing news and the financial markets. Give priority to those that aren't afraid to take a stand and recommend what's in your best interests. Observe a particular outlet or publication over time and consider if their guests and interviewees seem competent and objective.

I don't have a problem with opinion shows that are clearly labeled as such. The public definitely has an appetite for some of them; on the political left, you have programs on CNN and MSNBC. On the political right, FOX has some popular conservative opinion shows. I'm not suggesting that you or anyone else should watch or like such programs.

Political partisans tend to distort the news rather than report the news factually, and they may cause you to make more emotionally based decisions. Political partisans overstate the impact that the president and others can have over our economy and financial markets.

REMEMBER

Stay away from outlets that cater to advertisers or are driven by an ideological agenda.

Trust Yourself First

Look in the mirror. You'll see the best financial person you can hire and trust. What may be missing is enough education and confidence to make more and better decisions on your own, which this book can assist you with doing.

If you need help making a major decision, hire conflict-free advisors who charge a fee for their time. Work in partnership with advisors. Never turn over or abdicate control.

Invest in Yourself and Others

Don't get so wrapped up in making, saving, and investing money that you lose sight of what matters most to you. Invest in your education, your health, and your relationships with family members and friends.

Having a lot of money isn't worth much if you don't have your health and people with whom to share your life. Give your time and money to causes that better our society and our world.

Chapter **18**

Ten Things to Know about Investing Apps

M ost apps are offered by existing larger companies as another option for their customers to connect to and interact with what they offer. And, of course, companies would love for you to use their apps so they can continue to promote themselves to you and ensure that you remain a loyal customer. The investment companies you do business with — banks, mutual fund companies, brokerage firms, and so on — are no exception.

That said, you can also find some apps offered by smaller start-up companies that solely exist online and perhaps even only as an app. I urge you to be skeptical and extremely careful with such enterprises, for reasons I discuss later in this chapter.

Over time, the best new firms emerge and help improve the overall financial land-scape and your options. But I don't want you to be some small company's guinea pig. Given the choice between a start-up and a longer-standing, proven, success-ful investment company with good customer service, I bet you can guess which one will get my investment dollars.

With that as background, in this chapter, I offer advice for how to make the most out of using investing-related apps and sidestep common app pitfalls and prob-lems, as well as providing a short list of the best investment apps I've reviewed.

Beware of the General Dangers of Putting Apps on Your Cell Phone

Computer viruses, malware, and ransomware attacks have garnered more attention, but similar problems occur with smartphone apps. The worst of the lot can end up tracking and spying on you. Some are a scam and/or some sort of virus or malware.

Even if an app doesn't have these nefarious issues, you should also check out the background and agenda of any company offering an investment-related app and understand how such companies may be making money from the app. Most apps are nothing more than glorified advertising from the company behind the app. Sure, the product may dangle something seemingly helpful (such as free stock quotes), but ultimately you need to uncover the provider's agenda, track record, and reputation.

INVESTIGATE

Do your research on an app before downloading and beginning to use one. Check with more than one independent source and read independent reviews, especially those which are critical and less than flattering.

Use Apps Only from Proven Companies with Good Reputations and Longevity

Most of the companies I recommend in this chapter (and book) are companies with lengthy track records of success. For sure, technology is disrupting and changing many industries and companies. But that doesn't mean you should only do business with firms that exist solely online, in the cloud, and so on.

First, such companies are far more likely to be here today but gone tomorrow. Second, if you need actual customer service — such as talking with a real live person by phone — some of these newfangled firms simply don't provide such contact options. They may only offer email, which isn't ideal for resolving nuanced or mildly complicated problems. Finally, start-ups by definition lack a long-term proven track record.

TIP

Research the history of companies that you're considering doing business with. Download apps directly from the company's website so you're sure you're getting their actual app rather than a knock-off or a fraudulent one.

Consider the Alternatives to an App

Before downloading and using an app, you should question the need for it and consider the alternatives. Remember that the company behind the app wants to tie you to its company so you do more business with it. Is that your goal?

You likely have your phone with you *all* the time. Do you really want this app running and in your face *all* the time? Maybe, maybe not — think about it and examine the alternatives. Getting constantly changing investment prices on your phone every minute isn't going to make you a better investor.

Use the Best Personal Finance Apps to Have More to Invest

Unless you've been fortunate to earn a lot of money in a short period of time, received a large inheritance, or won the lottery, you likely want more money to invest. Some folks need extra help and hand-holding to lick the problem of over-spending, and some simply want to feel on top of where their money goes and do something constructive about it. Many websites and related apps purport to address this problem, but in reality they have massive conflicts of interest through the affiliate relationships (that is, kickbacks) they have with companies that they direct business to. Advertising is also a common problem.

REMEMBER

Some apps to date have overcome these problems, but things can change, so don't take my current recommendation in this space as a forever endorsement. That said, here are a few good options right now:

>> I like the Goodbudget app for its simplicity and practicality. The basic version provides you with up to one year of spending-tracking history in ten main categories (envelopes). A paid or premium version ($60 per year) gives you up to seven years of expense tracking with unlimited categories as well as email support. I suggest starting with the free version and then deciding later whether an upgrade is worth your while.

>> Some apps are simply designed to save you money. GasBuddy, for example, shows you the price for gasoline at various service stations in a local area. It's free for consumers to use.

>> Especially when you're going on lengthy car trips, car tolls can add up quickly. The Tollsmart Toll Calculator app is a low-cost app that enables you to compare toll costs for alternative routes. The Waze app can help with navigating traffic.

>> ShopSavvy enables you to shop across online and in-store retailers for specific products you enter or for which you scan a barcode.

Be Skeptical of Investing Apps Offering "Free" Trading

There are no free lunches in the investment world. The only way that a broker can offer free trades is by making money elsewhere. Brokerage firms that only exist as an app that I have reviewed have many problems, including poor customer service, limited account types, high fees for other basic services including simply closing your account, and so on. They simply have too many deficiencies and drawbacks, and they won't actually save you money in the long run compared with the best investment and brokerage firms I recommend in this book.

Review Current and Historic Financial and Economic Data

The St. Louis Fed's signature economic database — FRED, which stands for Federal Reserve Economic Database — is accessible through an app. Here's a rare case where you can have a wealth of data at your fingertips and not be bombarded with ads or plugs to buy things.

Are you curious how the latest unemployment rate compares with prior years and decades? Would you like to see how corporate profits stack up now compared with past economic cycles? How about understanding what the "financial stress index" is and how it has changed in recent months and years? You can see all this data and much more on the St. Louis FRED website.

Invest with Leading Fund Providers

Of course, many banks, investment companies, brokers, and so on have apps. So if you have a favorite investment firm or bank, check out what it offers. For its broad array of cost effective funds with solid long-term performance, I use Vanguard's app.

In addition to Vanguard, other major fund companies with quality offerings and apps include T. Rowe Price and Fidelity.

Tap into the Best Investment Brokerage Firms

Check out the apps offered by leading investment brokerage firms recommended in this book, such as E*Trade, Fidelity, and Charles Schwab. Also remember that the leading fund companies mentioned in the preceding section also have discount brokerage operations. Vanguard, E*Trade, Fidelity, and Schwab all offer no-commission online trading of stocks and ETFs.

Examine the Best Real Estate Apps

If you're looking for a home or basic types of investment real estate, the Real Estate App from realtor.com has the most comprehensive and up-to-date collection of listings. It includes a mapping feature that enables you to specify particular areas in which you want to see the homes for sale. Also, you can detail specific features of a home that interest you. If you're a renter, realtor.com also has an easy-to-use Rentals App.

Seek out Good Small-Business Apps

You can find lots of apps for small business. Among the better ones I've reviewed are the QuickBooks App and the Wave Accounting App for small businesses (not to be confused with the Waze app I mention earlier in the chapter for trip navigation). I also like Dropbox, a cloud-based service for storing and sharing documents, files, photos, videos, and so on.

Bonus Chapter

Taking Care with Health Insurance

When you're young and living under your parents' roof, you're unlikely to be concerned with health insurance. School-aged kids generally get their health insurance through a parent's coverage, a practice that's usually continued through college.

Welcome to the young-adult world of health insurance! Health insurance was in the news soon after the election of President Barack Obama in 2008 because he promised during the campaign, and then pushed for, a national health insurance program (Obamacare passed in 2010) mandated by the federal government.

Health insurance was front and center once again during the 2016 presidential election. Candidate Donald Trump promised over and over again that he would "repeal and replace" Obamacare with "something so much better." Once elected, President Trump soon discovered that the U.S. healthcare and health insurance industries are much more complicated than he realized, as is getting members of Congress to agree on a specific repeal-and-replace plan. "Now, I have to tell you, it's an unbelievably complex subject . . . Nobody knew healthcare could be so complicated," President Trump said in his second month in office.

I could have told Mr. Trump that the healthcare industry and reforming it is complicated — but he didn't ask me! In fact, I've had involvement with and interest in the healthcare and insurance industry since my first professional job after college as a management consultant. Most young adults are fortunate to not be big consumers of healthcare. But, because you never know what the future holds and people of all ages should get checkups and preventative care, this chapter discusses the best and most affordable ways to secure health insurance in your 20s and 30s. I also cover the ramifications of the healthcare bill (known as Obamacare) that was signed into law in 2010 and what possible changes may be coming in the future.

Making Sure You're Covered

Having health insurance is essential for nearly everyone, no matter your age. Many people get health insurance through their employers. Numerous people don't have coverage because it is or seems costly.

Historically, some people who can afford health insurance choose not to buy it because they believe they're healthy and they're not going to need it. Others who opt not to buy health insurance figure that if they ever really need healthcare, they'll get it even if they can't fully afford it.

WARNING

Although you may think you're healthy and don't need health insurance, think again. People without health insurance are more prone to put off getting routine and preventative care, which can lead to small problems turning into big ones. Besides this being an unwise approach to optimizing your health, it often costs more because of advanced illness, emergency room visits, and so on.

This section discusses transitioning from your parents' coverage to your own and how the healthcare laws help you get coverage.

Transitioning your coverage

Each state once had its own laws as far as health insurance coverage went, so there was no one-size-fits-all approach. In the past in most states, an adult child generally lost health insurance coverage under a parent's policy upon college graduation or when turning a particular age (for example, 25 or 26). Each state had a unique set of laws. Consider, for example, three state rules I pulled at random:

>> Connecticut required that group comprehensive and health insurance policies extend coverage to unwed children until the age of 26, provided they remained residents of Connecticut or were full-time students.

>> Florida allowed for dependent children up to age 25 who lived with a parent or were students, and those up to 30 who were also unmarried and had no dependent children of their own, to remain on their parents' insurance.

>> Wyoming allowed a child who was unmarried and a full-time student to remain on a parent's insurance up to age 23 if the parent was covered by a small group policy.

Then the Affordable Care Act, also known as Obamacare, was passed in 2010 so states had to amend their approach to conform with Obamacare's requirements — detailed in the next section, "Seeing how Obamacare changed your coverage."

So, what are the best ways to negotiate keeping health insurance coverage in your 20s without spending a small fortune for coverage? Here's my advice:

>> **Consider staying on your parents' policy until you secure full-time employment.** As soon as you're eligible for your employer's health plan, sign up for it. (You can and should offer to help pay for your share of the coverage if you're financially able to do so.)

>> **If you don't have access to your own coverage through your employer, look to COBRA.** The Consolidated Omnibus Budget Reconciliation Act (COBRA) enables you to stay on your parents' policy for up to 18 months from the time you lose coverage on that policy. Just be aware that you have to pay the full premiums.

>> **If you're self-employed, or your employer doesn't offer health coverage or the coverage isn't very good, get your own policy with a high deductible.** A deductible is the amount of medical claims you must first pay out of your pocket before insurance coverage kicks in. Check out the later section "Finding Your Best Health Plan" for advice. You can then sock money away in a health savings account (HSA) if you desire. See the section on HSAs later in this chapter.

Seeing how Obamacare changed your coverage

In 2010, Congress passed, and President Obama signed, two comprehensive healthcare reform bills that affect how you can get health insurance coverage. Summarizing thousands of pages of legislation in a concise space is challenging, but the reality is that the highlights that apply to young adults aren't that extensive.

Obamacare implemented the following changes to group health plans offered through employers:

>> Employers must offer coverage to their employees for their adult children up to age 26 who aren't eligible for coverage under another employer's health plan. So if your mother or father is covered under a group health plan, you may get coverage through that plan through age 26, even if you aren't a dependent for income tax purposes. The coverage isn't taxable to the employee or dependent.

>> Insurers may not impose lifetime limits on claims paid (annual limits became prohibited as of 2014).

>> Employers must offer minimum coverage to full-time employees or make payments to the government.

>> Group health plans must limit cost sharing and deductibles to those in a health savings account–eligible, high-deductible health plan.

>> Group health plans must remove all preexisting-condition exclusions on all participants.

Higher-income earners are subjected to some higher taxes to help pay for the health bill:

>> Single taxpayers with earned income above $200,000 and married couples filing jointly with earned income above $250,000 pay an extra 0.9 percent Medicare tax on wages and self-employment income in excess of these thresholds.

>> Taxpayers with modified adjusted gross income (MAGI) from any source (including investments) above these thresholds are subject to a 3.8 percent additional tax on the lesser of their net investment income (for example, interest, dividends, and capital gains) and the amount by which their modified adjusted gross income exceeds the thresholds.

Recent developments and likely future changes

Major changes to Obamacare can only occur when both the House and the Senate can get a majority to agree to those changes and the president is willing to go along as well. Efforts to "repeal and replace" Obamacare failed in 2017 in the Senate.

There have been a number of incremental changes to Obamacare in recent years including:

>> **Elimination of mandate (penalties):** Previously, if you didn't secure an Obamacare approved/mandated policy, you were forced to pay a sizeable financial penalty on your annual federal income tax return. That has since been eliminated.

>> **Short-term scaled-down plans allowed:** Health insurance plans that offer coverage for up to one year and renewability for a total of three years are allowed as short-term alternatives to Obamacare compliant plans.

>> **Open enrollment time frame modified:** The period each year when you can enroll in a new or different Obamacare health insurance plan has been changed to the 45-day period from November 1 through December 15.

>> **Expansion of subsidies:** The income levels at which Obamacare policies can be at least partially subsidized was expanded. See the subsidy calculator on the Kaiser Family Foundation website at https://www.kff.org/interactive/subsidy-calculator/.

>> **States allowed to have work requirements for Medicaid coverage:** Each individual state can choose to have work requirements, for those who are able, as a condition for being under the state's Medicaid program (health insurance program for lower-income people).

President Biden's election and the fact that he was vice president at the time of Obamacare's passage and Congress is also under his party's control (the mid-term elections in 2022 are likely to change that) may lead to changes to counteract some of the modifications that occurred under the prior administration's tenure.

Finding Your Best Health Plan

Most working-age folks obtain health insurance through their employer. Employer-provided coverage eliminates the hassle of having to shop for coverage from scratch. Also, thanks to the purchasing power of a group, employer-provided coverage may provide a higher level of benefits, given the cost, than individually purchased coverage.

If you're self-employed, out of work, or working for an employer that doesn't offer health coverage, you need to shop for and secure health insurance. And even if your employer does offer health policies, you may well have choices to make. In the following sections, I discuss the important issues to consider when selecting among available health insurance plans.

Selection of doctors and hospitals

Open-choice plans that allow you to use any doctor or hospital you want are less common and generally more expensive than *restricted-choice plans*, such as *health maintenance organizations* (HMOs) and *preferred provider organizations* (PPOs). These plans keep costs down because they negotiate low rates with selected providers.

HMOs and PPOs are more similar than they are different. The main difference is that PPOs still pay the majority of your expenses if you use a provider outside their approved list. If you use a provider outside the approved list with an HMO, you typically aren't covered at all.

TIP

If you want to use particular doctors or hospitals, find out which health insurance plans they accept as payment. Weigh whether the extra cost of an open-choice plan is worth being able to use the services of particular medical providers if they're not part of a restricted-choice plan. Also be aware that some plans allow you to go outside their network of providers as long as you pay a bigger portion of the incurred medical costs. If you're interested in using alternative types of providers, such as acupuncturists, find out whether the plans you're considering cover these services.

Plan benefits and features

Healthcare plans typically offer some important features. The following list identifies the key features to search for to ensure a quality plan at the most reasonable cost:

>> **Major medical coverage:** This includes hospital care, physician visits, and ancillary charges, such as X-rays and laboratory work. If you're a woman and you think you may want to have children, make sure your plan has maternity benefits.

>> **Deductibles and co-payments:** To reduce your health insurance premiums, choose a plan with the highest deductible and *co-payment* (the amount you pay when service is rendered, such as $10 to $30) you can afford. As with other

insurance policies, the more you're willing to share in the cost of your claims, the less you'll have to pay in premiums. Most policies have annual deductible options (usually $250, $500, $1,000, or higher) as well as co-payment options, which are typically 20 percent or so of the claim amount. With the passage of Obamacare and plans compatible with health savings accounts, many plans have a deductible of several thousand dollars. Insurance plans generally set a maximum out-of-pocket limit such as $1,000 or $2,000 on your annual co-payments. The insurer covers 100 percent of any medical expenses that go over that cap. Many HMO plans don't have deductible and co-payment options.

TIP

If you have existing health problems and you have a choice of group plans through your employer, consider plans with low out-of-pocket expenses. Because you're part of a group, the insurer won't increase your individual rates just because you file more claims.

>> **Lifetime maximum benefits:** Health insurance plans specify the maximum total benefits they'll pay over the course of time you're insured by their plan. The national health insurance bill signed into law in 2010 prevents insurers from setting lifetime maximums. If you're ever examining a short-term or other plan that is outside of the government-mandated plan network, keep in mind that with the high cost of healthcare, you should choose a plan that has no maximum or that has a maximum of at least $5 million. See the section "Seeing how Obamacare changed your coverage" earlier in this chapter.

Shopping for Health Insurance

Yes, health insurance is among the more complicated things to shop for, but it's like other products and services — there's a marketplace of providers competing for your business. This section explains how to unearth your best options and what to do in case you're ever denied coverage in the future.

Uncovering the best policies

When shopping for health insurance, you basically have two options: You can buy a health plan through an agent or you can buy directly from an insurer. When particular health insurance plans are sold both ways, buying through an agent usually doesn't cost more.

Obamacare, which includes a federal marketplace, provided a new way in some states to buy health insurance — through state-based exchanges.

If you're self-employed or you work for a smaller employer that doesn't offer health insurance as a benefit, get proposals from the larger and older health insurers in your area. Larger plans can negotiate better rates from providers, and older plans are more likely to be here tomorrow. Nationally, Blue Cross Blue Shield, Kaiser Permanente, Aetna, UnitedHealth, CIGNA, Assurant, and Anthem are among the older and bigger health insurers.

Many insurers operate in a bunch of different insurance businesses. You want an insurer that's one of the biggest in the health insurance arena and is committed to, understands, and has more experience in that business. If your coverage is canceled, you may have to search for new coverage.

Also check with professional or other associations that you belong to, as such plans sometimes offer decent benefits at a competitive price because of the purchasing clout they possess. A competent independent insurance agent who specializes in health insurance can help you find insurers who are willing to offer you coverage.

WARNING

Health insurance agents have a conflict of interest that's common to all financial salespeople who work on commission: The higher the premium plan they sell you, the bigger the commission they earn. So, an agent may try to steer you into higher-cost plans and avoid suggesting some of the cost-reducing strategies that I discuss in this chapter, such as opting for a higher deductible.

Dealing with Obamacare's high health insurance prices

When millions of health insurance policyholders had their plans canceled during the years when Obamacare (also known as the Affordable Care Act) was implemented, many of them faced big rate hikes when shopping for a replacement policy. That's because of the essential health benefits that, by law, must be included in health insurance policies. These benefits include maternity and newborn care, mental health and substance use disorder services, prescription drugs, and pediatric services (including dental and vision care), to give a partial list. In the past, you were able to pick and choose from plans that excluded some of these services and thus were less expensive.

Plus, Obamacare includes consumer protection provisions that have elevated prices. For example, it prohibits health insurance companies from limiting or excluding coverage related to preexisting health conditions. In order to absorb this cost and costs related to other provisions, insurance companies have raised rates substantially.

While many people faced much higher priced policies due to Obamacare, some folks qualify for government subsidies that help reduce the effective price of said policies. (Of course, this money doesn't come out of thin air; it comes from the federal government and therefore, taxpayers.)

Qualifying for a subsidy depends on your family income and how many children you have. Subsidies are available to qualified individuals and families whose incomes fall in the range of 138 percent to 400 percent of the poverty line (assuming they buy a policy on a government exchange). At the top of the spectrum for 2021, an individual making under $51,040 would be eligible for a subsidy, as would a family of four earning less than $104,800.

In recent decades, health insurance prices have consistently increased faster than the overall rate of inflation. That has continued under Obamacare. Here are a few tips for health insurance shoppers to make the most of their spending:

» If your plan is/was canceled, don't just go with the plan mentioned in the cancelation letter. Shop around. Contact an agent who focuses on health insurance plans and ask to see a side-by-side comparison of various plans. Check out other companies. If you're eligible for a subsidy, check out the exchanges. Chances are you'll find something more reasonable if you're willing to make trade-offs in the area of deductibles and out-of-pocket expenses.

» Be patient and do your homework. Talk to insurers and agents. Spend some time on the computer; the Affordable Care Act marketplace website is www. healthcare.gov. Ask friends and colleagues what they're doing. Although you do need to be mindful of enrollment deadlines, you don't want to rush into what is an important financial decision.

» If you go with a bronze plan, consider one that is compatible with a health savings account (HSA). A bronze plan may be best for people who are generally healthy. These have the lowest premiums. Of course, they also have the highest deductibles, which means that in the event you do get sick, you'll have to cover more of your costs out of pocket. And that is why it's important to select a bronze plan that's compatible with an HSA (not all of them are). I have always recommended HSAs as a great tax-saving strategy, and now that deductibles are so high, they make more sense than ever. After all, if you have to have a high deductible anyway, at least getting the tax break on the out-of-pocket expenses you have to pay makes sense. See the section, "Health Savings Accounts: Tax Reduction for Healthcare Costs," later in this chapter.

» Do what you can to get and stay healthy. Chances are you'll now be paying more out of pocket for non-preventative care, so good health should be your top priority. Of course, health insurance is needed because some conditions are unpreventable, but you can affect plenty of others with lifestyle improvements. Obviously, if you smoke, stop now; smoking is the only "preexisting condition" health insurance companies are allowed to charge you more for. But it's also important to eat healthfully, exercise, and lose weight if you need to. The healthier you are, the less you'll need to seek medical care — and the less you'll have to pay out of pocket for your care.

Handling insurance rejection

Before the passage and implementation of Obamacare, those with so-called pre-existing conditions sometimes got turned down when applying for health insurance or had to pay substantially higher premiums. A similar phenomenon happens with other types of insurance when you're deemed too great a risk. For example, you may have problems with getting life or disability insurance or have to pay a much greater price if you're not in the best of health.

When you try to enroll in a particular life or disability insurance plan (discussed in Chapter 15), you may be turned down because of current or previous health problems. That may happen (but isn't likely to) in the future with health insurance, depending on what happens with Congress and President Biden. If your current health causes you to be charged a high premium for life or disability insurance or be denied such coverage outright, try these strategies to find out why and get approved:

>> **Ask the insurer why you were denied.** If you're denied coverage because of a medical condition, find out what information the company has and determine whether it's accurate. Perhaps the company made a mistake or misinterpreted some information that you provided in your application.

TIP

>> **Request a copy of your medical information file.** Just as you have a credit report file that details your use (and misuse) of credit, you also have a medical information report. Once per year, you can request a free copy of your medical information file (which typically highlights only the more significant problems over the past seven years, not your entire medical history) by calling 866-692-6901 or visiting www.mib.com (click on "Request Your MIB Consumer File"). If you find a mistake on your report, you have the right to request that it be fixed. However, the burden is on you to prove that the information in your file is incorrect. Proving that your file contains errors can be a major hassle — you may even need to contact physicians you saw in the past because their medical records may be the source of the incorrect information.

INVESTIGATE

>> **Shop around.** Just because one company denies you coverage doesn't mean that all insurance companies will deny you. Some insurers better understand certain medical conditions and are more comfortable accepting applicants with those conditions. Although most insurers charge higher rates to people

with blemished medical histories than people with perfect health records, some companies penalize them less than others. An agent who sells policies from multiple insurers, called an independent agent, can be helpful because she can shop among a number of different companies.

>> **Find a job with an employer whose insurer doesn't require a medical exam.** Of course, this shouldn't be your only reason for seeking new employment, but it can be an important factor. If you're married, you may also be able to get into an employer group plan through your spouse's plan.

Health Savings Accounts: Tax Reduction for Healthcare Costs

Health savings accounts (HSAs) are terrific for reducing your taxes while saving money for healthcare expenses. They especially make sense if you're self-employed or an employee of a smaller company with no health plan or a high-deductible health plan.

An HSA is fairly simple: You put money earmarked for medical expenses into an investment account that offers tax-deductible contributions and tax-deferred compounding, just like a retirement account (withdrawals aren't taxed so long as the money is used for qualified healthcare expenses). For tax year 2021, you can sock away up to $3,600 for an individual account and $7,200 for a family account. To qualify for an HSA, you must have a high-deductible health insurance policy — at least $1,400 for individuals and $2,800 for families.

You don't have to deplete the HSA by the end of the year: Money can compound tax-deferred inside the HSA for years. If you qualify, you can begin to investigate an HSA through insurers offering health plans you're interested in or with the company you currently have coverage through (also see my website, www.erictyson.com, for the latest information on the best HSAs).

You may also be able to save on taxes if you have a substantial amount of healthcare expenditures in a year relative to your income. You can deduct medical and dental expenses as an itemized deduction on Schedule A to the extent that they exceed 10 percent of your adjusted gross income.

TIP

If you expect to have out-of-pocket medical expenses and can't qualify for an HSA because of your employer's plans, find out whether your employer offers a *flexible spending* or *healthcare reimbursement account.* These accounts enable you to pay for uncovered medical expenses with pretax dollars. If, for example, you're in a combined 35 percent federal and state income tax bracket, these accounts allow you to pay for necessary healthcare at a 35 percent discount. These accounts can also be used to pay for vision and dental care.

WARNING

Be forewarned of the major stumbling blocks you face when saving through medical reimbursement accounts:

» **You need to elect to save money from your paycheck prior to the beginning of each plan year.** The only exception is at the time of a "life change," such as marriage, a spouse's job change, divorce, the birth of a child, or a family member's death.

» **You also need to use the money within the year you save it.** These accounts contain a "use it or lose it" policy.

Index

About the Author

Eric Tyson is an internationally acclaimed and best-selling personal finance author, lecturer, speaker, and former advisor. Through his work, he is dedicated to teaching people to manage their money better and to successfully direct their own investments.

Eric is a former management consultant to businesses for which he helped improve operations and profitability. Before, during, and after this time of working crazy hours and traveling too much, he had the good sense to focus on financial matters.

He has been involved in the investing markets in many capacities for more than three decades. Eric first invested in mutual funds when he opened a mutual fund account at Fidelity in high school. With the assistance of Dr. Martin Zweig, a now-famous investment market analyst, Eric won his high school's science fair with a project on what influences the stock market. In addition to investing in securities over the decades, Eric has successfully invested in real estate and started and managed his own business. He has counseled thousands of clients on a variety of investment quandaries and questions.

He earned a bachelor's degree in economics at Yale and an MBA at the Stanford Graduate School of Business. Despite these impediments to lucid reasoning, he came to his senses and decided that life was too short to spend it working long hours and waiting in airports for the benefit of larger companies.

An accomplished freelance personal finance writer, Eric is the author of numerous best-selling books, including *For Dummies* books on personal finance, investing, mutual funds, and home buying (co-author), and is a syndicated columnist. His work has been featured and quoted in hundreds of national and local publications, including *Kiplinger's Personal Finance Magazine, Los Angeles Times, Chicago Tribune,* the *Wall Street Journal,* and *Bottom Line/Personal,* and on NBC's *Today Show,* ABC, CNBC, FOX, FOX Business, PBS's *Nightly Business Report,* CNN, CBS national radio, Bloomberg Radio, National Public Radio, and Business Radio Network. He's also been a featured speaker at a White House conference on retirement planning.

You can visit him on the web at www.erictyson.com.

Dedication

Before I get to the thank-yous, please allow me a *really* major thank-you and dedication.

This book is hereby and irrevocably dedicated to my family and friends, as well as to my former students, counseling clients, and customers, who ultimately taught me everything I know about how to explain financial terms and strategies so that all of us may benefit.

Author's Acknowledgments

First, I'd like to thank Linda Brandon and Tracy Boggier. Thanks also to Christy Pingleton for all of her fine editing! And thanks to everyone else who contributed to getting this book done well and on time.

A tip of my cap to our fine technical reviewer, Gary Karz, who helped to ensure that I didn't write something that wasn't quite right.

Publisher's Acknowledgments

Senior Acquisitions Editor: Tracy Boggier

Development Editor: Linda Brandon

Copy Editor: Christine Pingleton

Proofreader: Debbye Butler

Technical Editor: Gary Karz, CFA

Production Editor: Mohammed Zafar Ali

Cover Image: © hocus-focus/Getty Images

Leverage the power

Dummies is the global leader in the reference category and one of the most trusted and highly regarded brands in the world. No longer just focused on books, customers now have access to the dummies content they need in the format they want. Together we'll craft a solution that engages your customers, stands out from the competition, and helps you meet your goals.

Advertising & Sponsorships

Connect with an engaged audience on a powerful multimedia site, and position your message alongside expert how-to content. Dummies.com is a one-stop shop for free, online information and know-how curated by a team of experts.

- Targeted ads
- Video
- Email Marketing
- Microsites
- Sweepstakes sponsorship

20 **MILLION**
PAGE VIEWS
EVERY SINGLE MONTH

15
MILLION
UNIQUE
VISITORS PER MONTH

43%
OF ALL VISITORS
ACCESS THE SITE
VIA THEIR MOBILE DEVICES

700,000 NEWSLETTER
SUBSCRIPTIONS
TO THE INBOXES OF
300,000 UNIQUE INDIVIDUALS
EVERY WEEK

# of dummies

Custom Publishing

Reach a global audience in any language by creating a solution that will differentiate you from competitors, amplify your message, and encourage customers to make a buying decision.

- Apps
- Books
- eBooks
- Video
- Audio
- Webinars

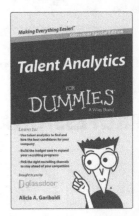

Brand Licensing & Content

Leverage the strength of the world's most popular reference brand to reach new audiences and channels of distribution.

For more information, visit dummies.com/biz

PERSONAL ENRICHMENT

Staying Sharp dummies

9781119187790
USA $26.00
CAN $31.99
UK £19.99

Facebook dummies
Carolyn Abram

9781119179030
USA $21.99
CAN $25.99
UK £16.99

Guitar dummies
Mark Phillips
Jon Chappell

9781119293354
USA $24.99
CAN $29.99
UK £17.99

Investing dummies
Eric Tyson, MBA

9781119293347
USA $22.99
CAN $27.99
UK £16.99

Beekeeping dummies
Howland Blackiston

9781119310068
USA $22.99
CAN $27.99
UK £16.99

Digital Photography dummies
Julie Adair King

9781119235606
USA $24.99
CAN $29.99
UK £17.99

Meditation dummies
Stephan Bodian

9781119251163
USA $24.99
CAN $29.99
UK £17.99

Pregnancy ALL-IN-ONE dummies
6 Books

9781119235491
USA $26.99
CAN $31.99
UK £19.99

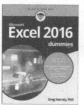
Samsung Galaxy S7 dummies
Bill Hughes

9781119279952
USA $24.99
CAN $29.99
UK £17.99

iPhone dummies
Edward C. Baig
Bob "Dr. Mac" LeVitus

9781119283133
USA $24.99
CAN $29.99
UK £17.99

Crocheting dummies
Karen Manthey
Susan Brittain

9781119287117
USA $24.99
CAN $29.99
UK £16.99

Nutrition dummies
Carol Ann Rinzler

9781119130246
USA $22.99
CAN $27.99
UK £16.99

PROFESSIONAL DEVELOPMENT

Windows 10 dummies
Andy Rathbone

9781119311041
USA $24.99
CAN $29.99
UK £17.99

AutoCAD dummies
Bill Fane

9781119255796
USA $39.99
CAN $47.99
UK £27.99

Excel 2016 dummies
Greg Harvey, PhD

9781119293439
USA $26.99
CAN $31.99
UK £19.99

QuickBooks 2017 dummies
Stephen L. Nelson, MBA, CPA, MS in Taxation

9781119281467
USA $26.99
CAN $31.99
UK £19.99

macOS Sierra dummies
Bob "Dr. Mac" LeVitus

9781119280651
USA $29.99
CAN $35.99
UK £21.99

LinkedIn dummies
Joel Elad, MBAs

9781119251132
USA $24.99
CAN $29.99
UK £17.99

Windows 10 ALL-IN-ONE dummies
10 Books
Woody Leonhard

9781119310563
USA $34.00
CAN $41.99
UK £24.99

SharePoint 2016 dummies
Rosemarie Withee
Ken Withee

9781119181705
USA $29.99
CAN $35.99
UK £21.99

Fundamental Analysis dummies
Matt Krantz

9781119263593
USA $26.99
CAN $31.99
UK £19.99

Networking dummies
Doug Lowe

9781119257769
USA $29.99
CAN $35.99
UK £21.99

Office 2016 dummies
Wallace Wang

9781119293477
USA $26.99
CAN $31.99
UK £19.99

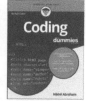
Office 365 dummies
Rosemarie Withee
Ken Withee
Jennifer Reed

9781119265313
USA $24.99
CAN $29.99
UK £17.99

Salesforce.com dummies
Liz Kao
Jon Paz

9781119239314
USA $29.99
CAN $35.99
UK £21.99

Coding dummies
Nikhil Abraham

9781119293323
USA $29.99
CAN $35.99
UK £21.99

dummies.com

dummies
A Wiley Brand

Learning Made Easy

ACADEMIC

9781119293576
USA $19.99
CAN $23.99
UK £15.99

9781119293637
USA $19.99
CAN $23.99
UK £15.99

9781119293491
USA $19.99
CAN $23.99
UK £15.99

9781119293460
USA $19.99
CAN $23.99
UK £15.99

9781119293590
USA $19.99
CAN $23.99
UK £15.99

9781119215844
USA $26.99
CAN $31.99
UK £19.99

9781119293378
USA $22.99
CAN $27.99
UK £16.99

9781119293521
USA $19.99
CAN $23.99
UK £15.99

9781119239178
USA $18.99
CAN $22.99
UK £14.99

9781119263883
USA $26.99
CAN $31.99
UK £19.99

Available Everywhere Books Are Sold

dummies.com